The Foundations Under Attack

The Roots of Apostasy

Michael de Semlyen

Dorchester House Publications

Dorchester House Publications
P.O. Box 67
Rickmansworth
Herts WD3 5SJ
England

Copyright © 2006 Dorchester House Publications

All rights reserved. No part of this publication may be reproduced, stored in a retrieval system, or transmitted in any form or by any means - mechanical, electronic, photocopying, or otherwise - without the prior written consent of the publisher.

Short extracts may be quoted for review purposes.

All Scripture quotations are from the Authorised Version of the Bible, unless otherwise noted.

ISBN 978 0 9518386 1 7
EAN 9780951838617

Front cover graphics from top to bottom, left to right, include the following illustrations: the Bible, Martin Luther, Jonathan Edwards, martyrdom of Stephen, Polycarp and Christians in Roman Stadium, and Charles Haddon Spurgeon.

Typeset and printed by
Freedom Print
Holmer Green, Bucks HP15 6QT

CONTENTS

Preface	v
Foreword	vii
Introduction	ix
PART I - HISTORY AND PROPHECY	**1**
Chapter 1 - The Historical View of Prophecy and Antichrist	3
Chapter 2 - Futurism – Leapfrogging History – The Wiles of the Devil	11
Chapter 3 - The Counter-Reformation – The Source of the Futurist View of Prophecy	17
Chapter 4 - Futurism Devised across the Centuries by the Jesuits	23
Chapter 5 - Historicist Expositors of the Nineteenth Century	33
Chapter 6 - Islam in Prophecy	35
PART II - THE KING JAMES BIBLE AND MODERN VERSIONS	**47**
Chapter 7 - The Proliferation of Modern "Bibles"	49
Chapter 8 - The Modern Versions – Origins and Influences	59
Chapter 9 - The Textual Controversy	65
Chapter 10 - Bible Verse Comparisons	73
PART III - ARMINIANISM: A MAN-CENTRED GOSPEL	**97**
Chapter 11 - The Origins of Arminianism	99
Chapter 12 - Catholicism and Arminianism in England and France During the Sixteenth and Seventeenth Centuries	119
Chapter 13 - "New Revivalism" Charles Finney, D.L.Moody, and a Man-Centred Gospel	135
Chapter 14 - The Pentecostal and Charismatic Movements	145
Chapter 15 - The Abandoning of the Protestant Reformed Religion	153
Epilogue	**163**
A. "Notes from a former Charismatic to Christians in the Charismatic Movement"	164
B. Papal Rome and the EU	179
C. The Foundations Under Attack: The Roots of Apostasy	201
D. The Monarchy In Peril	219
E. How Understanding the Doctrine of Election Changed My Life: Testimony of a New York Homemaker	230
Acknowledgements	**232**

Preface

"The Anti-Historical Church and Nation"

~

"We don't usually in this century go back to the 13th century to decide how we should continue to run things." So said Mrs. Barbara Mills, the Director of Public Prosecutions, in supporting restrictions on trial by jury in July 1993. "Magna Carta was enormously important in its day, but we aren't still in 1215, and talk of 'inalienable rights' is largely irrelevant.'" As a Sunday Telegraph editorial observed, "… the problem with Mrs. Mills and her kind is not that they are historically inaccurate but that they are anti-historical."

In a small booklet, *The Monarchy in Peril*, published by Spirit of '88 in 1994, and included in the appendix of this book, it was argued that our country's participation in the Maastricht Treaty is anti-historical. It is hard to represent this treaty, at odds with the hard-learned lessons of our past, as anything but an irresponsible abandoning of our tried and tested constitution centred on the Protestant Throne. Ironically, lessons from that same spurned thirteenth century and the unhappy reign of King John have caused many who look to learn from such things to draw another comparison.

Two years before Magna Carta, in 1213, King John, under considerable pressure from across the channel, had ignominiously placed the crown of England at the feet of the Pope's legate. On the very same date, May 21, in 1993, the Maastricht bill passed through the House of Commons after its Third Reading. Her Majesty's Accession Oath was dispensed with, as the "Crown in Parliament" was in a very real sense laid at the feet of those who rule in Brussels.

Ironically, it was two other men named John—the Prime Minister, John Major, and the late Leader of Her Majesty's Opposition, John Smith—who were primarily responsible for this.

With Parliament's assent to Maastricht, Britain carelessly threw away the true crown jewels and discarded those great principles centred on the institution of Monarchy and the Protestant Throne, which have safeguarded and guided our integrity and very existence as a nation for several centuries.

The years have passed, and another government is in power, one now led by a Prime Minister who is contemptuous of our nation's institutions, and whose "New Labour" administration is thoroughly anti-historical. Maastricht has led on to Amsterdam, Amsterdam to Nice, and Nice to the proposed EU Constitution, signed by Tony Blair, but stalled by its rejection by French and Dutch voters.

Restrictions on trial by jury have been extended. "Habeas corpus", the presumption of innocence in our justice system, would not long survive the implementation of *Corpus Juris*. *Magna Carta*, fount of our freedoms, scarcely merits mention in our professedly "free" press, nor does *The Bill of Rights*. The prospect of our ancient liberties being altogether subsumed into a Roman-Catholic-dominated federal Europe[1], anti-historical as this would be, looms large.

Foreword

The current controversy between the KJV in English and the modern bible versions is the same old conflict fought by the early church with the Gnostics and in the Middle Ages by the Waldensians with the Papists; as well as by the Protestants with the Jesuits in the sixteenth century. The battle over God's Word, its providential preservation, and the correct identification of Antichrist is a crucial one. It is the spiritual battle fought by followers of Christ against followers of Antichrist, the true faith against the counterfeit, the Reformation versus the Counter-Reformation.

The abandoning of the Protestant identity of our nation is reflected in the loss of patriotism and by an increasing disregard for our history and heritage. There has been departure from the certainties of our only truly Protestant and Authorised Bible, now replaced by a plethora of corrupted modern versions, and further undermined by the repudiation of the doctrines of grace by a man-centred gospel. The rejection through the centuries of the old orthodoxy by influential Arminians such as Archbishop Laud, John Wesley, and Charles Finney paved the way for the successes of the Counter-Reformation and the "ecumenical" acceptance of the old spiritual enemy, the Church of Rome. Through it all we no longer know quite who we are and what we stand for. Our established Church is losing its identity, as is our nation. Together with our sovereignty and independence, we are abandoning our hard-won freedoms; and few people know or seem to care.

The King James Version of the Bible was conceived at the Reformation and given birth soon after in 1611. The Revised Version of the Bible of 1881, which has spawned the many modern versions, was the product of an era during which Darwinism, Liberalism, Higher Criticism, and the Romanising Oxford Movement were in fashion among opinion formers in the Church. That revised

Bible has proven to be an historic break-through for the Counter-Reformation. Largely lost in its rendering is the prophetic and historical identification of Papal Rome as the Antichrist. The differing renditions of the Scriptures, based on manuscripts that were rejected by the Reformation, obscure and conceal the true meaning of the prophetic passages; instead exonerating Rome and substituting a Futurist identification of Antichrist. The importance of Church history therefore is difficult to overestimate. Faced with such widespread ignorance in today's church, we set out in this book to demonstrate just how important the knowledge of history is. For if we ignore the lessons of History we are destined to repeat its mistakes.

Introduction

"New Lamps for Old"

~

A feature of the future-orientated times in which we live is a remarkable lack of knowledge of history, especially among younger people. In the age of the sound bite and the TV image, for most people there is little time for reading books of any kind, and even less patience for the application and study that history requires. Besides, the spirit of the age reassures us that we've graduated from our past. What is now, and even more what is to come is seen as innately superior to what was then; after all, we have evolved as well as progressed. In this spirit, the twentieth century's doyen of consumerism, Henry Ford, made his best-known contribution to twentieth-century thought by announcing that, "History is more or less bunk."[3] Orwellian "designer babies" are now joining designer cars and clothes. New products in a new age are conditioned with a new philosophy and life-style, and we can dismiss the past.

Sadly, this subtle and alluring new thinking has greatly affected the church. Very few Christians have more than a scant knowledge of Church history or of the precious legacy of our Christian heritage handed down to us by our forefathers. The Charismatic movement is convinced, in step with the New Age movement, that the Lord is "doing a new thing." Renewal, it is thought, has rescued us from our past, from the unpleasantness, the strife and the bloodletting. The old conflicts over doctrine and error are no longer relevant nor is the

---

[3] Court record, *Chicago Tribune* libel case, 1919, quoted by Samuel T. Williamson, *Saturday Review*, January 22, 1955, as an entry in the book by George Seldes: *The Great Quotations*, 1983, Citadel Press, p. 253.

recollection of them acceptable. The mere use of the word *heresy*, a word that is so central in all of Church History, has been deemed divisive, as well as intolerant and unloving, and has nearly been eliminated from the modern versions of the Bible.[4] Today, the term *heresy* could hardly be more "politically incorrect."

Despite a wealth of evidence in Scripture to the contrary, many Christians, especially those in the Charismatic movement, are convinced that the Lord is "doing a new thing." The verse of Scripture often used for justifying this view is Isaiah 43:19, which says, *"Behold, I will do a new thing; now it shall spring forth; shall ye not know it? I will even make a way in the wilderness, and rivers in the desert."*

But the teaching of the Word of God again and again points us back to our past, to our roots and heritage, as well as reminding us that *"there is no new thing under the sun."*[5]

> *"And they that shall be of thee shall build the old waste places: thou shalt raise up the foundations of many generations; and thou shalt be called, The repairer of the breach, The restorer of paths to dwell in."*[6]

Isaac knew where to find the living water. *"And Isaac digged again the wells of water, which they had digged in the days of Abraham his father; for the Philistines had stopped them after the death of Abraham: and he called their names after the names by which his father had called them."*[7] *"For thou, O God, hast heard my vows: thou hast given me the heritage of those that fear thy name."*[8] And that great Scripture from Jeremiah: *"Thus saith the LORD, Stand ye in the ways, and see, and ask for the old paths, where is the good way, and walk therein, and ye shall find rest for your souls. But they said, We will not walk*

---

[4] The King James Version has the word *heresy* (or *heretic*) in five different books of the New Testament; the NIV, in only one (2 Peter 2:1).
[5] Ecclesiastes 1:9b
[6] Isaiah 58:12
[7] Genesis 26:18
[8] Psalm 61:5

therein."[9] New lamps are preferred to old.

Like Church, like nation, we feel that we have little or nothing to learn from so much that was unsavoury in our past, when tolerance and unity were in such short supply. There is no need to think or talk about the old battles for the faith, nor for our children to learn about them in school. We need no longer "walk in the old ways."

This was not so in previous centuries. Followers of Christ believed that it was essential to be well informed and knowledgeable about the past in order to maximise understanding of the Scriptures. They were convinced that without history they could not understand prophecy, and without Scripture they would have only a superficial understanding of history.

It is the belief of this writer that the future-orientation and modernising motive of the church and the world today has, to a considerable extent, stemmed from the conversion of most of the church from historicism to futurism—that is, from an historical to a futurist understanding of Bible prophecy.

As this book will attempt to show, the abandoning of the interpretation of Scripture as revealed in History has taken place only during the past one and a half centuries or so. Before then Christians were much less prone to speculate about future events, which they regarded as in the province of God alone. They were more inclined then to look back into history for the fulfilment of Bible prophecy, and to look forward in expectancy to the return of the Lord.

History may be seen as "His Story", the revealing throughout the Christian era of the work of the Holy Spirit in the world, through the church of the Lord Jesus Christ and through His Word. As such, its study was held in great respect, and gave much encouragement, most especially to those who placed their faith in Him.

> *"We have heard with our ears, O God, our fathers have told us, what work thou didst in their days, in the times of old."* [10]

---

[9] Jeremiah 6:16
[10] Psalm 44:1

therein."[9] New lamps are preferred to old.

Like Church, like nation, we feel that we have little or nothing to learn from so much that was unsavoury in our past, when tolerance and unity were in such short supply. There is no need to think or talk about the old battles for the faith, nor for our children to learn about them in school. We need no longer "walk in the old ways."

This was not so in previous centuries. Followers of Christ believed that it was essential to be well informed and knowledgeable about the past in order to maximise understanding of the Scriptures. They were convinced that without history they could not understand prophecy, and without Scripture they would have only a superficial understanding of history.

It is the belief of this writer that the future-orientation and modernising motive of the church and the world today has, to a considerable extent, stemmed from the conversion of most of the church from historicism to futurism—that is, from an historical to a futurist understanding of Bible prophecy.

As this book will attempt to show, the abandoning of the interpretation of Scripture as revealed in History has taken place only during the past one and a half centuries or so. Before then Christians were much less prone to speculate about future events, which they regarded as in the province of God alone. They were more inclined then to look back into history for the fulfilment of Bible prophecy, and to look forward in expectancy to the return of the Lord.

History may be seen as "His Story", the revealing throughout the Christian era of the work of the Holy Spirit in the world, through the church of the Lord Jesus Christ and through His Word. As such, its study was held in great respect, and gave much encouragement, most especially to those who placed their faith in Him.

> *"We have heard with our ears, O God, our fathers have told us, what work thou didst in their days, in the times of old."* [10]

---

[9] Jeremiah 6:16
[10] Psalm 44:1

29 October 2004 - Prime Minister Tony Blair and Foreign Secretary Jack Straw sign the European Constitution treaty under the dominant bronze statue of Pope Innocent X. (1645-49).

[Preface p.vi]

Photo courtesy of The Daily Mail web site: <http://www.dailymail.co.uk/pages/live/articles/news/news.html?in_article_id=323962&in_page_id=1770&ct=5>

US President George W. Bush, First Lady Laura Bush, and former US Presidents George Bush and Bill Clinton before the Catafalque of Pope John Paul II at his funeral on April 4, 2005.
"...*With whom the kings of the earth have committed fornication*..."
[Epilogue: 'Papal Rome and the EU' p179]

Photo from the Christian Today web page:
<http://www.christiantoday.com/news/church/last.mourners.queue.to.see.pope.john.paul.ii.before.funeral/461.htm>

Her Majesty, who at her Coronation promised "to maintain to the utmost of her power the Laws of God, the true profession of the Gospel and the Protestant Reformed religion established by law" visits Pope John Paul II, wearing black, which is symbolic of the Anglican Church's submission to the Church of Rome.

[Epilogue: 'The Monarchy in Peril' p.219]

Photo courtesy of <http://boston.com/news/specials/pope/galleries/retrospective?pg=10> The Boston Globe.

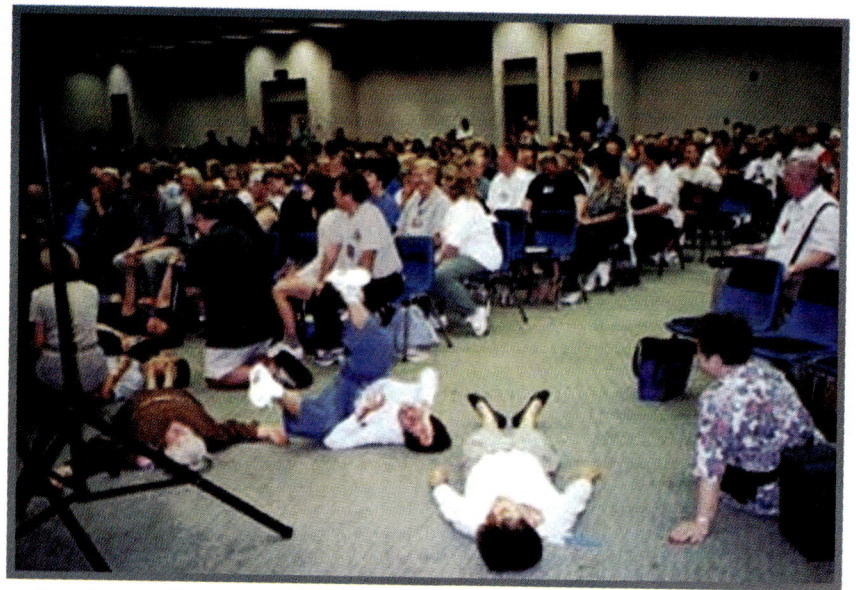

People at an Ecumenical Charismatic session, laughing hysterically, barking like dogs, grunting like pigs and rolling on the floor.
http://www.traditioninaction.org/bkreviews/A_012br_CloseUps_Guimaraes.htm

Charismatic priests from many different movements meet at the Vatican October 1990. Source: *Inside the Vatican*, March 1996
[Chapter 14: 'The Pentecostal and Charismatic Movements' p145]

PART I
HISTORY AND PROPHECY

Chapter 1

The Historical View of Prophecy and Antichrist

There are two great truths that stand out in the preaching that brought about the Protestant Reformation—the *"just shall live by faith"*[1] (not by the works of Romanism or any other religion) and "the Papacy is the Antichrist revealed in Scripture." It was a message for Christ and against Antichrist. The entire Reformation rested on this twofold testimony. In losing the second, unquestionably we have done injury to the first; ecumenical Christianity and "new evangelicalism" provide abundant testimony to this.

Iain Murray in his book *The Puritan Hope* described the Reformers as "unanimous in their belief" that the Papal system is both the *"man of sin"*[2] and the Babylonian whore of which Scripture forewarns. Rome was the great Antichrist, and so firmly did this belief become established that it was not until the nineteenth century that evangelicals seriously questioned it.[3]

Victorian Bible scholar Dr. Grattan Guinness ringingly declared, "Thousands of martyrdoms have sealed the testimony against the Papal antichrist, and on this testimony rests the Reformation. To reject it is to reject the foundation of the noblest and divinest work which has been wrought in this world since the day of Pentecost."[4]

The Protestant or Historical interpretation of prophecy views the

---

[1] Romans 1:17; Galatians 3:11; Hebrews 10:38 (and Habakkuk 2:4: *"the just shall live by his faith"*)
[2] 2 Thessalonians 2:3
[3] Iain Murray: *The Puritan Hope*, Banner of Truth.
[4] H.Grattan Guinness: *Romanism and the Reformation*, (First Edition 1887, p/b edition 1999), Our Inheritance Publications 1999, 130 South Coast Road, Peacehaven, East Sussex BN10 8RD

prophecies of Daniel, Paul, and John as fully and faithfully laying out the entire course of Christian history; and sees the Book of Revelation as a pre-figuration in detail of the chief events affecting the church and Christendom. "*A great cloud of witnesses*"[5] has given testimony to the correctness of this view. Wycliffe, Huss, Savonarola, Luther, Calvin, Melancthon, Zwingli, Tyndale, John Rogers, Latimer, Ridley, Hooper, Cranmer, John Foxe, Bunyan, the translators of the King James Bible, the men who published the Westminster and Baptist Confessions of Faith, Sir Isaac Newton, Wesley, Whitefield, Jonathan Edwards, Matthew Henry, and (more recently) Spurgeon, Bishop J.C. Ryle, Hudson-Taylor. and Dr. Martyn Lloyd-Jones—these men, among countless others, steeped and soaked in Scripture, recognised the office of the Papacy, the Vicar of Christ, as "*the man of sin*", the new face of the old paganism that is "*MYSTERY, BABYLON*"[6] in the Bible. They saw it all in the Scriptures; it was quickened to them. They saw the counterfeit bride, the Harlot that would be judged at the end of history. All of them were immensely burdened for the souls of those in bondage to such an evil and corrupt system and imprisoned in what Luther called "the Babylonian Captivity of the Church." They knew that it was their duty to view the Church of Rome as God views her and stand clearly against all her heresies. If they were right about this then, they are still right today. God's Word does not change, **and** Rome has since added to her many heresies.

What Is Historicism?

The Historicism Research Foundation has a helpful summary on historicism on its web site:
> "In brief, Historicism teaches that biblical predictions are being fulfilled throughout history and continue to be fulfilled today. The Book of Revelation is a pre-written history of the Church from the time of its writing to the future Second Advent of Christ, which shall usher in the new heaven and new earth."

---
[5] Hebrews 12:1
[6] Revelation 17:5

Historicists agree on the following unique concepts:
- The "Year-Day" principle of prophetic language defines a day of symbolic time as representing a year of actual historic time.
- The "Time, Times, and Half a Time", "3½ years", "1260 days", and "42 months" time period, which occurs seven times in Daniel and Revelation, is understood by Historicists to be fulfilled in history.
- All Historicists believe that the Papacy is that Antichrist, the Man of Sin of 2 Thessalonians 2, and the Beast of Revelation 13.
- Historicists generally agree that Revelation 9 speaks of the Muslim scourge which afflicted Christendom.[7]
- All Historicists agree that the book of Revelation prophesies the history of the Church from the Apostolic era to the future Second Advent of Jesus Christ.
- The Historicist interpretation was the standard interpretation from Wycliffe to Spurgeon (spanning 500 years) and is known as the Protestant interpretation, in distinct contrast to Preterism and Futurism which were Jesuit interpretations contrived during the Counter-Reformation.

Additionally, the Reformation confessions, including the Irish Articles (1615), the original Westminster Confession of Faith (1646), the Savoy Declaration (1658), and the London Baptist Confession (1688), have adopted the Historicist interpretation.[8]

The "Little Horn" of Daniel

The Reformers also identified the Papacy as the persecuting *"little horn"* of Daniel 7. John Wycliffe asked, "Why is it necessary in unbelief to look for another Antichrist?" In the seventh chapter of Daniel, Antichrist is forcefully described by a horn arising in the time of the fourth kingdom, which will *"wear out the saints of the most High."*[9] The Reformers believed, as do many Christians today, that

---
[7] See Chapter 6, "Islam in Prophecy."
[8] <http://www.historicism.net/>
[9] Daniel 7:25

the little horn of Daniel 7[10] had risen out of the fourth beast, the Roman Empire, and had sprung up among the ten kingdoms into which Imperial Rome was divided[11]. The little horn is *"diverse"* or different from the other kingdoms.[12] The Papacy proved to be different from the other kingdoms, claiming spiritual as well as temporal power. The little horn has *"a mouth speaking great things."*[13] Over the centuries the Papacy has repeatedly laid claim to rule the world as Christ's representative. It has also claimed to speak with infallibility on matters of faith and doctrine as well as continuing to insist, that "there is no salvation outside the Church of Rome."[14]

In Daniel's dream, the little horn *"had eyes"* and his *"look was more stout than his fellows."*[15] The Pope, who lays claim to the keys of the kingdom of heaven, is said to watch over more people than any other leader. He is responsible for the spiritual oversight of more than one billion people across the world today.

The little horn *"made war with the saints and prevailed against them"*[16] and would *"wear out the saints of the most High*

---

[10] Daniel 7:24 "And the ten horns out of this kingdom are ten kings that shall arise: and another shall rise after them; and he shall be diverse from the first, and he shall subdue three kings." Rev. E. B. Elliott, M.A., says: "I might cite three that were eradicated from before the Pope out of the list first given; viz., the Heruli under Odoacer, the Vandals, and the Ostrogoths." *Horae Apocalypticae,* Vol. III, p. 168, Note 1. London: 1862.

[11] These were the following: the Angles and Saxons in Britain; the Franks in all Gaul north and west of the River Moselle; the Alemanni in North Switzerland, Swabia, Alsace, and Lorraine; the Burgundians in west Switzerland and the valleys of the Rhone and Saone in southeast Gaul; the Visigoths in southwest Gaul and Spain; the Suevi in that part of Spain which is now Portugal; the Ostrogoths in Pannonia, what is now Austria; the Lombards in Noricum, between the Ostrogoths and the Alemanni; the Heruli in Italy; and the Vandals in North Africa, with capital at Carthage.

[12] Daniel 7:7,19,23-24

[13] Daniel 7:8

[14] Boniface VIII: Unam Sanctum

[15] Daniel 7:20

[16] Daniel 7:21

...... and they shall be given into his hand until a time and times and the dividing of time."[17] This part of the prophecy was comprehensively fulfilled over the many centuries of Papal Rome's ruthless persecution of Bible-believing Christians—through the Dark Ages, during the Inquisition, and right up to the French Revolution. Evangelicals, frequently referred to as belonging to "fundamentalist sects", are persecuted in Roman Catholic countries today.

The little horn would *"think to change times and laws."*[18] The Papacy has changed both human laws and divine laws. It has annulled and abrogated the laws of kings and emperors and, relatively recently, in 1870, declared itself infallible in defiance of Scripture. It has presumed to annul marriages, too, and to ordain a celibate "Priesthood" in place of the biblical model of married pastors. Not only laws but also times have been changed. The calendar of Pope Gregory has replaced the calendar of Emperor Justinian. There are all the many different "Saints'" days, and we have both Christ's Mass, Christmas, to celebrate our Lord's birth and the pagan goddess Astarte's festival, Easter,[19] for His death and resurrection.

1260 "Year-days"

In prophetic language, a day of symbolic time represents a year of actual, historic time.[20] The "Time, Times, and Half a Time" (also rendered "3^1/$_2$ years" or "42 months") time period, which occurs seven times in Daniel and Revelation, is understood by Historicists to be fulfilled in history. Futurists interpret this as a literal 3^1/$_2$ years. Historicists, utilising the "Year-day" principle, interpret this as 1260 years (one month being equal to thirty days).

The interval from the Pope-exalting decree of the emperor Phocas, AD 607, to the Revolution of 1848 and formal deposition of the Pope, on 8 February 1849, spans 1260 years or 3^1/$_2$ day-years (with 1260 lunar years passing from the Papal Decree of Phocas to

---

[17] Daniel 7:25
[18] Daniel 7:25
[19] See Chapter 10, "Bible Verse Comparisons", Comparison Number 1.
[20] Ezekiel 4:6

the Revolution of 1830).

The Man of Sin and the Mystery of Iniquity

The picture that emerged from Daniel's dream was clear for those guided by the Holy Spirit at the time of the Reformation, as it had been to the early Christians. There seems to have been a remarkable consensus of understanding among the church fathers as well as the Reformers. According to the *Encyclopaedia Britannica*, during those first centuries, "Christians universally believed that the power that was retarding the revelation of the Antichrist was the Roman Empire."[21]

They equated the little horn with the *"man of sin"* and the Antichrist. They knew that *"the mystery of iniquity"* already at work in Paul's day[22] would follow the fall of the Roman Empire. It was widely understood that the Apostle, writing to the Thessalonians, wrote **mysteriously**, that *"he[23] who letteth will now let, until he be taken out of the way"*, **because** he was referring to Imperial Rome. Had he been more explicit and spelled out his belief, that the Empire which was restraining the Antichrist would fall at some indeterminate time, he would surely have brought the Christians, especially the Thessalonians, into conflict with the ruling power.

The following quotes[24] from the exposition of chapter 2 of 2 Thessalonians by prominent early Church Fathers illustrate the general Christian identifying of the restraining power.

- Irenaeus (AD 130-202) - On the dismemberment of the Empire now in existence [the Roman Empire] the catastrophe will occur.
- Tertullian (AD 160-250) - What is the restraining power? What but the Roman State?

---

[21] "Antichrist", in the Encyclopaedia Britannica, 1961 ed., vol. 2, p. 60.
[22] 2 Thessalonians 2:3-7
[23] Some new Bible versions, including the *New King James Version* translate this (2 Thessalonians 2:7) as *He* (not *he*), which clearly means the Holy Spirit, thereby allowing only for a futurist interpretation and a pre-tribulation rapture.
[24] Russell R. Standish and Colin D. Standish: *The Rapture and the Antichrist*, Hartland Publications, Rapidan, VA 22733 USA

- Lactantius of Gaul (A.D. 240-320) - Beseech the God of Heaven that the Roman State might be preserved, lest more speedily than we supposed the hateful tyrant [the man of sin] should come.
- Chrysostom (A.D. 345-407) - As Rome succeeded Greece, so Antichrist is to succeed Rome.
- Jerome (A.D. 342-420) - All ecclesiastical writers have delivered to us that when Rome is to be destroyed, ten kings will divide the Roman world among them and then will be revealed the Man of Sin.[25]

Others such as Augustine of Hippo (A.D 354-430), Cyril of Jerusalem, Theodoret of Antioch, and Hippolytus of Rome all believed that the antichrist would emerge with the fall of the Roman Empire. Nearly fifteen hundred years later, even Roman Catholic convert, Cardinal John Henry Newman, felt obliged to admit that "the withholding power, mentioned in 2 Thessalonians 2:6 was the Roman Empire. I grant this, for all the ancient writers speak of it."[26]

---

[25] All five quotes from The Church Fathers are referenced in Samuel J. Cassels, Christ and Antichrist, Philadelphia Presbyterian Board of Publication. 1846
[26] Cardinal J.H. Newman, *Discussions*, 49

Chapter 2

Futurism – Leapfrogging History – The Wiles of the Devil

"For we wrestle not against flesh and blood, but against principalities, against powers, against the rulers of the darkness of this world, against spiritual wickedness in high places."[1]

How then was the historical understanding of Scriptural prophecy lost to so much of the church?

Futurism, cleverly devised by Spanish Jesuit scholarship, was able to accomplish this in a fashion that is difficult not to admire. Such an accomplished counterfeit, which would involve a counterfeit church, a counterfeit bible and a counterfeit prophecy of antichrist, may have been foreseen by the Apostle John, "... *and when I saw her I wondered with great admiration.*"[2]

It is important to realise that scholars—both Roman Catholic as well as Protestant—have agreed as to the Jesuit origin of the Futurist school of prophecy. The Roman Catholic "Truth Society" has described the Futurist School as that "founded by the Jesuit Ribera in 1591, which looks for Antichrist, Babylon, and a rebuilt temple in Jerusalem, at the end of the Christian Dispensation."[3]

The second school of interpretation—the Praeterist (or Preterist) scheme—has been defined by the same Roman Catholic Truth Society as that, "founded by the Jesuit Alcasar in 1614, and

---

[1] Ephesians 6:12
[2] Revelation 17: 6b
[3] Rev. G.S. Hitchcock, DD (Doctor of Sacred Scripture, Rome): *The Beasts and the Little Horn,* November 1911

explaining the book of Revelation by the fall of Jerusalem in 70 AD or by the fall of pagan Rome in 410 AD."[4]

Both systems of interpretation, originated by the Counter-Reformation, succeeded in divorcing the *antichrist*, revealed as *the man of sin, the little horn*, and *the Mother of Harlots*, from the here and now and from mediaeval and modern history. Between them these two schemes manage to avoid the entire period of more than fifteen centuries of the Papacy. They do so by stopping short of its beginnings in the fifth century and then by projecting forward from today into the unknown future.

Futurism denies that the dynasty of Popes is the Antichrist and points instead to a future individual world ruler at the end of the age. It thus postpones most of the prophetic predictions of Scripture including almost all the Book of Revelation into a fragment of time in the indefinite future. Ribera and later Futurist scholars determined that Daniel's seventieth week should be separated from the first sixty-nine and projected forward to the end of time, thus establishing "the futurist gap."[5]

If we were to look ahead to a world leader who is yet to appear, our expectancy would inevitably be governed by the shaping of this event and not to the coming of the Lord. The Reformers and like-minded Christians before and since were described as "those who love the coming of the Lord." If we are to live in a manner that Scripture clearly requires, in the daily expectation of the Lord's return[6], how can it be that there is supposed to be so much unfulfilled prophecy in the Bible?

The result of this, inevitably, is that our guard is dropped. Vigilance is rare and few watchmen are at their posts.

Today's extraordinary paradox is that so many in the church say they believe in the imminent Second Coming, and yet interpret the prophecy of the Antichrist, which **must be fulfilled** before the Lord

---

[4] Ibid.

[5] See further explanation under the subheading "The Seventy Weeks" in this chapter.

[6] The Lord told His disciples, "...*be ye also ready: for in such an hour as ye think not the Son of man comes*" (Matthew 24:44), and the Apostle Paul told the Thessalonians: "... *let us not sleep, as do others; but let us watch ...* (Thessalonians 5:6).

returns, to take place sometime in the indefinite future.[7] This ambivalent thinking surely has much to do with the decline of holiness in the church today.

The Antichrist in the Historicist Protestant understanding is the longstanding spiritual enemy of the people of God, not discernible to the world but clearly recognised in Scripture and in history. Praeterism's Antichrist pre-dates the fall of the Roman Empire, is an individual persecuting ruler, and has often been identified as Nero. Futurism looks forward to the end of the age for Antichrist's appearance as a world dictator who will covenant with the Jews and then persecute them and the rest of the world in the great tribulation. The futurist system set out expressly to shield the Papacy from the identification of Antichrist and to counter the established historical view.

The historical view sees the prophecies in Daniel, the letters of Paul and John, and the Revelation as fully and faithfully laying out the entire course of Christian history. In contrast, the Praeterist view sees them as having been fulfilled before the fall of the Roman Empire, while the Futurist view sees them as dealing with a new scenario, within a future fragment of time at its close, after what has become known as "the futurist gap."

The Seventy Weeks

As the new Futurist system evolved during the nineteenth century, the fragment of time predicted as the period of the great tribulation became identified in Scripture with "Daniel's seventieth week." To this end, this week of seven day-years is detached from the previous sixty-nine weeks and pitched forward to a time still in the future, revealing "the futurist gap." Ribera, the father of Jesuit Futurism, had postulated this in his scheme. For Ribera, "prophecy stopped with the fall of the Roman Empire only to resume at the time of the

---

[7] The Futurist Pre-Tribulation Rapture theory provides for the departure of the church before the world ruler antichrist makes his entrance to begin a seven-year tribulation period. Dispensational Futurism is not to be confused with historic pre-millennialism, which believes in a visible reign of Christ in glory on earth with the risen saints for one thousand years, but not a two-stage second coming begun by a "secret rapture" (nowhere to be found in the New Testament).

Rapture. It was as though God put a giant rubber band on the Messianic time measure ... this is exactly the scenario used by Hal Lindsey and a multitude of other prophecy teachers."[8] This supposed gap of around two thousand years or more is a concept which, apart from Ribera, had found very little support throughout all of church history until a South American Jesuit's theories were taken up and developed at the time of the Oxford Movement. The gap has no Scriptural support, seems to be arbitrary and illogical and stretches the meaning of the Hebrew translation into grammatical inconsistency.

The modern versions' translations of Scripture undoubtedly favour the futurist gap theory. A comparative study reveals how the great prophetic passage in Daniel 9:24-27 calls for an entirely different interpretation in the new Bibles—relating to both Christ and Antichrist, rather than, as indicated in the Authorised Version, to Christ alone. In fact, the eclipse of the historical interpretation of prophecy was, very likely, a determining motive in the move to replace the Authorised Bible in the nineteenth century. This consideration and the wide disparity in the translation of key passages, between the Authorised Version following the received or majority text, and the new versions with their favoured selections from differing eclectic Greek texts, is the subject of much of the second part of this book.

Seventy, in Scripture, is a number of special significance, signifying completeness. The children of Israel, the family of Jacob that went into Egypt were **seventy**.[9] The Lord commanded Moses to appoint **seventy** elders to help him bear the burden of the people.[10] He sent out **seventy** other disciples also ahead of His own ministry.[11] He commanded his disciples to forgive each other "*seventy times seven times*".[12] The Babylonian captivity was to last **seventy** years.[13] Then Daniel, who understood by Jeremiah the expiration of the seventy years of the captivity, was employed to make known to the church another more glorious release, at the end

---

[8] Robert Caringola, *Seventy Weeks: The Historical Alternative*, p.35.
[9] Exodus 1:5
[10] Numbers 11:16
[11] Luke 10:1
[12] Matthew 18:22
[13] Jeremiah 25:11,12

of seventy, not years, but weeks of years.[14]

> *"Seventy weeks are determined upon thy people and upon thy holy city, to finish the transgression, and to make an end of sins, and to make reconciliation for iniquity, and to bring in everlasting righteousness, and to seal up the vision and prophecy, and to anoint the most Holy.*
>
> *"Know therefore and understand, that from the going forth of the commandment to restore and to build Jerusalem unto the Messiah the Prince shall be seven weeks, and threescore and two weeks: the street shall be built again, and the wall, even in troublous times.*
>
> *"And after threescore and two weeks shall Messiah be cut off, but not for himself: and the people of the prince that shall come shall destroy the city and the sanctuary; and the end thereof shall be with a flood, and unto the end of the war desolations are determined.*
>
> *"And he shall confirm the covenant with many for one week: and in the midst of the week he shall cause the sacrifice and the oblation to cease, and for the overspreading of abominations he shall make it desolate, even until the consummation, and that determined shall be poured upon the desolate."*[15]

This great prophecy of completeness is centred on Jesus Christ and His cross and was completely and perfectly fulfilled when, after three and a half years of His ministry, He was cut off in death in the middle of the seventieth week of seven years. He confirmed the covenant with His blood of the new covenant (testament), finished transgression and made an end of sins, caused the sacrifice and oblation to cease with His complete and perfect once-for-all sacrifice, reconciled His people to Himself, brought in everlasting righteousness imputed to the believer, and sealed up the vision and the prophecy at the precise time in history defined by Daniel. The

---

[14] Daniel 9:2
[15] Daniel 9:24-27

confirmation of the *covenant "upon thy* [Daniel's] *people"* for the week of seven years was fulfilled by the Lord's ministry before the cross and the apostles' ministry for three and a half years afterwards[16], specifically proclaiming the gospel to *"the lost sheep of the house of Israel."*[17]

The remainder of this prophecy of the complete work of God is fulfilled finally with another "seventy"—AD 70—when the people of the prince that shall come (the predicted Messiah) will destroy Jerusalem and the Temple, in judgement, with a vast Roman army (with a "flood"). The Son of God lamented as he looked ahead once more to the destruction and desolation of His own—as a hen her errant chicks—knowing what lay ahead. Again and again the rebellious children of Jerusalem had been chastised for their transgressions by the invasions of foreign armies. The Lord of Hosts, the Prince, was the One who sent them. The great tribulation of that time would be carried out once more by the pagan armies of the World Empire of the day. This time, those armies would come from Rome. In Old Testament times the terrible judgements of the Lord had been carried out by Assyria, Babylon, and neighbouring nations. This was *"the abomination of desolation, spoken of by Daniel the prophet,"* the Roman host of idol-worshipping Gentiles who would *"stand in the holy place"*[18] in Jerusalem, which would be *"compassed with armies"* and from which believers would be enabled to make their escape.

---

[16] No seven-year agreement was to be made by the Antichrist with the Jews to enable them to rebuild the temple and offer sacrifices which will be broken after three and a half years so that the sacrifices cease—no "futurist gap."

[17] John 1:31, Matthew 10:5-6

[18] Matthew 24:15,16

Chapter 3

The Counter-Reformation – The Source of the Futurist View of Prophecy

The Roman Catholic institution had been rocked and shaken by that great movement of the Spirit, as the new printing presses poured out Bibles, books, and tracts, and the great truths of the gospel swept across the Western World. Salvation by grace alone through faith alone, the supremacy of the Bible, and the church's identification of the Papacy as the Antichrist revealed in Scripture, were transforming the religious and political map of Europe. Germany, the Scandinavian countries, Holland, Switzerland, and England had become Protestant. France, Poland, Bavaria, Austria, and Belgium were swinging that way as well. In consternation the Papacy looked around in every direction for help. The Lord, in His mysterious sovereignty, allowed the desperate prayers of the Roman Church to be answered in the person of the remarkable man who was to lead the Counter-Reformation, Ignatius Loyola, born in the very same year as Martin Luther (1483).

Martin Luther[1] and Ignatius Loyola[2]

---

[1] Illustration courtesy of What Saith the Scripture: <http://www.whatsaiththescripture.com/Stories/The.Conversion.of.Luther.html>
[2] Illustration courtesy of Loyola University Chicago: <http://www.luc.edu/jesuit/ignatius.bio.html>

The Council of Trent (1545-1564) was called to take drastic measures to deal with the crisis. The Jesuit Order, established by Loyola in 1540 and instituted to prosecute the Counter-Reformation, dominated the Council. Accommodation or compromise with the spread of Protestantism was not on the agenda. Anthony Froude, Regius Professor of History at Oxford University in the 1890s, described the Council:

> "It met no longer with a pretense of desiring peace, but to equip and renovate the Roman Communion for the reconquest of its lost dominions. It met to split nations into factions; to set subjects against their sovereigns and sovereigns against subjects. The history of Europe for a hundred years was the history of the efforts of the Church, with open force or secret conspiracy, with all the energy, base or noble, which passion or passionate enthusiasm could inspire, to crush and annihilate its foes. No means came amiss to it, sword or stake, torture chamber or assassin's dagger. The effects of the Church's working were seen in ruined nations and smoking cities, in human beings tearing one another to pieces like raging maniacs, and the honour of the Creator of the world befouled by the hideous crimes committed in His Name."[3]

The Jesuits, founded and led by Ignatius Loyola, were utterly single-minded in their determination to re-establish the divine rule of Rome and bring about the infallibility of the Pope. As author Benjamin Wilkinson has suggested:

> "Ignatius Loyola came forward and may well have said in substance to the Pope: 'Let the Augustinians continue to provide monasteries of retreat for contemplative minds; let the Benedictines give themselves up to the field of literary endeavour; let the Dominicans retain their responsibility for maintaining the Inquisition; but we, the Jesuits, will capture the colleges and the universities. We will gain control of instruction in law, medicine, science, education, and so weed

---

[3] Anthony Froude: Lectures on the Council of Trent, p. 335.

out from all books of instruction, anything injurious to Roman Catholicism. We will mold the thoughts and ideas of the youth. We will enroll ourselves as Protestant preachers and college professors in the different Protestant faiths. Sooner or later, we will undermine the authority of the Greek New Testament of Erasmus, and also of those Old Testament productions, which have dared to raise their heads against tradition. And thus will we undermine the Protestant Reformation.'"[4]

Even all of this would not be enough, however. The printing and widespread distribution of the Word of God was rendering persecution less effective, and sometimes even counter-productive. *"All that walk godly in Christ Jesus shall be persecuted;"*[5]; *"Precious in the sight of the Lord is the death of His saints."*[6] The newly published Scriptures encouraged true Christians greatly, showing plainly the great privilege accorded to servants of Christ, being chosen to suffer for the Master, and showing, too, the source of the persecution. *"And I saw the woman drunken with the blood of the saints, and with the blood of the martyrs of Jesus..."*[7] Luther's *Babylonian Captivity of the Church* underlined the truth revealed throughout Scripture of the identity of *"MYSTERY, BABYLON THE GREAT, THE MOTHER OF HARLOTS AND ABOMINATIONS OF THE EARTH."*[8]

The Battle for God's Word

Pursuing and punishing "heretics" (true believers) was counter-productive. It was clear that the Counter-Reformation needed to take on the very Word of God itself. The Jesuit Bible of 1582, the *Douay-Rheims Version,* brought out to combat the much loved *Tyndale Version,* like the Roman Catholic Spanish Armada six years later, succeeded in making little impact on a Protestant people nurtured on the solid food of the pure Word and utterly convinced of

---

[4] Our Authorised Bible Vindicated: Benjamin G. Wilkinson, Ph.D.
[5] 2 Timothy 3:12
[6] Psalm 116:15
[7] Revelation 17:6a
[8] Revelation 17:5

the identity of Antichrist. The Jesuits concluded that it was essential to devise a counter-system of interpretation that would nullify the revelation in Scripture of the Antichrist identity of the Papacy. However, this was easier said than done. The Word of God, providentially preserved through the centuries, was jealously guarded by His saints.

Harvard Bible scholar, Edward F. Hills, wrote about the cosmic spiritual warfare waged throughout the Christian era in graphic terms:

> "The history of the New Testament text is the history of conflict between God and Satan. Soon after the New Testament books were written, Satan corrupted their texts by means of heretics and misguided critics whom he had raised up. However, these assaults on the integrity of the Word were repulsed by the providence of God, who guided true believers to reject these false readings and to preserve the true text in the majority of New Testament manuscripts. At the end of the Middle Ages this true text was produced in print and became the *Textus Receptus* (the Received Text), the foundation of the glorious Protestant Reformation."

> "But Satan was not defeated. Instead, he staged a clever comeback by means of 'naturalistic New Testament textual criticism'. Old corrupt manuscripts, which had been discarded by the God-guided usage of the believing Church, were brought out of their hiding-places and re-instated. Through naturalistic textual criticism, also the fatal logic of unbelief was set in motion. Not only the text but also every aspect of the Bible and of Christianity came to be regarded as a purely natural phenomenon. And today thousands of Bible-believing Christians are falling into this devil's trap through their use of modern-speech versions, which are based on naturalistic textual criticism and so introduce the reader to the naturalistic point of view. By means of these modern-speech versions Satan deprives his victims of both the shield of faith and the sword of the Spirit and leaves them unarmed and helpless before the terrors and temptations of this modern apostate world. What a clever comeback! How Satan must be hugging himself with glee over the seeming success of

his devilish strategy."[9]

The critics that Dr. Hills refers to were the mainly German "higher critics" of the Counter-Reformation who attacked the Received Text and exalted the Alexandrian text. Among these critics were Sclhleiermacher, Griesbach, Wellhausen, Tischendorf, and Tregelles. They were the new Gnostics[10] who helped build the shaky foundations of the bible intended to replace the Authorised Version.

The adoption of the Futurist system of prophecy in the period leading up to the 1881 Revised Edition of the Bible undoubtedly increased the pressure in the demand for revision. Spurred on by Newman and other leaders of the Oxford Movement, the Anglo-Catholic led Revising Committee were intent on assisting the re-interpretation of great prophetic passages of antichrist such as the Apostle Paul's description of the *man of sin* of 2 Thessalonians 2. Clearly the proposed new bible was designed to less readily lend itself to the Protestant reformed prophetic portrayal of the Papal Antichrist.

Futurism Aided by Modern Versions of the Bible

The Futurist interpretation of the Bible has gained further currency and authority as a result of the modern versions that have proliferated during this last century. The many variations among different renderings of the prophetic passages of Scripture have inevitably caused doubt about their true meaning. When in doubt, it is natural to avoid controversy. The historical view, that the Papacy is clearly revealed in Scripture, is controversial. Almost without exception, the translators of the new bibles have held to a Futurist theology. Their translations inevitably reflect this. The familiar wording of the Authorised Bible has been replaced in most modern versions to an extent that makes it difficult to recognise the "man of sin" or the "little horn" of Daniel as did our forefathers in Christ. As part two of this book will seek to show, the new translations or modern versions, in marked contrast to the Authorised Version, have so altered the

---

[9] Edward F. Hills: *The King James Version Defended*, 1984, 4th edition, reprinted 1988, Christian Research Press.
[10] Alan O'Reilly: *O Biblios*, Covenant Publishing Ltd.

Scriptures identifying the Papacy and Romanism, that the traditional Historicist and Protestant view is difficult to sustain. No wonder so few evangelicals hold to it today!

This impoverishes true history. Although the Bible clearly directs us in many different ways to *"remember the things of old"*, we rarely do so today. *"One generation shall praise thy works to another, and shall declare thy mighty acts,"*[11] wrote the psalmist, but our magnificent Christian heritage is virtually discarded. Many of the great deeds of God of the past, including the deliverances in England of 1588 and 1688 and the selfless sacrifice of countless martyrs of the faith, have become an embarrassment for those who now wish to offer and receive a "love gospel" unhindered by uncomfortable truths.

---

[11] Psalm 145:4

Chapter 4

Futurism Devised across the Centuries by the Jesuits

The Futurist interpretation of prophecy was originally propounded by the Spanish Jesuit scholar Francisco Ribera and was developed by the eminent Jesuit "Saint" and apologist, Cardinal Bellarmine, at the end of the sixteenth century. Ribera's ingenious scheme was part of the spiritual counter-attack known as the Counter-Reformation, the spearhead of Rome's fight-back against the growing threat posed by the Protestant Reformation.

The sixteenth-century Futurist theories of Ribera, which projected forward all but the first five chapters of the Book of Revelation into the future, and pointed forward to an individual and political Antichrist, found little favour with Protestants for approaching two and a half centuries. However, the Jesuit theories had laid the groundwork for the radical departure from the widely accepted historicist view.

Ribera's ideas were further developed in a book, first published at the beginning of the nineteenth century, which has exercised inestimable influence on the church right up to the present day. The book, which was written in Spanish, was called *The Coming of the Messiah in Glory and Majesty*. It laid the basis for "dispensationalist futurism" and originated the theory of the two-stage Second Coming. It was written under the name Ben Ezra, who represented himself as a scholarly Jewish convert to Christ seeking enlightenment for his Jewish brethren.

Although the Church of Rome distanced itself from Ben Ezra, and even banned his book in some countries, it seems highly probable that this was a deception perpetrated by the Jesuits, comparable in ingenuity and scope with any of the many elaborate wiles and schemes that have been devised in the long history of the Papal institution. It may be helpful and instructive to give but one other important example in history of this kind of deception.

For four centuries before the Reformation, the Church of Rome built up her pretensions on what are known as the "Decretals of Isidore", a fictitious collection of Bulls and Rescripts supposedly issued by the Bishops of Rome during the first three centuries of the Christian era. The decretals were said to evidence the authority of the popes of that early age. They were supposed to represent the fruit of the researches of Isidore of Seville, one of the most learned bishops of the ninth century, given to the world two centuries after Isidore's death. In the general ignorance that characterised that "Golden Age" of the Church of Rome, the Decretals were everywhere accepted as authentic, and men beheld with awe the power wielded by Peter and his immediate "successors." During the Reformation the genuine history of these centuries was examined, the forgery was discovered, and the "Decretals of Isidore" exposed, vying with "The Donation of Constantine" as the most audacious imposture ever palmed off on an unsuspecting world. Yet for four centuries they did their work, and Rome reaped the benefit.[1]

Rabbi Juan Josafat Ben Ezra was in fact the assumed name of Emmanuel Lacunza, a Chilean of Spanish descent. He was a Jesuit, who joined the order at the age of sixteen and had risen within it to be a zealous superintendent of the Noviciates, before embarking on the task of writing the four volumes of *The Coming of the Messiah in Glory and Majesty*. Had not his true identity been discovered and much later been made known through his untimely and mysterious death, the Christian world would have continued to believe, as many still do, that he was a Messianic Jew. With the Jews of his day marginalised by the Roman Church, this identity was ideal for gaining acceptance from Protestants. There can be little doubt that it was for the consumption of Protestants that this elaborate Jesuitical deception was prepared. To get them to begin dabbling in the theory of a future Antichrist was worth a vast amount of time and labour to the Church of Rome. The Protestants would

---

[1] Duncan McDougall, M.A. *'The Rapture of the Saints'*, <http://www.historicist.com/articles2/saints.htm>

have been impressed by the exclusion of the book by Rome and its listing among banned books, which were very often their favoured reading. Apart from the sheer scope and breadth of scholarship of the book, they also may have been perhaps cleverly won over by aspects of Ben Ezra's eschatology that were in step with the beliefs of the Reformers, but out of step with Rome. For example, Lacunza's scheme postulated not a single individual, but a world-wide organisation, as Antichrist.

In 1816, fifteen years after his death, the Diplomatic Agent of the Republic of Buenos Aires published the first complete Spanish edition of Lacunza's work in London. Ben Ezra's real identity, that being a son of the Mother Church from Chile rather than a Jewish Rabbi, must have been known to the publishers, but at that time had to be concealed in Protestant England. An English edition of Lacunza's book translated by Edward Irving appeared in 1827. Irving, described as the forerunner of the charismatic movement[2], was a highly intelligent and zealous Scottish preacher whose once Presbyterian congregation applied to join the Church of Rome and developed into the "Catholic Apostolic Church." Irving learned Spanish in record time in order to translate and publish Lacunza's book. In doing so he became an ardent advocate of Lacunza's prophetic views and with flaming oratory preached the Secret Rapture and a **second** Second Coming of Christ with His saints in glory after the seven-year reign of Antichrist. This is thought to be the first time in the whole history of the church that anyone taught that the saints would be "caught up" or raptured **secretly**. It had not previously been considered part of the true faith once given to the saints.

The idea was originated in *The Coming of the Messiah in Glory and Majesty,* the manuscript of which was published in London, Spain, Mexico, and Paris between 1811 and 1826. Lacunza had written, "When the Lord returns from heaven to earth upon His coming forth from heaven, and much before His arrival at the earth, He will give His orders, and send forth His command as King and God omnipotent: with a shout ('by the order') with the voice of the archangel, and with the trump of God. At this voice of the Son of God, those who shall hear it, shall forthwith arise, as saith

---

[2] Arnold Dallimore: *The Life of Edward Irving*, Banner of Truth.

the evangelist Saint John 'those who hear shall live.'"[3] Here may be found for the first time, with the selective use of Scripture, the concept of "the secret rapture" (the saints to meet their Lord in the air without the world knowing), perhaps prompting the Voice from heaven (and the ecstatic utterance of a young girl named Margaret McDonald) that is said to have commanded Irving to begin preaching the "secret rapture of the saints." Then follows the appearance of the individual world ruler, "the Antichrist", who will swiftly emerge as the world dictator and revive the old Roman Empire as a ten-nation confederacy. He will make a covenant with the Jews, involving the rebuilding of the temple and the reinstitution of animal sacrifices and promising peace and safety; then break it and launch the great tribulation prior to the return of Christ with his saints. Thus, at odds with Scripture, Christ's second (or third) coming is dated, and the day will be known to the world several years in advance.

The Seed is Sown

The Diplomatic Agent made a copy of Irving's translation of Lacunza's book, with its Futurist elements, available to the library of the Archbishop of Canterbury. In 1826, Dr. S.R. Maitland, the scholarly librarian to the Archbishop, published the first of a series of tracts on futurist prophecy, *An Enquiry* into the generally accepted year-day view of the 1260 days of Daniel and Revelation. Probably not realising that he was advancing the theories of a Jesuit, he adopted the ideas of Rabbi Ben Ezra, a Jewish convert, as it seems likely he believed Lacunza to be. He also adopted the concept of a future personal Antichrist, a world ruler, again presumably unwittingly, from the earlier work of Ribera.

The *Catholic Emancipation Act* was enacted in 1829, and the Jesuits were again active, having been allowed back into England. In 1833 the Tractarian or Oxford Movement was launched. Dr. Maitland's publications and those of William Burgh and Anglican Professor James Todd, both members of the faculty of Trinity College, Dublin, provided the spiritual fire-power and the theological foundations needed to help launch the new movement. Its leaders included John Henry Newman, who building on the foundations laid

---

[3] Juan Josafat Ben Ezra: *The Coming of the Messiah in Glory and Majesty*, 1833, William Curry Junior & Co., pp. 10-11.

by Maitland and especially by Todd's large treatise, wrote on the future Antichrist in several of his Oxford Tracts. He and fellow Futurists Sir Robert Anderson and Reverend Michael Baxter were able to argue that the tracts showed that Protestants had unjustly represented the Papacy as the Antichrist of Scripture and that the Reformation had gone much too far. The new reading of Scripture confirmed them in their partiality towards ritualism and Romanism. The sense of injustice and outrage aimed at the Reformed faith spurred them on in adopting Roman Catholic doctrine and practice as well as blinding them to its errors.

The Brethren, newly formed in Dublin in 1827, and in particular J.N. Darby, one of the founding fathers of the movement, an Anglican High Churchman who had been "rocked in the cradle of Tractarianism,"[4] also acclaimed the "great discovery" of Maitland and Irving as a divine revelation. Significantly, "J.N. Darby and Edward Irving both attended lengthy meetings on the study of Bible Prophecy at Powerscourt House in Ireland. Topics discussed included the 1260 day-years, the gifts of the Spirit, Antichrist, and, very probably, the secret rapture that would precede Antichrist's appearance."[5]

Directed by Darby's Tractarian background and instincts, the early Brethren, based in Plymouth, outdid the Oxford Movement in the publishing of tracts, many of which were directed to the foretelling of future events, most particularly the exciting prospect of the secret pre-tribulation rapture. Scottish Hebrew and Gaelic scholar Duncan McDougall in his booklet *The Rapture of the Saints* described what took place:

> "'Here was a tree to be desired to make one wise,' the foretelling of future events which Christians could never have discovered for themselves by the most diligent study of the Bible. This detailed story of the coming Antichrist and all that he was to do had all the subtle attraction of clairvoyance

---

[4] Duncan McDougall, M.A. *The Rapture of the Saints*, <http://www.historicist.com/articles2/saints.htm>

[5] Leroy Edwin Froom: *The Prophetic Faith of Our Fathers Vol.3*, Review and Herald Publishing
  Association, Takoma Park, Washington, DC.

or crystal-gazing. It enabled people to read between the lines of their Bible many things that their own ministers had never discovered, and so to become wise, very wise, above that which is written. It placed them on a pedestal from which they could look down on the very pastors who had led them to Christ."[6]

In this fashion the carefully devised seeds of Futurism, patiently planted by the Counter-Reformation over a period of more than two centuries, had grown into a theological tree with many heretical branches, which, by and large, deny the fulfilment of prophecy until right at the very end of the Christian era. History, foretold by God the Holy Spirit, had been declared redundant by the preaching and teaching of Irving, Maitland, and Darby, and before them by the scholarship of the Jesuits Ribera, Bellamine, and Lacunza. As former Secretary of the Protestant Truth Society and author Albert Close wrote in 1916, "... So the Jesuits have enticed our Theological professors and the Plymouth Brethren to fire high over the head of the great Antichrist, at their two mythical Antichrists; one in the past, the Praeterist, the other in the future, the Futurist Antichrist. Between these two schools the whole Christian Ministry has been mixed up, and is practically sitting on the fence. Few ministers now preach from Daniel or the Revelation."[7]

By no means did all of the early Brethren, the majority of whom were ardent and committed Christians, embrace the new theories. Many were carried along by the tide of enthusiasm for the new teaching for a time, but changed their view when they learned of its origins. This was the experience of the eminent Greek scholar, S. P. Tregelles, who said of the secret rapture, "... it came not from Holy Scripture, but from that, which falsely pretended to be the Spirit of God." He was later excommunicated from the Brethren.

Given the impact of the theological colleges and the wider church of the new Higher Criticism in the climate of advancing humanism and Darwinism, it is not surprising that, in the years that followed, the new understanding of Bible prophecy spread as swiftly as it did. Early in the twentieth century, the popular Scofield Reference Bible,

---

[6] Duncan McDougall: *The Rapture of the Saints*.
[7] Albert Close: *Antichrist and his Ten Kingdoms*

which like so many other bibles today is filled with scholarly footnotes, incorporated Futurist theology into its Dispensationalist scheme in such a convincing way that few were able to distinguish it all from the inspired Scriptures. Dispensationalist Futurism has subsequently spread widely in evangelical circles, especially among Charismatics. As *Evangelical Times* writer John C. J. Waite has pointed out, "Dispensationalism has propagated the notion that the Old Testament Prophets have nothing to say about the church; that in fact they have only to do with Israel. The Church Age is regarded by some as a kind of parenthesis. Even those who do not accept the dispensational theory (of the Bible being divided up into up to seven distinctive dispensations...) have been affected unconsciously by this approach."[8]

As we have already seen, this has contributed much to the neglect of the study of Church History. Dispensationalist Futurism, in restricting so much of Scripture to Israel and the Jews, has seriously weakened the spiritual armoury of the church. Thus the Antichrist portrayed in Old and New Testaments is deemed not necessarily to come out of the church. But the Bible is entirely about Christ, and those who belong to him - not those who reject Him.

Thus it was that *sola scriptura*, the Word and only the Word, the axiom of Luther and the matrix of the Reformation, was put to one side by the many who took to the exciting new teaching. With the Antichrist yet to appear and the Papacy vindicated from its accusers, the authority of Scripture was enhanced among those who sought reconciliation with Rome. The Counter-Reformation, so hostile and confrontational towards heretics in the past, had emerged with a new face and a new strategy. The stage was being set for reunion with Rome. True, a new Bible would be required, to firmly establish Futurism within a revised text and undermine the faith of Protestants with a corrupted translation. The basis was being laid for the twentieth-century ecumenical movement. The stakes were high indeed. A few years before the Revising Committee (headed by Anglo-Catholics Westcott and Hort) produced the new Bible, Cardinal Manning, the leader of Catholicism in England (and, like Newman, a convert from the Church of England), spoke to the Jesuit "fathers" in stirring fashion, calling them to battle and unmistakably

---

[8] *Evangelical Times*, November 1993

laying out the strategy for the twentieth century.

> "Great is the prize for which you strive. Surely a soldier's eye and a soldier's heart would choose by intuition this field of England. None ampler or nobler could be found. It is an head of Protestantism, the centre of its movements and the stronghold of its power. Weakened in England, it is paralysed elsewhere. Conquered in England, it is conquered throughout all the world. Once overthrown here, all else is but a war of detail. All the roads of the world meet in one point, and this point reached, all the world is open to the Church's will."[9]

But it was not all one-way traffic—at least not in the nineteenth century. The historical view of Prophecy was, as we have seen, widely and well presented. Gifted and godly preachers like Charles Spurgeon, Grattan Guinness, and J. C. Ryle spoke out uncompromisingly; and books and tracts were published, matching the output of the Tractarians and the Brethren. Ryle, the first Bishop of Liverpool, saw what was happening as clearly as Cardinal Manning and the Jesuits:

> "The subject I now touch upon is of deep and pressing importance, and demands the serious attention of all Protestant Churchmen. It is vain to deny that a large party of English clergy and laity in the present day are moving heaven and earth to reunite the Church of England with the idolatrous Church of Rome. The poor Church of England stands on an inclined plain. Her very existence, as a Protestant Church, is in peril. I hold, for one, that this Romish movement ought to be steadily and firmly resisted. I regard it as a most mischievous, soul-ruining, and unscriptural movement. To say that re-union with Rome would be an insult to our martyred Reformers is a very light thing; it is far more than this: it would be a sin and an offence against God! Rather than be

---

[9] Edmund Sheridan Purcell: *Life of Cardinal Manning,* London: Macmillan 1896.

re-united with the idolatrous Church of Rome, I would willingly see my own beloved Church perish and go to pieces. Rather than become Popish once more, she had better die! Unity in the abstract is no doubt an excellent thing: but unity without truth is useless. ... When Rome has repealed the decrees of Trent, and her additions to the Creed, when Rome has recanted her false and unscriptural doctrines, when Rome has formally recanted image-worship, Mary-worship and transubstantiation; then, and not till then, it will be time to talk of reunion with her. Till then I call on all Churchmen to resist to the death this idea of reunion with Rome. Till then let our watchwords be, No peace with Rome! No communion with idolaters!"[10]

Bishop J.C. Ryle[11] and Charles Haddon Spurgeon[12]

Spurgeon saw the danger too. "It is the bounden duty of every Christian to pray against Antichrist, and as to what Antichrist is no sane man ought to raise a question. If it be not the Popery in the Church of Rome there is nothing in the world that can be called by that name. ... Popery is contrary to Christ's Gospel, and is the

---

[10] Bishop J.C.Ryle: *Knots Untied*, pp. 327-328.
[11] Illustration of J.C. Ryle courtesy of The Reformed Theology Source <http://www.reformedtheology.ca/author_quotes.htm#Ryle>
[12] Illustration of Charles Spurgeon courtesy of Born Today <http://www.born-today.com/Today/06-19.htm>

Antichrist, and we ought to pray against it." He pointed to the cost of commitment to the truth. "If a man be earnest about Truth, he will be sectarian. When we cease to strive, seek, contend and maintain the Truth, it will cease in our land and error alone shall reign." The Westminster and Baptist Confessions of Faith of his day took the same position with respect to the Scriptural identity of the Papacy. When the Metropolitan Tabernacle was being built in 1859, Spurgeon placed the newly reprinted *Baptist Confession of Faith* under the foundation stone. [13]

A generation earlier Lord Shaftesbury and other Protestant leaders had vigorously opposed the reconstitution of a Roman Catholic hierarchy for England and Wales, which they regarded as "Papal aggression". Shaftesbury sounded a warning, "Let us turn our eyes to that within, from Popery to Popery in the bud; from the open enemy to the concealed traitor."[14]

---

[13] Iain Murray: *Spurgeon and Hyper-Calvinism*: 1995, Banner of Truth.
[14] E.Hodder: *Life and Work of Lord Shaftesbury*, vol.2, pp. 332-3

Chapter 5

Historicist Expositors of the Nineteenth Century

Dr. H. Grattan Guinness, in his review of Post-Reformation interpreters, recorded his belief that the false futurist writings of the Jesuits Ribera and Bellarmine had been ably answered by Brightman and Mede in the seventeenth century and by Isaac Newton in the first half of the eighteenth century.

Joseph Mede's most excellent exposition of Revelation was approved and printed by the Puritan Parliament in 1641, and at the same time the Westminster Confession of Faith endorsed the historical interpretation of prophecy. Sir Isaac Newton followed Mede and the Puritan writers and futher advanced the comprehension of prophecy. The vastness of his genius led him to the most extensive views of things natural and Divine. He studied nature as a whole, history as a whole, chronology as a whole, and (in connection with these) prophecy as a whole.[1]

In 1842, Rev. Edward Bickersteth, hymn writer and author of the well respected book, *The Trinity,* who later in life became Bishop of Exeter, joined with Professor T. R. Birks in founding *The Prophecy Investigation Society*. Earlier, in 1839, Bickersteth had issued a warning against mixing doctrines and speculative prophetic interpretation, couched in temperate language:

> "The variety of new systems of the Apocalypse is a serious evil, and it is to be hoped that the present list of books may help to check this evil. Men of talents, and imagination, and

---

[1] *Romanism and the Reformation*: H.Grattan Guinness, (First Edition 1887, p/b edition 1999), Our Inheritance Publications 1999, 130 South Coast Road, Peacehaven, East Sussex BN10 8RD

piety, are in danger of forming to themselves a system of the Apocalypse, without any careful study of even leading writers who have gone before them. With great ingenuity they turn the figures of this book to their own views, and build up a beautiful theory; parts of which may indeed be true; but not having cautiously gone over the ground, nor duly considered the researches of their predecessors, they lose the benefit of lengthened experience, and the Church loses that full benefit, which their ability and piety might have imparted. The warnings against false prophets (Matthew 24:21-24) may reach both authors and readers—the danger of a false interpretation of prophecy, calculated to deceive the very elect."[2]

Birks, in his *First Elements of Sacred Prophecy*, was more forthright. He warned of the dangers of rejecting, "without distinction, the maxims in the interpretation of the sacred prophecies generally received by the Protestant churches, ever since the time of the Reformation." He referred to "several late writers" (including Burgh, Maitland, and Todd).

"They agree in few points, except in rejecting the conclusions of all previous expositors; and maintain that nearly the whole of Daniel's prophecies and those of the Apocalypse are unfulfilled. Now, if the theories of these writers are entirely groundless, the responsibility, which they have incurred, is very great, and the effects of their error might prove extremely fatal to the Church. The strongest bulwark against the revived zeal of the Romish Church will have been taken away when it is most needed; and the danger of a renewed apostasy will have been fearfully increased … … the light which the Word of God has thrown on half the whole period of the Church's history will have been quenched in darkness; and her hopes for the future, by a perplexed and fallacious

---

[2] Blakey Moor: *Brief Survey of Prophecies Fulfilled during the Century*, p.63: Blackburn, Durham and Sons, The Evangelical Library, 78 Chiltern Street, London W.1. Also *Bickersteth on the Prophecies*: 1839 edition, p 379.

application of irrelevant prophecies, be involved in a chaos of fanciful conjectures and inextricable confusion."[3]

Apart from Bickersteth and Birks, the principal historical expositors of the nineteenth century were Albert Barnes, Grattan Guinness, Christopher Wordsworth (the Bishop of Lincoln), Dr. A. J. Gordon in the United States, and Rev. E. B. Elliott. Elliott is widely recognised as the greatest among them.

Elliot's four-volume exposition, *Horae Apocalypticae*[4], was published in 1844. C. H. Spurgeon, who was himself an Historicist, or a "Continuist" as he called it, described Elliot's work as "the standard work on the Apocalypse." A monument of both historical and theological scholarship, *Horae Apocalypticae* traces the main streams of interpretation, handed down through the centuries by *"that great cloud of witnesses"* and illuminated by the Holy Spirit through the light of history. It shows with a wonderful weight of evidence in lingering detail how the Book of Revelation has been fulfilled right up to the sixth vial in chapter 16.[5]

E. B. Elliott also wrote of the new Futurist scheme, "It has a great advantage over every other form of interpretation in that it is not chained down by the facts of history. It can draw on unlimited powers of fancy, wherewith to devise in the dreamy future whatever may seem to fit the sacred prophecy."

Elliott went on to show, "the insuperable difficulties attending the Futurist scheme—how it sets language, grammar, and context at

---

[3] T. R. Birks: First Elements of Sacred Prophecy, 1843, London.

[4] Literally, "Hours with the Apocalypse"

[5] Historicists, writing then and now about that important period of church history in Victorian Britain, have identified it with the sixth vial Revelation prophecy. The rising apostasy, the assault of Darwinism, and Liberal "higher critical" scholarship; along with the downgrade of doctrine, the Oxford Movement, the advancing Romanising agenda in the Anglican Church, and the adoption of futurism (all leading to the 1881 revision and corruption of the Scriptures); prompt them to cite the Scripture in Revelation 16:13-14. *"And I saw three unclean spirits like frogs come out of the mouth of the dragon, and out of the mouth of the beast, and out of the mouth of the false prophet; for they are the spirits of devils, working miracles, which go forth unto the kings of the earth and of the whole world ..."*

defiance; how inconsistency marks it from beginning to end; how erroneous is their conception of antichrist, how self-contradictory and illogical; how opposed to History, Scripture, and the Ancient Fathers is the Futurist view of the religion of Antichrist ... but that it is, even intellectually speaking, a mere rude and commonplace conception of Satan's predicted masterpiece of opposition to Christ, compared with what has been actually realised and established in the Papacy. The Papal system is beyond anything that the Futurists have imagined, or ever can imagine, the very perfection of Anti-Christianism."[6]

---

[6] Rev. E.B. Elliott quote from Baron Porcelli: *The Antichrist: His Portrait and History,* The Historicism Research Foundation Inc.

Chapter 6

Islam in Prophecy

Many historicists see the two legs of Nebuchanezzar's image in Daniel 2 as referring to the divide of the post-Christian Roman Empire into the Western Empire under the Papacy and the Eastern Empire under Islam. The Historicist interpretation of the fifth trumpet in the book of Revelation (chapter 9:1-11) reveals the emergence of Islam in Arabia under Mohammed and the devastating early campaigns and conquests of his followers against Christendom.

Rev. E. B. Elliott's commentary of this passage describes an antichrist spirit ruthless in its savagery. At the same time he demonstrates how the Muslim "locust hordes" were used as an instrument of God's judgement on the "Christian" idolatry of Byzantium. The fulfilment of prophecy can repeat itself. As the twenty-first century's apostate Christendom falls away into idolatry and secularism, it is instructive for us, confronted by the same malign spirit, to be reminded **by Scripture** of the roots of Islam and its savage and sustained onslaught on apostate Christendom in the seventh and eighth centuries.

ISLAM in REVELATION - Chapter 9:1-11 - the Fifth Trumpet

(From the Historical interpretation by Rev. E. B. Elliott)

> 1. *And the fifth angel sounded, and I saw a star fall from heaven unto the earth: and to him was given the key to the bottomless pit.*
>
> 2. *And he opened the bottomless pit; and there arose a smoke out of the pit, as the smoke of a great furnace; and the sun and the air were darkened by reason of the smoke of*

the pit, as the smoke of a great furnace; and the sun and the air were darkened by reason of the smoke of the pit.

3. And there came out of the smoke locusts upon the earth: and unto them was given power, as the scorpions of the earth have power.

4. And it was commanded them that they should not hurt the grass of the earth, neither any green thing, neither any tree; but only those men which have not the seal of God in their foreheads.

5. And to them it was given that they should not kill them, but that they should be tormented five months: and their torment was as the torment of a scorpion, when he striketh a man.

6. And in those days shall men seek death, and shall not find it; and shall desire to die, and death shall flee from them.

7. And the shapes of the locusts were like unto horses prepared unto battle; and on their heads were as it were crowns like gold, and their faces were as the faces of men.

8. And they had hair as the hair of women, and their teeth were as the teeth of lions.

9. And they had breastplates, as it were breastplates of iron; and the sound of their wings was as the sound of chariots of many horses running to battle.

10. And they had tails like unto scorpions, and there were stings in their tails: and their power was to hurt men for months.

11. And they had a king over them, which is the angel of the bottomless pit, whose name in the Hebrew tongue is Abaddon, but in the Greek tongue hath his name Apollyon.

In his Thirteenth Lecture, Elliot interprets this passage as follows:

I. First as the peculiar country and people whence it was to originate. The locust, the groundwork of the symbol, is wholly Arabic. It was the "*east wind which brought the locusts*" on Egypt (Exodus 10:13)—a statement distinctly pointing to Arabia, as to the land upon the east of Egypt. The Syrians, we are told by Volney, "have remarked that locusts come constantly from the deserts of Arabia." The terms *Arab* and *locust* are in Hebrew almost the same. The symbol is used elsewhere in Scripture with like appropriateness: "They [the Midianite Arabs] came as grasshoppers," meaning locusts. (Judges 6:5)

Great peculiarity attached to these monsters in the vision before us; they were half **beast**, half **man.** Their coming, locust-like, in destructive swarms, is in accordance with the figure; but their shape was like **horses.** The horse was peculiarly Arabian, and seems to indicate hordes of cavalry; they were, it is said, "*prepared for battle*." They had teeth like **lions**—savage destroyers of life—and they resembled **scorpions** in their poison stings, implying that they would be the tormentors of those whose lives they spared. The scorpion is of the same native locality; witness the words of Moses, when reminding the Israelites of God's goodness to them throughout their forty years' wanderings: "Who led thee through that great and terrible wilderness, wherein were fiery serpents and scorpions?" (Deuteronomy 8:15) Thus the zoology is all Arabian.

Next, as to the human appearance of these locusts: their *faces like men*, their *hair as the hair of women*. What people could be thus pictured? ... There was a nation to which the whole of the descriptive symbol was literally applicable. Pliny, St John's contemporary, speaks of the Arabs as wearing the turban, having the hair long and uncut, and with the moustache too on their upper lip – "that venerable sign of manhood," as Gibbon calls it. In the Arabian poem *Antar*, written about Mahomet's time, we find the beard and moustache, the long-flowing hair and the turban, all specified as characterizing the appearance of the Arab. And the turban of the Arab was often noted as a crown. So Ezekiel spoke of "Sabeans [Arabs] from the desert, with beautiful crowns on their heads." (Ezekiel 23:42) The *breastplates of iron* worn by these creatures are also noted in the vision. The Saracens' policy was to wear defensive armour, their coats of mail being repeatedly mentioned by historians. Thus, on the whole, these concurrent symbols point to Arabia as the country whence the woe was to originate. And if we turn from prophecy to history, we find, at the opening of the seventh century, a fact notoriously verifying the prediction. A mighty Saracen or Arab invasion is the chief event, which it records.

II. But what of the *abyss,* out of which those locusts are said to have issued? The word is often used in Scripture with reference to Hell, or the place of the departed wicked. And in the New Testament it is likewise introduced as *"the deep,"* into which the devils entreated of our Lord that they might not be sent; and in the Revelation as *"the bottomless pit,"* where *"that old serpent, the devil"* is bound. Moreover, as the natural light of the sun is a fit emblem of the spiritual illumination that comes down from the God and Father of lights, so may we infer that whatever is described as darkening the atmosphere, even as smoke from a pit, must be meant in the opposite sense of a moral or spiritual pollution. This smoke, then, in the Apocalyptic vision, we consider to be an emanation from Satan issuing from the pit of hell; i.e., some system of false religion, which should obscure truth, or dim the light of heaven.

And was it even so? Did it so happen, at this particular juncture, that such a system of pestilent error rose up? And if so, did it take its rise from Arabia? To these enquiries we reply, Who has not heard of Mahomet, that false prophet; and of the spread of his too popular creed? This deadly evil came out from Arabia at the very time we speak of—a creed the invention of fanaticism and fraud. In its system the blessed God is described as cruel and unholy; and in its morals, pride, ferocity, superstition and sensuality, are held up for admiration, and show palpably where it had its origin. It was just after embracing Mahometan principles that the Saracens, as "locusts from the abyss," issued forth on Christendom. It was the adoption of this creed, the creed of Mahomet, that made them what they were, that united these hordes as one, that gave them the impulse to fly locust-like to propagate their faith over the world, and that imparted to them, as to raging lions of the desert, their destructive fury of fanaticism. Their scorpion venom was thereby prepared to torment such of the Christians as they should bring under their yoke, while the hope of gross licentiousness to be indulged in both here and hereafter, added sensualism to their ferocity. Well does the Saracen history accord with the prophetic emblem concerning them!

III. We have to observe the peculiar nature of the commission, *"Hurt not the grass or trees, but only those men who have not God's seal on their foreheads."* Mahomet expressly declared that his mission was against "idolaters;" and such he considered Christians. But in urging forward his followers against them, the Caliph Aboubeker did but fulfil the precept of the prophet when he gave the command, "Destroy no palm trees, nor any fields of corn: cut down no fruit trees, nor do any mischief to cattle." It was the dictate of policy, not of mercy; for by following this plan the Saracens, soon after their conquest, had formed flourishing countries round them. It was a marked peculiarity; for in other invasions, as the Gothic, fire, sword, and devastation tracked the invader's progress, and was accordingly prefigured in the Apocalyptic imagery: but with the Saracens it was the very reverse; and this reverse still more connects it with the prediction now before us.

IV. We have so far identified this passage with the Arabian heresy and irruption, that the inference we clearly deduce, is that Mahomet was the *star*, or ruler, adhered to. But why is this imposter referred to as a *star*? And why still more, since success followed his course for such a length of time, is he said to be *a fallen star*? To answer this question we must trace Mahomet's history back to his birth. His origin was princely, being descended from one of the noblest families in Arabia. Gibbon says, "The grandfather of Mahomet and his lineal ancestors appeared in foreign and domestic transactions as the princes of their country." They were, in the view of the Syrian Greeks, as among the stars on the political horizon. But just after the prophet's birth his father died; and soon after, his grandfather. Then the governorship of Mecca and keys of the Kaaba (or holy place of religion among the Arabians) attached to the office, passed into another branch of the family. Thus Mahomet became a *star fallen* from power. He says of himself, that at the opening of the seventh century, "he was a desolate orphan." He was indeed fallen, when as a poor widow's servant, he used to traffic in the markets of Damascus.

Mahomet, however, was imbued with a spirit calculated to struggle against, and triumph over misfortune. ... About three miles from Mecca was a cave called Hera; it was a secret and desolate spot. There he withdrew every year to consult, as he said, a spirit who was wont to visit him in his solitary hours, and hold converse with him. Gibbon well calls it, "The spirit of fraud and enthusiasm, whose abode was not in heaven, but in the mind of the prophet." This cave has aptly suggested to interpreters the idea of *the pit of the abyss,* whence the pestilential fumes and darkness were seen to issue. When, privately at first, and then more publicly, he began to announce his creed, for awhile his uncle and the elders of the city affected to despise the orphan's presumption. They chased him from Mecca, and his flight marks in history the era of the *Hegira,* A.D.622. Seven years afterwards was seen in Mecca's streets one to whom all bowed down in honour; whose words the multitudes revered; to whose command armies were obedient; who swayed the minds of men that they yielded implicit faith in his wild or crafty imagination. The "fallen star" had come forth again. The key of office was restored to him. The fugitive missionary was enthroned as the prince and the prophet of his native country. ... Even so in allusive contrast it is written in Revelation, "The key of the abyss" was given to him; and truly the smoke that arose, upon his opening, was as the pestilential fumes and darkness of hell.

"There came out locusts on the earth." It was in A.D.629 that the Saracens first issued from the desert, and proclaimed war against Christendom. The year 639 saw Syria subdued, and the Muezzin, calling to prayer, soon after sounded from a mosque built on the site of Solomon's temple. There he is still heard to this very day, when the appointed hour comes round for remembering the prophet. The subjugation of Egypt followed quickly on that of Syria; then some few years after, that of the African province; then, at the commencement of the eighth century, that of Spain. All this was within the limits of Roman Christendom, and consequently within the sphere of the Apocalyptic vision. But beyond this their conquests extended far and wide with terrible rapidity. Two short statements from history will give some idea of the progress of the Saracens, and of the desolations caused by them; of whom it might be said, as was said of the desolating force mentioned in Joel. *"The land is as the garden of Eden before them, and behind them a desolate wilderness."* (Joel 2:3). The one—that in ten years, from A.D.634 to 644, they had reduced 3600 castles to ruins, destroyed 4000 churches and had built 1400 mosques for the exercise of the religion of Mahomet. The other—that at the end of the first century of the Hegira, the Arabian Empire had been extended from the confines of India and Tartary to the shores of the Atlantic.

Bitterly did the Christians feel the scorpion's sting. They were deprived of the use of their arms, and like slaves of old, made to pay annually a life-redemption tax. They were required to stand up always in the presence of their tyrants, and were called by the names of opprobrium, as "infidel dog", "Christian dog", etc. In further token of contempt to their religion, to which the Christians still clung in fond attachment, no new churches were permitted to be built; no church bells to be rung; while the scoffing Moslem had free access, even during divine worship, to all those which were allowed to exist. Insults of the grossest kind were continually offered to Christian females; and undefinable acts of oppression practised on all. Every inducement was offered to apostasy; and the punishment of death was inflicted on any, who, after apostasy, again professed the Christian faith.

These *locusts*, it is said, had a *king over them,* whose name was *"Abaddon," or the "Destroyer."* Mohammed professed that the "spirit of the cave" had dictated to him the Koran; this was accordingly the law that governed the Saracens. The Caliphs, or chief governors, held rule only as vicars of the false prophet. What the doctrine of the book was, as acted out by them, appeared on the field of battle. There, when we see not only the loss of bodily life resulting, but also the ruin of souls from the poisonous precepts of Mohammedism, we cannot find more a fitting title to express the perpetuation of the prophet's character in each successive Caliph, than that of the "Abaddon," the "Destroyer" of Christians! There was, however, a term and limit prescribed to these *locusts*, both as to effect and as to duration. For observe, they were not to kill, i.e., to annihilate the men of Roman Christendom as a political body; but *"only to torment them."* And this woe was to last 150 days; i.e., in prophetic language, 150 years. ...

Observe now what had been the length of time occupied in these transactions. We date from the period when Mahomet publicly announced his mission to propagate his religion by violence and with the sword: a mission, which made his followers a woe to all countries, but especially to Christendom. The destroying commission might be said to commence at that period, when Mahomet, addressing his assembled followers, enquired, "Who will be my lieutenant?"

Ali, called by him "the Lion of God," replied, "O prophet, I will be thy lieutenant. Whoever rises against thee I will dash out his teeth, tear out his eyes, break his legs, rip him open. I am the man. I will be thy vizier."

Mr. Hallam justly observes: "These words of Mahomet's illustrious disciple are, as it were, a text upon which the commentary extends into the whole Saracenic history."

Thus then, reckoning from A.D.612 to A.D.762, when the Caliphate was removed to Baghdad, we find the intervening period to be precisely 150 years. To two remarkable coincidences, which occurred during this period, we should give attention. It has been observed that the apostasy of the Church was the assigned and predicted cause of this judgment. Now Mahomet's asserted commission was especially directed against idolaters; and it was in that character, as an idolatrous people, that Christendom appeared when the Saracen woe fell upon it. Up to the close of the seventh century the reproach of image-worship might seem deservedly to give cause for the scourge which they suffered under the Moslem sword; but about the year 717, the Isaurian family ascended the throne of Constantinople. For sixty years its princes, supported by many real Christians, though opposed by the Popes and the masses of the people, resisted image-worship and endeavoured to overthrow it. Mark then—it was during this period of resistance to the error that the Saracen horde received its first defeat at Constantinople.

Again in A.D.754 Constantine Copronymus called a council in order to condemn the idolatrous image-worship. It passed a solemn judgment against it: and, behold, it was the very next year that the Caliphate was divided, and the intensity of the Saracenic woe was brought to an end. But alas! The efforts of these emperors availed but little. In the year 781, the Queen Irene succeeded to the throne, having murdered her image-destroying husband. She convened what is called the seventh general council; and by a solemn act of the Catholic Church, the worship of images was declared lawful. Just then the Saracenic woe seemed for a time to revive. The Arab forces swept through Asia Minor into Greece, again and again bearing down all before them. Was there in all this no warning from God? The Eastern Church, however, persisted. In A.D.842 the struggle ended under the reign of the Empress Theodora, and image-worship became indisputably established. Through the ninth and tenth centuries it so continued; yet such was the long-suffering of God, no judgment seemed to follow.

But the time of retribution came at last.

Here we close, as far as regards this vision. But a fact or two, relative to the downfall of the Saracenic power, may be added. Luxury, we have said, weakened its strength. In A.D.841, the Caliph, distrusting his guards, was forced to hire a protective force of 50,000 Turks. These, like the Praetorian guards at Rome, in their turn became tyrants, and accelerated the sinking of the Saracens. ... The Persians, in A.D.934, stripped the Caliph of Baghdad of all temporal power, and left him only the title of Pontiff of Islamism. In the west, a century after, the Saracens were driven out; and though they continued as marauders, and even gained victories in Crete and Sicily, the *woe* might be said to have passed from Christendom.

One woe is past; and, behold, there come two woes hereafter (Revelation 9:12-19)[7]

The sixth trumpet's first woe was again soon to fall on idolatrous Eastern Christendom. Vast numbers of Turkmans, or Turks, from the area of the Caspian sea and the Euphrates, converted to the new all-conquering religion and "animated by the same spirit of hell," as Elliot describes it, waged "a holy war against the infidels" of Greek Christendom, occupying and settling all of Asia Minor. The second woe of the sixth trumpet culminated in the fall of Constantinople when history records *a third part of the men were killed* (Revelation 9:18).

---

[7] Rev. E. B. Elliott: *Horae Apocalypticae*

PART II
THE KING JAMES BIBLE AND MODERN VERSIONS

Chapter 7

The Proliferation of Modern "Bibles"

During the last century the Church has preached a watered-down Gospel from a seemingly unending range of "bibles", each of which differs from the other, sometimes radically. Until the closing years of the nineteenth century, "the people of the Book" were convinced that in the King James or Authorised Version they had the Word of God. They saw it as infallible; they had no doubt of its inerrancy. Preachers and their congregations approached the Scriptures with great reverence, "Thus saith the Lord." This was the authorised Bible; it was rare for anyone to question that which was universally accepted as the Word of God. There was no serious alternative to the King James for most of three hundred years. Rival editions, and there was no shortage of these, fell flat on their face before the majesty of the King James. Although custom and language changed, the King James Bible did not. Indeed there was no real case for change, and for most people the idea of change was unthinkable. It was widely regarded then as the Word of God in English.

If today, because of the prevalence of all the other translations, it is no longer seen as this, then which particular version has taken its place? If there is not to be any one version but a combination or synthesis of all versions, and there are more than one hundred and fifty of them, the number rising fast; then who is to choose the true Scriptures and discard the false? If there were to be no one trustworthy version with a just claim to be the Word of God, then we would have to conclude that we worship a God who is either careless or powerless to keep His Word pure through the ages. The very question posed repeatedly in today's pulpits by the words "depending on what version you are using" reminds us of man's first questioning of God's Word, "... *has God said?*"[1] The existence of so many differing versions is a major problem for evangelism, **especially to Muslims** and others of different religions or cults who have their own scriptures.

The footnotes that are to be found in new versions, including the NIV, the RSV, the NASB, the NEB, and the Good News, question the choice of manuscript[2] and cast doubt on the authenticity of the Scriptures. Verses or parts of verses and whole passages are omitted with an explanatory footnote, or often without one. The inevitable consequence of this is the undermining of Scripture's claim to be absolute Truth. ... "*Thy word is truth.*"[3]

How can we claim that God's Word is inerrant and infallible and at the same time admit that there are errors in every translation and that we don't possess a Bible that we can trust? We are not just being inconsistent and illogical; much more serious—we are in direct conflict with Scripture. Scripture declares emphatically that God will preserve His Holy Word **pure** in all ages. He has done so in the Authorised King James Version, the complete Word of God and the Final Authority in all matters of faith and practice.

"The words of the Lord are pure words: as silver tried in a furnace of earth, purified seven times."[4]

"Thy word is very pure: therefore thy servant loveth it."[5]

That purity is patently missing in popular new versions such as the NIV and the Good News, as we shall show in our section comparing selected key verses of Scripture. The Bible clearly supports the doctrine of verbal inspiration. Dr. Napier Malcolm asks, "How can we say that each word of the Bible (that is, the Hebrew and Greek originals) is inspired of God and true when different Bibles say different things? The modern versions are based on the belief that not every word of our present Bibles is necessarily true.

---

[1] Genesis 3:1
[2] This is done by including the phrase "some early manuscripts have..." in those footnotes.
[3] John 17:17
[4] Psalm 12:6
[5] Psalm 119:140

The translators believe that God may have inspired the original, but He has not preserved the original."[6]

Preservation of God's Word

Again and again God's providential preservation of His Word is promised in the Bible:

"... Thou shalt keep them (the words of the Lord), O Lord, thou shalt preserve them from this generation for ever."[7]

"For ever, O Lord, thy word is settled in heaven."[8]

"Heaven and earth shall pass away, but my words shall not pass away."[9]

"Being born again, not of corruptible seed, but of incorruptible, by the Word of God, which liveth and abideth for ever."[10]

"The grass withereth, the flower fadeth: but the Word of our God shall stand for ever."[11]

Men of great faith of the past have admitted their difficulty in explaining those things regarding inspiration and inerrancy, which are hard to be understood. But, as Bishop Ryle pointed out, "We may rest assured that the difficulties which beset any other theory of inspiration are tenfold greater than any which beset our own." Ryle's high view of Scripture reflected his belief that the Authorised Version that he used was preserved inspired, infallible and inerrant, and entirely trustworthy.

---

[6] *British Church Newspaper*, December 24, 2004.
[7] Psalm 12:7
[8] Psalm 119:89
[9] Matthew 24:35
[10] 1 Peter 1:23
[11] Isaiah 40:8

The Bible as God's Word

"This Bible is God's Bible," insisted C. H. Spurgeon, "and when I see it, I seem to hear a voice springing up from it, saying, "I am the book of God; man, read me. I am God's writing; open my leaf, for I was penned by God;' ... ... Oh, book of books! And wast thou written by my God? Then will I bow before thee. Thou book of vast authority! ... ... for he has written this book himself, ... let us love it; let us count it more precious than much fine gold. ... ... I plead with you, I beg of you respect your Bibles, and search them out, ... go home and read your Bibles,..."[12]

As internationally recognised New Testament textual critic Edward F. Hills argued, "In regard to Bible versions, then, we follow the example of the Apostles and the other inspired New Testament writers. Just as they recognized the Septuagint as the providentially appointed translation of the Hebrew Old Testament into Greek, so we recognize the King James Version and the other great historic translations of the holy Scriptures as providentially approved. Hence we receive the King James Version as the providentially appointed English Bible. Admittedly this venerable version is not absolutely perfect, but it is trustworthy. No Bible-believing Christian who relies upon it will ever be led astray. But it is just the opposite with modern versions. They are untrustworthy, and they do lead Bible-believing Christians astray."[13]

Dr. B. B. Warfield and countless others have tried to devise a theory of the special providential preservation of the Scriptures which leaves room for naturalistic New Testament textual criticism. But this is impossible, for the two concepts are mutually exclusive. Naturalistic New Testament criticism requires us to treat the text of the New Testament like the text of any other book, in other words, to ignore or deny the special providential preservation of the Scriptures. Hence if we really believe in the Scriptures' special providential preservation then we cannot follow the naturalistic method of New Testament textual criticism.

---

[12] A Sermon (No. 15) delivered on Sabbath Evening, March 18, 1855, by the Reverend C.H. Spurgeon at Exeter Hall, Strand.
<http://www.ccel.org/ccel/spurgeon/sermons01.xiv.html>
[13] Edward F. Hills: *The King James Version Defended*, Christian Research Press, PO Box 2013, Des Moines, IA 50310

Dr. Hills, in his book, *The King James Version Defended*, pointed to six principles in support of this view:

- The Old Testament text was preserved by the Old Testament priesthood and the scribes and scholars that grouped themselves around that priesthood.
- When Christ died upon the cross, the Old Testament priesthood was abolished. In the New Testament dispensation, every believer is a priest under Christ the great High Priest. Hence, the New Testament text has been preserved by the universal priesthood of believers, by faithful Christians in every walk of life.
- The Traditional Text, found in the vast majority of the Greek New Testament manuscripts, is the true text because it represents the God-guided usage of this universal priesthood of believers.
- The first printed text of the Greek New Testament represents a forward step in the providential preservation of the New Testament. In it the few errors of any consequence occurring in the Traditional Greek Text were corrected by the providence of God, operating through the usage of the Latin-speaking Church of Western Europe. In other words, the editors and printers who produced this first printed Greek New Testament text were providentially guided by the usage of the Latin-speaking Church to follow the Latin Vulgate in those few places in which the Latin Church usage rather than the Greek Church usage had preserved the genuine reading.
- Through the usage of Bible-believing Protestants God placed the stamp of His approval on this first printed text, and it became the Textus Receptus. It is the printed form of the Traditional Text found in the vast majority of the Greek New Testament manuscripts.
- The King James Version is an accurate translation of the Textus Receptus. On it God has placed His stamp of approval through the long continued usage of English-speaking believers. Hence it should be used and defended today by Bible-believing Christians.[14]

---

[14] Ibid.

"Not only do English speaking Christians own in the King James version the greatest translation of the Bible ever produced in any language, called 'The miracle of English prose', but also the greatest literary masterpiece ever authored. 'It's language,' one said, 'we reserve for God.' Its power, sweep and breathtaking authority transcends all other works, while its Elizabethan eloquence, antiquated yet timeless, speaks more profoundly and intimately to our heart than our modern day tongue."[15]

Difficult to Read

An answer to those who protest that the Authorised Bible is too difficult for the modern reader to read, with all its archaic terms and turn of phrase, was provided by the much-respected expository preacher, the late Dr. D.M. Lloyd-Jones who was quoted in *'The Majority Text: Essays and Reviews in the Continuing Debate'*:

"Yet we are told - it [the Bible] must be in such simple terms and language that anybody taking it up and reading it is going to understand all about it. My friends this is sheer nonsense. What we must do is educate the masses of the people up to the Bible, not bring the Bible down to their level. One of the greatest troubles today is that everything is being brought down to the same level; everything is cheapened. The common man is the standard of authority; he decides everything, and everything has to be brought down to him ... ... What we need is therefore, not to replace the Authorized Version ... We need rather to reach and train people up to the standard and language, the dignity and the glory of the old Authorized Version."[16]

Prince Charles, who does not seem to have understood the main message of the Bible, and much needs the prayers of God's people at this time, sought to express in simple fashion something of the lofty inaccessibility and majesty of so much of Scripture, in contrast with the banalities of the Alternative Service Book: "The Word of God is

---

[15] Rev. Charles Salliby: *If the Foundations Be Destroyed,* Pine Hill Press Inc. Freeman, SD 57029
[16] Theodore P. Letis: *The Majority Text: Essays and Reviews in the Continuing Debate*, Institute For Biblical Textual Studies, Grand Rapids, MI 49503, pp. 103-104.

supposed to be a bit over our heads. Elevated is what God is."[17] If he becomes King, providing his Coronation Service remains the same, he will be required to assent to a higher view of Scripture than this. His mother, Her Majesty Queen Elizabeth, at her accession, swore her Coronation Oath affirming that the Bible is "the most valuable thing that this world affords. Here is wisdom. This is the Royal Law. These are the lively oracles of God."

To those who continue to argue that the Authorised Version is hard to understand, and that we therefore need modern versions, author Alan O'Reilly asks in his book, *O Biblios,* how it is that its text caused the English people to become a Bible loving people— "the people of the book"—in the words of the historian Green.[18]

The marvellous fact is that the *King James Bible* **is** comprehensible to the untrained mind. In many parts of the "Bible belt" in the United States today the great majority of ordinary grass roots Christians would use no other version. The same applies in African countries where both the King James and another version have been used. There is simply the widespread recognition that the KJV has clarity and authority that is not found in other versions. Apart from its magnificent use of language the Authorised Bible flows rhythmically and **has actually proved far easier to learn than other translations.**

As American Creation Scientist, Henry M. Morris, author of *The Genesis Project*, has written, "The English of the King James is not nearly so archaic or difficult to follow as its critics allege. In fact, it is in general written in a much simpler vocabulary, with a higher percentage of one and two syllable words, than almost any of the new translations. The honest reader will find it at least as easy to understand as any other." Dr. Hills maintains that "the English of the King James Version ... is not a type of English that was ever spoken anywhere. It is biblical English...."[19]

However, the ultimate criterion is not the ease with which we can read it, rather it is the purity of the text. The King James translators

---

[17] Excerpt from a chapter contributed to by the Prince of Wales to *The Real Common Worship*, published to protest against the new Anglican Prayer Book.
[18] *O Biblios - The Book,* p. 32.
[19] *King James Version Defended*, p. 218.

were of a calibre and breadth of scholarship surely unmatched in the world today, and they were entirely submitted to the Scriptures, which they regarded as sacred and inerrant. They approached the work of translation with great reverence attested to by their handling of the Greek and Hebrew texts, placing each word and phrase precisely as they perceived was intended by the Holy Spirit. There is a consistent faithfulness in their approach to the original text, which is testified to by the use of Italics when words are added in the English translation. [20]

The question that we need to ask of our Bible is "is it inspired by the spirit of God who leads us into all truth or is it just the product of scholarship, reason and research?" We shall be trying to show the importance of an awareness of the crucial and often startling and shocking differences between the King James and the modern versions; and we do urge the reader to take a little time to study the section which follows which compares translations.

In arguing the case for the *King James Version*, we do not suggest that those Christians who use it are necessarily more spiritual, better informed, more faithful in prayer, more competent in expounding the Word or more zealous in reaching out to sinners than those who use another version. Nor is this an excursion into what some call "bibliolatry" but is a serious attempt to encourage discernment in the use of Bible versions. We walk in a minefield of deception as the version comparisons in the section at the end of this chapter and elsewhere in this book are intended to demonstrate.

Different Greek Manuscripts

One misconception among Christians today needs to be cleared up. The belief that all modern versions are simply revisions of the Authorised Version in more up-to-date language is incorrect. Such revisions do exist, but the great majority of modern versions use translations **from entirely different Greek manuscripts**. The underlying Greek text of the King James Version of the New Testament is called the *Textus Receptus* or Received Text. It derives from what is known as the "Majority Text", so named because

---

[20] Nor did they carry out their undertaking in secret, as did the translators of the Revised Version of 1881, as we shall show in the following chapter under the subheading "The Textual Controversy."

approaching 95% of all existing manuscript evidence supports this text. It was first printed in Basel, in 1516, under the editorship of Erasmus and was the text most relied on by the Protestant Reformation in England and in Europe. It was reproduced in many editions in the sixteenth century, and the 1611 King James translation was largely based on Theodore Beza's Fourth Edition of 1588.

The modern translations are mainly based on the "Minority Texts", which were presented to the world as alternatives to the *Textus Receptus (TR)* at the end of the nineteenth century. We recognise the sincerity, the weight of argument and the thoroughness of scholarship of textual critics who support these "rediscovered manuscripts." We respect, too, the carefully reasoned arguments that seek to invalidate the *TR*, although we do not accept their conclusions. The simple fact is that the originals or "autographs" are not to be found, and therefore the evidence relating to the integrity of codices or manuscripts is highly complex. This author is in no way qualified to enter into it. He simply looks to set out the facts, and without concealing his confidence in God's providential role in preserving His Word and providing it in English, invites the reader to look more closely into these things.

Chapter 8

The Modern Versions – Origins and Influences

The 1881 committee that produced the Revised Version, the mother of the majority of today's modern versions, was unimpressed with the weight of the evidence supporting the Received Text, which had been used for English translations by William Tyndale, John Rogers, and Miles Coverdale, as well as later by the 1611 translators.

The Revising Committee and the Minority Texts

Led by Anglo-Catholic Cambridge Professors Westcott and Hort, the 1881 Revising Committee convinced most of the Church that the "Alexandrian" and "Western" Greek texts should replace the Received Text where the versions differed. Arguing that these Minority Texts were the oldest and therefore the most accurate and pure,[1] they often substituted what may well have been the third

---

[1] Textus Receptus Traced Back to the Year AD 350 - Surprisingly, of all people, Dr. Hort, testifies to the fact, to which all authorities must agree, that the Greek New Testament of the Textus Receptus type can be traced back very positively to the year AD 350 and is as old as any known manuscript. Hort says; "The fundamental text of the late extant Greek MSS [manuscripts] generally is beyond all question identical with the dominant Antiochian or Graeco-Syrian text of the second half of the fourth century. The community of text implies, on genealogical grounds, a community of parentage; the Antiochian Fathers and the bulk extant MSS written from about three or four to ten or eleven centuries later must have had, in the greater number of extant variations, a common original, either contemporary with or older than our oldest extant MSS, which thus lose at once whatever presumption of exceptional purity they might have derived from their exceptional antiquity alone," – *Hort's Introduction,* p.92. This gives a greater antiquity to the *TR* than to the Greek Text of the Revised Version.

century corrupted text of Origen, Eusebius, and Jerome whenever the manuscripts differed. These texts had been rejected by the church fathers of the Antioch School and were also rejected by the Protestant Reformers.

Origen, the best known leader of the Alexandrian School, and now very much back in fashion in our theological colleges, taught that Christ was a created being—divine, but in a lesser sense than the Father—although at the same time he did teach the doctrine of the eternal generation of the Son. Steeped in Gnosticism, he edited a six-column Bible called the *Hexapla,* with a different version of the Bible in each column, and was continually changing Bible verses to accommodate his own philosophical and mystical ideas. Dr. Philip Schaff, who became head of both American Revising Committees (Old and New Testaments) as we shall see, shared many of Origen's Gnostic ideas and wrote of Origen, "his predilection for Plato led him into many grand and fascinating errors."[2]

The fifth column of the corrupted *Hexapla* was copied by Eusebius for Emperor Constantine's new State Church in AD 331. *Sinaiticus* and *Vaticanus*, the two key Greek New Testament manuscripts used in the 1881 Revised Bible, may well have derived directly from this source or even have been two of the fifty prepared by Eusebius and others at that time. Many textual authorities believe that Jerome's Latin Vulgate Bible, favoured always by the Church of Rome, also originated from this family of manuscripts, as it is largely in agreement with the Minority Texts.

One of the newly authenticated manuscripts, *Codex 'B'* or *Vaticanus*, discovered in 1481 in the Vatican library in Rome and kept there ever since, was of central importance to the revising work. Erasmus, who, along with Beza, Stephanus, and the Elzevirs, edited the *Textus Receptus*, had had access to *'B'*, also known as *Vaticanus*, at the beginning of the Reformation, but had rejected it.[3] Manuscripts of the same stable were available to the 1611 translators too, but they also refused to make use of them. Yet to these manuscripts the Westcott and Hort Committee assigned

---

[2] Schaff: *History of the Christian Church*, Vol. II, p. 291.
[3] Profesor E.C. Bissell: *Historic Origin of the Bible*, p. 84.

supremacy. American New Testament scholar, Dr. Herman C. Hoskier, who in 1913 had written the lengthy volume *Codex 'B' - A Study and Indictment*, is quoted as saying, "We always come back to '*B*', as Westcott and Hort is practically '*B*'. My thesis then is that '*B' (Vaticanus)* and *Aleph (Sinaiticus)* and their forerunners, with Origen, who revised the Antioch text, are Egyptian revisions current between AD 200 and 400 and abandoned between 500 and 1881, merely revived in our day." In fact there are over three thousand differences between *Aleph Sinaiticus* and *B Vaticanus* in the Gospels alone.[4]

Westcott and Hort

Bruce Foss Westcott and Fenton John Anthony Hort, both brilliant and respected scholars of their day, were dominant on the 1881 Revising Committee. We can learn much about their views and theological positions from their letters and biographies published by their respective sons. Both Cambridge professors were liberal theologians of the new higher critical school, who were greatly influenced by the Oxford Movement, the forerunner of the Ecumenical movement within the Church of England. Both men were anti-Protestant, sacerdotalist, and had pronounced leanings to Mariolatry.

Professor Westcott wrote to the Archbishop of Canterbury, "It does not seem to me that the Vaudois [the Waldensians] claim an ecclesiastical recognition. The position of the small Protestant bodies on the Continent is no doubt one of great difficulty. But our church can, I think, only deal with churches growing to fuller life."[5] Hort wrote to Westcott, on September 23, 1864, " I believe Coleridge [Samuel Taylor Coleridge, the poet] was quite right in saying that Christianity without a substantial church is vanity and disillusion; and I remember shocking you and Lightfoot not so long ago by expressing a belief that 'Protestantism' is only parenthetical and temporary."[6] Hort harboured a lifetime hatred of the Received Text, which as early as 1851 he described as "vile, leaning on late

---

[4] Dr. Alan O'Reilly: *O Biblios – The Book,* The Covenant Publishing Co., Ltd.
[5] Westcott: *Life of Westcott:* Vol. II, p. 53.
[6] Hort; *Life of Hort: Vol. II*, p. 30.

manuscripts" and "villainous".[7]

Bruce Foss Westcott and Fenton John Anthony Hort[8]

Professor Westcott wrote in another letter to the Archbishop of Canterbury, "I wish I could see to what forgotten truth Mariolatry bears witness."[9] He saw the Virgin as another manifestation of God. In writing to his fiancée in 1847 about his religious experiences in France, he described a small oratory housing a life-size "Pieta" (Madonna and dead Christ) with place only for one person to kneel. "Had I been alone I could have knelt there for hours."[10]

Professor Hort, who called the doctrines of evangelicals "perverted rather than untrue", described himself as "a staunch sacerdotalist" and declared that "the pure Romish view of the sacraments seems to me nearer, and more likely to lead to the truth than the evangelical. ... We dare not forsake the sacraments or God will forsake us." He also had been "persuaded for many years that Mary-worship and Jesus-worship have very much in common in their causes and results."[11]

---

[7] Ibid: Vol. I, p. 211.
[8] Illustration of Bruce Foss Westcott and Fenton John Anthony Hort courtesy of: Westcott and Hort Resource Centre <http://www.tegarttech.com/wh/index.html>
[9] Westcott: *Life Of Westcott,* Vol. II, p. 50.
[10] Ibid: Vol. I, p. 81.
[11] Hort: *Life of Hort*, Vol. I, p. 400 and Vol. II, pp. 49 & 50.

Both men rejected the substitutionary nature of Christ's atonement. In line with Roman Catholic dogma they believed that it was not through Christ's death that He atoned for sin, but through the Incarnation. As Hort wrote to Westcott in 1860, "Certainly nothing could be more unscriptural than the modern limiting of Christ's bearing our sins and sufferings to his death; but indeed that is only one aspect of an almost universal heresy."[12]

Both men favoured the Darwinian hypothesis and the new Old Testament higher criticism and were opposed to a literal interpretation of the first three chapters of the book of Genesis. Neither Westcott nor Hort ever stated that the Bible was verbally inspired or inerrant. Professor Westcott's pioneer work on subjecting the sacred text to critical and sceptical analysis helped to usher in the school of modernism and the work of well-known liberal scholars, like Wellhausen, Karl Barth, Bultmann, and more recently Hans Kung, Dr. John Robinson (author of *Honest To God*), and David Jenkins, who, like Westcott, was a former Bishop of Durham.

---

[12] Hort: *Life of Hort*, Vol. 1, p. 430 [letter to Westcott, October 15, 1860].

Chapter 9

The Textual Controversy

In the Preface of the NIV we read, "the Greek text used in translating the New Testament was an eclectic one." *Eclectic* refers to the practice of using a number of differing manuscripts to select verses or portions of Scripture at the sole discretion of those scholars appointed to the task. The Preface further explains, "the translators made their choice of readings according to accepted principles of New Testament textual criticism." The "accepted principles" refer to those laid down for posterity by Westcott and Hort. The controversial theories of these two men have determined the accepted method of New Testament criticism for the twentieth and twenty-first centuries and beyond.

Unlike 1611, when there was total unanimity among the group of scholars—godly men who were sold out for Christ and who worked entirely in the open—the 1881 committee, **which met secretly**, was not united. One indicator as to why unity was not achieved was the inclusion of a Unitarian at the insistence of both Westcott and Hort. They had both made this a resigning issue. The minority, dissenting view was publicly represented by John Burgon, Dean of Chichester, a strenuous upholder of the Majority (Byzantine) Text, the *Textus Receptus,* which he called the Traditional Text. Burgon, who is ranked among Victorian textual scholars alongside Tregelles, Scrivener, and Tischendorf, was sufficiently challenged by the Oxford Movement's assault on the Scriptures to dedicate his life to the defence of what he regarded as the infallible Word of God. He believed that the traditional text was the true text, which by perpetual tradition, generation by generation, had been handed down by God's grace and providence, unfailingly, from the time of the apostles. God had fulfilled His promise to preserve His Word.

"I am utterly disinclined to believe," wrote Dean Burgon, "that after 1800 years, 995 copies out of every thousand, suppose, will prove untrustworthy; and that the one, two, three, four or five that remain ... will be found to contain what the Holy Spirit originally inspired. I am utterly unable to believe, in short, that God's promise has so entirely failed, that at the end of 1800 years much of the text of the Gospel had in point of fact to be picked out of a wastepaper-basket by a German critic [Professor Tischendorf] in the convent of St Catherine."[1]

In his book *Revision Revised,* Burgon wrote in the dedication to his friend Viscount Cranbrook:

"My one object has been to defeat the mischievous attempt, which was made in 1881 to thrust upon this Church and Realm a revision of the Sacred Text, which recommended though it be by eminent names, I am thoroughly convinced, and am able to prove, is untrustworthy from beginning to end. The English (as well as the Greek) of the newly revised version is hopelessly at fault. It is to me simply unintelligible how a company of scholars can have spent ten years in elaborating such an unsatisfactory production. Their uncouth phraseology and their jerky sentences, their pedantic obscurity and their unidiomatic English, contrast painfully with the 'happy turns of expression, the music of cadences, the felicities of the rhythm' of our Authorised Version.

---

[1] Professor Tischendorf's account states that *Sinaiticus* was discovered among other manuscripts stored in St. Catherine's Roman Catholic convent near Mount Sinai in Egypt.

Dean John Burgon[2]

"The transition from one to the other, as the Bishop of Lincoln[3] remarks, is 'like exchanging a well-built carriage for a vehicle without springs, in which you get jolted to death on a newly mended and rarely traversed road.' But the Revised Version is inaccurate as well; exhibits defective scholarship, I mean, in countless places.

"It is, however, the systematic depravation of the underlying Greek which does so grievously offend me; for this is nothing else than the poisoning of the 'River of Life' at its sacred source. Our Revisers, (with the best and purest intentions, no doubt) stand convicted of having substituted for them fabricated readings, which the Church has long since refused

---

[2] Illustration of John Burgon courtesy of The Dean Burgon Society
<http://www.deanburgonsociety.org/DeanBurgon/whowasdb.htm>
[3] Christopher Wordsworth (1807-1885), Bishop of Lincoln, author of *Is The Papacy Predicted by St Paul?* and *Rome Babylon and the Apocalypse,* both available from Dorchester House Publications

to acknowledge, or else has rejected with abhorrence; and which only survive at this time in a little handful of documents of the most depraved type. ... We venture to assure the reader without a particle of hesitation that Aleph [Sinaiticus], B [Vaticanus], and D [Bezae] are three of the most scandalously corrupt copies extant; exhibit the most shamefully mutilated texts which are to be met with; and have become by whatever process (for their history is wholly unknown) the depositaries of the largest amount of fabricated readings, ancient blunders and intentional perversions of truth which are discoverable in any known copies of the word of God."[4]

However Dean Burgon's views and those of the Bishop of Lincoln failed to carry the day and the "revised editions" were published in Britain and the United States to widespread acclaim. The stakes in that momentous controversy simply could not have been higher. "If Burgon was right and Hort wrong, then Hort pulled off the tour de force of all time," was one commentator's summary of what had taken place. If this were so, it would prove to be, in Burgon's words, "the most astonishing, as well as the most calamitous literary blunder of the Age."

The American Revision Committees – Dr. Philip Schaff

The American Revised Version and its Committees followed on from the radical work of its English counterpart. As in England, two companies were formed for Revision—one for the Old Testament, the other for the New Testament. Bishop Ellicott and Dr. Angus of the English Revision Committee asked Dr. Philip Schaff to take the lead in America and in conjunction with them he selected the other committee members, drew up the provisional draft of the Constitution and organised the first American meeting. He often travelled to England to confer with Ellicott, Westcott, and Hort. Like the two Cambridge Professors who were dominant on the English committee, Schaff was the prime mover for all the work of both Old Testament and New Testament Committees in America and chaired them both. One Old Testament Committee member, Dr. T.W.

---

[4] Dean Burgon: *Revision Revised*

Chambers, remarked that, "the Christian public is indebted to Philip Schaff more than to all other persons together."[5]

Dr. Philip Schaff[6]

Dr. Schaff's theology seems to have been as deviant from orthodoxy as that of his two colleagues in England, Westcott and Hort. Like both English professors he was a liberal evolutionist, and he also declared himself a follower of the pantheistic German theologian Schleiermacher, whom he described as "the greatest theological genius since the Reformation."[7] His life's work, *The History of The Apostolic Church,* begun in 1853, reveals theories and doctrines so startling that several leading theological journals in America and Canada denounced them as anti-Scriptural and anti-Protestant. In classifying the sources of history, he puts in the first rank "the official letters, decrees and bulls of Popes," pronouncing them "pure, original utterances of history."[8]

Schaff was twice tried for heresy by his denomination and taught

---
[5] David Schaff, *Life of Philip Schaff*
[6] Illustration of Dr. Philip Schaff courtesy of: The Theologian
<http://www.theologian.org.uk/churchhistorynecessityofreformation.html>
[7] *Princeton Review,* January 1854, p. 168.
[8] *New Brunswick Review,* May 1854, p. 20.

at the very liberal Union Seminary. As chairman of the revision committee, Dr. Schaff not only was greatly influenced by Westcott and Hort, but also by the Unitarians Ezra Abbot and Joseph Thayer, of Harvard, as well as other liberals whom he placed on the committee. Most new versions since that time have adopted the same presuppositions as did those 19th century revisers.[9]

The unease about the suitability of Dr. Schaff as Head of the American Standard committee was expressed in the 1854 *New Brunswick Review*. "Through the misty drapery of Dr. Schaff's philosophy, every essential feature of the papal system stands forth with a prominence so sharply defined, as to leave doubt impossible and charity in despair," said one reviewer. The following quotation from contemporary writers of standing present the danger of Schaff's teachings:

> "It is quite time that the churches of our country should awake to the extent and the tendencies of this movement in the midst of American Protestantism. After a series of advances and retractions, strongly resembling the advances of the Tractarian party in England, we have at length a bold avowal of the 'Primacy of Peter', the fundamental and test doctrine of the Papacy, followed by a concession of every vital point of Christianity—Church, Ministry, Worship, Sacraments, and the Right of Private Judgment—to Romanism, and that, too, *while the name and the forms of Protestantism are* (as far as possible) *studiously retained.*"[10]

Dr. B. G. Wilkinson, in his 1930 book, *Our Authorized Bible Vindicated,* described the Gnostic influence that could be traced from Origen and the third-century corrupted text through to the Oxford Movement, Newman, and the textual bias of the Revisionists in England and America:

> "As the Vaticanus and Sinaiticus are evidently the product of Gnosticism, what would be more natural than that the

---

[9] Dr. Henry Morris: *A Creationist's Defence of the King James Bible* <www.icr.org/bible/kjv.htm>
[10] *New Brunswick Review*

Catholicism of Newman and the Gnosticism of his followers, who now flood the Protestant churches, would seek, by every means possible, to reinstate in leadership Gnosticism's old title-papers, the Vaticanus and Sinaiticus? Cardinal Newman believed that tradition and the Catholic Church were above the Bible. Westcott and Hort, great admirers of Newman, were leaders of the Revision Committee. ... Dr. Schaff sat in the *Parliament of World Religions* in Chicago, in 1893, and was so happy among the Buddhists, Confucianists, Shintoists, and other world religions, that he said that 'he would be willing to die among them.' The spirit of the Revisionists on both sides of the ocean was an effort to find the Word of God by the study of comparative religions. This is the spirit of Gnosticism; it is not true faith in the inspiration and infallibility of the Bible."

The Effect of Textual Criticism on Contemporary "Bibles"

Few Christians are aware of how in many respects the *New International Version* (NIV) is very much closer to the *New World Translation* (NWT), the Bible of the Jehovah's Witnesses, than it is to the King James. The same verses at odds with those in the KJV are again and again to be found in both versions. The same omissions are made, except that whereas the NIV often records the verse omitted as a footnote, the NWT leaves it out altogether. As Reverend Charles Salliby writes in his 1994 book *If the Foundations Be Destroyed,* "the NIV is clearly an 'Interdenominational (and ecumenical) masterpiece' that can cross any church threshold and make all within happy with whatever they believe. With this translation you could prove or disprove the Virgin Birth, or indeed the Deity of Jesus. ... Something to ponder: I do not know of one Christian who uses a *New World Translation* nor have I ever heard that such a Christian exists. Have you? Yet the NIV, whose contents so closely resemble those of the NWT, is the best selling Bible in the English speaking world today. If that is not a paradox, what is?"[11]

Not many Christians are aware of the extraordinary views held

---

[11] Charles Salliby: *If the Foundations be Destroyed*

and expressed by Dr. Robert Bratcher, chief translator of the Good News Version, published in 1966 by the American Bible Society. In 1953 Dr. Bratcher had written in a Brazilian Baptist publication that, "Jesus Christ would not enjoy omniscience. That is an attribute of God. ... Jesus did not claim He and the Father to be one — which would be absurd."[12]

In a letter to Julius C. Taylor, Dr. Bratcher wrote, "Of course I believe what I wrote in *The Journal Batista* of July 9th 1953." In 1981 he is quoted as saying: "Only willful ignorance or intellectual dishonesty can account for the claim that the Bible is inerrant and infallible... ... To invest the Bible with the qualities of inerrancy and infallibility is to idolatrize it, to transform it into a false god."[13]

The uproar following these and other remarks was such that Dr. Bratcher apologised in a press release. However, his apology was made because he had offended people, not in any way a retraction of the content of the many things that he had written and said. Dr Bratcher, of course, as Westcott and Hort before him, is fully entitled to his beliefs and enjoys the freedom under Christ to express them. However, such liberal beliefs **must inevitably influence the interpretation and translation of Holy Scripture,** and have done so, as we shall demonstrate.

Without venturing any deeper into the complex controversy among textual critics regarding the integrity of the different Greek manuscripts and their deployment in the many new versions, we simply seek to present comparisons of the English translations that speak for themselves.

---

[12] O Jornal Batista [The Baptist Journal], July 9, 1953, under the "Questions & Answers"
[13] The Baptist Courier, April 2, 1981.

Chapter 10
Bible Verse Comparisons

Just thirty examples follow, out of many hundreds of instances in which the new translations seriously diminish the divinity of Christ and undermine the Atonement. The new versions are also markedly ecumenical, lending support to Roman Catholic teaching and dogma, as will be shown; and for this reason they have surely been an important factor in the recent rapid advance of the inter-church process. We have discussed earlier that the modern versions lend themselves more readily to futurism, to a two-stage Second Coming, and to a world ruler Antichrist to appear after the rapture of the saints. Daniel's *"seventy weeks"* is translated with an unmistakable antichrist "prince" to fit the futurist thinking of the Oxford movement, of Newman, of Westcott and Hort, and of so many others who have exonerated the papacy from Scripture's identification.

We believe that conservative evangelicals are correct when they insist that the KJV is the only **Protestant** Bible in common use in our language. We are not aware of any instances of the KJV weakening the translation in any way in relation to the standing of Christ, His divinity, His name, His blood or His sacrifice. Even those who have set out to argue the superiority of the new translations have not cited instances of the KJV in any way undermining the great truths of the Gospel. Where opponents of the Authorised Bible point to what may seem to be obvious error in the translation they are often mistaken. Perhaps the best example of this is *Easter* in Acts 12.

1. Acts 12:3-4

KJV (King James Version)	"And because he [King Herod] saw it pleased the Jews, he proceeded further to take Peter also. *Cont'd*

	(then were the days of unleavened bread.) And when he had apprehended him, he put him in prison, and delivered him to four quaternions of soldiers to keep him; intending **after Easter** to bring him forth to the people."
NIV (New International Version)	"When he saw that this pleased the Jews, he proceeded to seize Peter also. This happened during the Feast of Unleavened Bread. After arresting him, he put him in prison, handing him over to be guarded by four squads of four soldiers each. Herod intended to bring him out for public trial **after the Passover.**"

Those who oppose the concept of a perfect Bible seize on the translation of *Easter* for the Greek word *pascha* as clear proof of the imperfection of the KJV. After all, in twenty-eight other appearances in the New Testament *pascha* is translated *Passover*. However, *Easter* is correct and *Passover* incorrect. Easter derives from the ancient pagan festival of Astarte, or Ishtar, the female goddess, known in the Bible as the *"queen of heaven"* (Jeremiah 7:18; 44:17 & 25). Herod was a pagan Edomite and would therefore observe Easter in honour of Astarte, not the Passover. The key to the correct translation is the sequence of events. Verse 3 tells us that Herod imprisoned Peter during the days of unleavened bread which were **after** the Passover[1] with the intention of holding a public trial after his own festival of Easter. The Passover preceded the events of Acts 12. Scripture does not use the term "Passover" to refer to the entire period[2].

The Deity of Christ

2. Acts 8:36-38 (Verse 37 removed.)

KJV	"And as they went on their way, they came unto a certain water: and the eunuch said, See, here is water; what doth hinder me to be baptized? **And Philip said, If thou believest with all thine**

---
[1] Exodus 12:13-18
[2] "The Feast of Unleavened Bread" is the form used, for example Mark 14:12

	heart, thou mayest. And he answered and said, **I believe that Jesus Christ is the Son of God.** And he commanded the chariot to stand still: and they went down both into the water, both Philip and the eunuch; and he baptized him."
NIV	"As they traveled along the road, they came to some water and the eunuch said, "Look, here is water Why shouldn't I be baptized?" And he gave orders to stop the chariot. Then both Philip and the eunuch went down into the water and Philip baptized him."
Good News	"As they traveled down the road, they came to a place where there was some water, and the official said, 'Here is some water. What is to keep me from being baptized?' The official ordered the carriage to stop, and both Philip and the official went down into the water, and Philip baptized him."

This verse, one of the outstanding testimonies to the deity of Christ in the Bible, is missing altogether from the text of the new versions. It appears as a footnote in both the Good News and in the NIV.[3] Yet, the Church fathers Irenaeus and Cyprian mention it in the second and third centuries, **well before** the *Vaticanus* and *Sinaiticus* **codices came into existence.**

3. Micah 5:2 (Jesus' origins "from ancient times"?)

KJV	"...yet out of thee shall he come forth unto me that is to be ruler in Israel; whose goings forth have been from of old, **from everlasting.**"
NIV	"... out of you will come for me one who will be ruler over Israel, whose origins are from of old, **from ancient times.**"
NWT (New World Translation)	"...from you there will come out to me the one who is to become ruler in Israel, whose origin is from early times, **from the days of time indefinite.**"

---

[3] The NIV point to "some late manuscripts" and the Good News to "some manuscripts" that add verse 37.

This great prophecy refers to the eternal Son of God who has no origin.[4] Both the NIV and the Jehovah's Witness NWT blasphemously describe the Lord Jesus Christ as a created being.

4. 1 John 5:7-8 (Verse 7 removed; verse 8 rearranged.)

KJV	"For there are three that bear record in heaven, **the Father, the Word, and the Holy Ghost: and these three are one. And there are three that bear witness in earth,** the Spirit, and the water, and the blood: and these three agree in one."
NIV	"For there are three that testify: the Spirit, the water and the blood; and the three are in agreement."
Good News	"There are three witnesses: the Spirit, the water, and the blood; and all three give the same testimony."

The NIV, Good News and almost all other modern versions omit verse 7, which says, *"For there are three that bear record in heaven, the Father, the Word and the Holy Ghost, and these three are one."* Additionally verse 8 is divided to conceal this omission.

Known as "the Johannine Comma", this verse and its inclusion in the Bible has been at the centre of considerable controversy for a long time, and the arguments against it are formidable. However, there is surely no verse in Scripture that more clearly defines the Trinity and the divinity of Christ. For Jehovah's Witnesses and Mormons it is unanswerable, unless they can marshal the arguments of the "naturalistic" and "higher" textual critics, or argue that it wasn't divinely inspired.

The omission of the last twelve verses of Mark's Gospel in the Westcott and Hort versions, which record in the footnote that "the two most reliable early manuscripts do not have Mark 16:9-20", was comprehensively challenged by John Burgon, Dean of Chichester, who wrote to the Revision Committee:

---

[4] John 1:1: *"In the beginning was the Word, and the Word was with God, and the Word was God."*

"With the exception of the two uncial manuscripts that have just been named (Vaticanus and Sinaiticus), there is not one Codex in existence... ...which leaves out the last twelve verses of Mark... ...Not only have you on countless occasions thrust out words, clauses and entire sentences of genuine Scripture, but you have been careful that no trace should survive of the fatal injury you have inflicted. I wonder you were not afraid. Can I be wrong in deeming such a proceeding sinful? Has not the Spirit Pronounced a tremendous doom (in Revelation: 22:19) for those who do such things?"[5]

Later on, in 1883, Burgon, the principal dissenter of the 1881 Revising Committee, gave a second solemn warning to posterity,

"A hazy mistrust of all Scripture has been insinuated into the hearts and minds of countless millions, who in this way have been forced to become doubters—yes, doubters—in the Truth of Revelation itself. One recalls sorrowfully the terrible woe denounced by the author of Scripture on those who minister occasions of falling to others: *'It must needs be that offences come, but woe to that man by whom the offence cometh'*"[6]

Also missing from Mark's Gospel is the second part of verse 11 of chapter 6, the Saviour's solemn warning, as shown below.

Mark 6:11

KJV	"And whosoever shall not receive you, nor hear you, when ye depart thence, shake off the dust under your feet for a testimony against them. **Verily I say unto you, It shall be more tolerable for Sodom and Gomorrha in the day of judgment, than for that city.**"

---

[5] John Burgon: *The Last Twelve Verses of Mark,* Bible for Today, 900 Park Ave., Collingswood, NJ 08108.
[6] John Burgon: *Revision Revised*

NIV	"And if any place will not welcome you or listen to you, shake the dust off your feet when you leave, as a testimony against them."
The Message	"If you're not welcomed, not listened to, quietly withdraw. Don't make a scene. Shrug your shoulders and be on your way."

5. Matthew 5:44 (Verse from the Sermon on the Mount is mutilated.)

KJV	"But I say unto you, Love your enemies, **bless them that curse you, do good to them that hate you, and pray for them that despitefully use you**, and persecute you."
NIV	"But I tell you: Love your enemies and pray for those who persecute you."

6. 1 Timothy 3:16

KJV	"And without controversy great is the mystery of godliness: **God was manifest in the flesh**, justified in the Spirit, seen of angels, preached unto the Gentiles, believed on in the world, received up into glory."
NIV	"Beyond all question, the mystery of godliness is great: **He appeared in a body**, was vindicated by the Spirit, was seen by angels, was preached among the nations, was believed on in the world, was taken up in glory."
NWT	"Indeed, the sacred secret of this godly devotion is admittedly great: '**He was made manifest in the flesh**, was declared righteous in spirit, appeared to angels, was preached about among nations, was believed upon in [the] world, was received up in glory.'"

This verse clearly reveals the divinity of Jesus Christ. The Authorised translation describes Christ as truly God; the NIV translation could hardly be more banal. Widely seen as the most serious corruption of God's pure and holy Word (which one would expect to find in the Jehovah's Witness bible). Believers who use the NIV are handicapped in evangelising Jehovah's witnesses.

According to Burgon, out of 254 copies of Paul's Epistles known to the 1881 Revision Committee, no less than 252 preserved the expression "God was manifest" with only the favoured two differing with "he who was manifested (the revisers first translation). The 1882 choice of wording was influenced by the Unitarian member of the Committee who declared himself entirely satisfied with the translation.

7. Daniel 3:25

KJV	"He answered and said, Lo, I see four men loose, walking in the midst of the fire, and they have no hurt; and the form of **the fourth is like the Son of God**."
NIV	"He said, 'Look! I see four men walking around in the fire, unbound and unharmed, and **the fourth looks like a son of the gods.**'"
NWT	""He was answering and saying: 'Look! I am beholding four able-bodied men walking about free in the midst of the fire, and there is no hurt to them, and **the appearance of the fourth one is resembling a son of the gods.**'"
Good News	"'Then why do I see four men walking around in the fire?' he asked. 'They are not tied up, and they show no sign of being hurt—and **the fourth one looks like a god.**"

The KJV describes the fourth man in the fiery furnace as *"like the Son of God"*. One edition of the Good News Version translates this as *"like an angel"*. In the NIV, the NWT, The Good News footnote, and several other versions it is *"like a son of the gods."* The difference is very considerable.[7]

8. Matthew 8:2

KJV	"And, behold, there came a leper and **worshipped him,** saying, **Lord,** if thou wilt, thou canst make me clean."
Good News	"Then a man suffering from a dreaded skin disease came to him, **knelt down before him,** and said, '**Sir,** if you want to, you can make me clean.'"

In this one short verse, Christ's divinity is twice lessened by The Good News Version. The word worshipped, referring to Jesus during His ministry, is used six times in the Authorised Version of the Gospel of Matthew but only once in The Good News.

9. Zechariah 13:6

KJV	"And one shall say unto him, **What are these wounds in thine hands?** Then he shall answer, Those with which I was wounded in the house of my friends."
NIV	"If someone asks him, '**What are these wounds on your body?**' he will answer, 'The wounds I was given at the house of my friends.'"
NWT	"And one must say to him, '**What are these wounds [on your person] between your hands?**' And he will have to say, 'Those with which I was struck in the house of my intense lovers.'"
RSV	"And if one asks him, '**What are these wounds on your back?**' he will say, 'The wounds I received in the house of my friends.'"

---

[7] Genesis 6:2-6: *"That the sons of God saw the daughters of men that they were fair; and they took them wives of all which they chose. And the LORD said, My spirit shall not always strive with man, for that he also is flesh: yet his days shall be an hundred and twenty years. There were giants in the earth in those days; and also after that, when the sons of God came in unto the daughters of men, and they bare children to them, the same became mighty men which were of old, men of renown. And GOD saw that the wickedness of man was great in the earth, and that every imagination of the thoughts of his heart was only evil continually. And it repented the LORD that he had made man on the earth, and it grieved him at his heart."*

The prophetic reference to the crucifixion has been removed from the NIV and other modern versions.

Washed in the Blood of the Lamb (?)

10. Revelation 1:5

KJV	"…Unto him that loved us, **and washed us** from our sins in his own blood."
NIV	" … To him who loves us **and has freed us** from our sins by his blood,"
Good News	" … He loves us , and by his death he **has freed us** from our sins…"

The NIV, the Good News and almost all other modern versions nowhere have the believer "washed in the blood of the lamb." Thus the majority of Christians now sing "O happy day—when Jesus washed my sins away" without Biblical warrant.

The Virgin Birth

11. Luke 2:33 (Jesus—the Son of God or the son of Joseph?)

KJV	"And **Joseph and his mother** marvelled at those things which were spoken of him."
NIV	"**The child's father and mother** marveled at what was said about him."
The Message	"**Jesus' father and mother** were speechless with surprise at these words."

Besides this change in verse 33 (in the NIV and most of the new versions), in verse 43, "*Joseph and His mother*" becomes "*his parents*". In both places the Greek text contains the word *Joseph*. It is translated as Joseph thirty-three times in the New Testament. It is difficult to avoid the conclusion that there seems to have been a deliberate attempt to undermine the Virgin Birth, which is nowadays called into question by many leading liberals in the Church of England and elsewhere.

12. Isaiah 7:14

KJV	"...Behold, **a virgin shall conceive, and bear a son**, and shall call his name Immanuel."
Good News	"...**a young woman who is pregnant will have a son** and will name him 'Immanuel.'"
NIV	"...**The virgin will be with child and will give birth to a son**, and will call him Immanuel."

In The Good News Version this famous Messianic prophecy does not predict the Virgin Birth. Any young pregnant woman may have a son, but the Virgin Birth is unique. Of a total of fourteen occasions when the word *virgin* is used in the Greek and in the KJV, the Good News has eleven times substituted different words, i.e., *girl, young woman, young girl* and *unmarried*.

The NIV translation of Isaiah 7:14 is *"The virgin will be with child..."* as it is also in Matthew 1:23. The use of the definite article points to **The** Virgin Mary, the "Mother of God", and the "Queen of Heaven" of Roman Catholicism.

Roman Catholic Doctrine supported by Ecumenical Translations

13. Matthew 1:25

KJV	"And knew her not **till she had brought forth her first-born son**: and he called his name JESUS."
NIV	"But he had no union with her **until she gave birth to a son**. And he gave him the name of Jesus."
The Message	"But he did not consummate the marriage **until she had the baby**. He named the baby Jesus."

The NIV and most other modern versions, to uphold Roman Catholic teaching of the perpetual virginity of Mary, omit *first-born*.

14. John 1:42 (Peter—the Rock or the Little Stone?)

KJV	"...Thou art Simon the son of Jona: thou shalt be called Cephas, which is by interpretation, **A stone**."
Good News	"...'Your name is Simon son of John, but you will be called Cephas,' (This is the same as Peter and means **'a rock.'**)"
The Message	"He immediately led him to Jesus. Jesus took one look up and said, 'You're John's son, Simon? From now on your name is Cephas' (**or Peter, which means 'Rock'**)."

Whereas the KJV translates the name Peter as "a stone", *The Good News*, *The Message*, and some other modern versions translate it as "rock."

Much of the new authority recently gained by the Roman Catholic Church, based on the ancient claim of the Popes to be the successors of Peter, rests on these new translations. *The Good News* is seen as an ecumenical bible; the *Revised New English Bible*, a recent addition to the many revisions, is also an ecumenical bible, translated by both Protestant and Roman Catholic scholars. According to the International Bible Society, the *NIV, RSV, NASV, Good News* and *RNEB* New Testaments are all based on the United Bible Society/Nestle-Aland Greek eclectic text. Prominent among the scholars that produced this text in its second and third editions was His Eminence Cardinal Carlo Maria Martini, Archbishop of Milan, a Jesuit and the Vatican's leading Greek scholar, who had long been among the favourites to succeed John Paul as Pope. Many "new evangelicals" see the wide distribution of these "ecumenical Bibles", based on "a common text" authorised by the Vatican, as an essential step towards reunion with Rome.

15. John 6:55

KJV	"For my flesh is **meat indeed** and my blood is **drink indeed**."
NIV	"For my flesh is **real food** and my blood is **real drink**."
Good News	"For my flesh is **the real food**; my blood is **the real drink**."

The KJV translation emphasis on "indeed" carries the meaning "true" which is the closest to the Greek Received Text. The new translations suggest "the real presence", the dogma of Roman Catholicism which was the central and crucial issue of the sixteenth-century Reformation in England. Most of the martyrs of the faith chose to die in denying that there is "real food" or "real drink" in the sacrament of the Lord's Supper. They insisted that there is the true spiritual nourishment received in the heart by faith with thanksgiving.

16. Matthew 24:23

KJV	"Then if any man shall say unto you, Lo, here is Christ, or there; believe it not."

This has long been interpreted, as warning against "the real presence" and "the Blessed Sacrament" which is "reserved for adoration" in Roman Catholic and many Anglican Churches. The "real presence" is being brought back into currency again in a different form among professing Protestant churches through the summoning or calling down of the Holy Spirit to effect healing and other signs and wonders or "to practise the real presence of God with us."

17. Matthew 19:17

KJV	"And he said unto him, **Why callest thou me good**? there is none good but one, that is, God:..."
NIV	"**'Why do you ask me about what is good?'** Jesus replied. 'There is only One who is good.'"

The Church of Rome calls all that have been beatified or canonised "good". They are to be venerated and often their relics are to be adored. This is an example of a **"dynamic equivalence"** translation in the NIV—the ecumenical translator not accepting from the plain text what he believes simply cannot be there.

18. Matthew 6:7

KJV	"But when ye pray, **use not vain repetitions**, as the heathen do:…"
NIV	"And when you pray, **do not keep on babbling like pagans**,…"
Good News	"When you pray, **do not use a lot of meaningless words**, as the pagans do,…"

Repetitious prayers like the "Hail Mary" can be said without censure from the new versions.

19. James 5:16

KJV	"Confess your **faults** one to another, and pray one for another, that ye may be healed…"
NIV	"Therefore confess your **sins** to each other and pray for each other so that you may be healed.…"

Here we find the new biblical warrant for the Roman Catholic sacrament of the Confessional.

20. 2 Peter 1:20-21

KJV	"Knowing this first, that **no prophecy of the Scripture is of any private interpretation.…**"
Good News	"Above all else, remember that **no one can explain by himself a prophecy in the Scriptures...**"
CEV (Contemporary English Version)	"But you need to realize that **no one alone can understand any of the prophecies in the Scriptures…**"

In other words prophecy is not an expression of the personal opinion of the prophet, but of God, through His Spirit. The Good News translation renders a totally different meaning to these verses by beginning, "No one can interpret any prophecy of Scripture by himself..."

The Apostle was teaching us how prophecy was **given**. This and other modern versions tell us how it should be **received**. The Church of Rome's position that the individual **must not exercise private judgement** in interpreting Scripture but submit to the authority of Mother Church, the Magisterium, is supported by this translation. As Kansas City Jesuit Professor, H. Willmering, recently wrote in *The Catholic Community,* "it is of prime importance to know that prophecy of Scripture is not subject to private interpretation by every individual, as the false teachers assume it is." It will not have escaped the reader that the issue here is that very issue at the heart of the Protestant Reformation—the authority of the Bible over the authority of the Church, or the authority of the Church over the Bible.

21. 2 Thessalonians 2:7

KJV	"... For the mystery of iniquity doth already work: only **he** who letteth will let until **he** be taken out of the way."
NKJV	"... For the mystery of lawlessness is already at work**,** only **He** who now restrains will do so until **He** is taken out of the way."

The New King James Version, **although considerably closer than other modern versions**, is not the KJV in updated language. Nor is it faithful to the Received Text. Like other modern versions it reflects the views and interpretations of its translators and is eclectic in its choice of manuscript renderings, often preferring the corrupted minority texts to the received text.[8]

---

[8] Some new Bible versions, besides the *New King James Version* translate this as He (not he), which clearly means the Holy Spirit. This only allows for a futurist interpretation and a pre-tribulation rapture. See Chapter 1, "The Historical View of Prophecy and Antichrist"; Subheading "The Man of Sin and Mystery of Iniquity."

22. 2 Thessalonians 2:10

KJV	"And with **all deceivableness of unrighteousness** in them that perish; because they received not the love of the truth, that they might be saved."
NIV	"and in **every sort of evil that deceives** those who are perishing. They perish because they refused to love the truth and so be saved."

The coming of the *"man of sin"* was to be with *"all deceivableness of unrighteousness."* As J.A. Wylie, Victorian author of *The History of Protestantism* wrote, "Let us mark the phrase. It is a very remarkable one. It is used in no other place; it is employed to describe no other system; it describes the great apostasy and it alone. It is not simply 'deceivableness,' nor is it simply 'unrighteousness', it is the 'deceivableness of unrighteousness,' nay, it is the all-deceivableness of unrighteousness.

"Paganism was a system of deceivableness. It was the worship of a false god, under the pretence of being the worship of the true God, but popery is deceivableness on a scale far beyond that of paganism. The one was a counterfeit of the religion of nature; the other is a counterfeit of the Gospel. Popery has a god of its own—him, whom the canon law calls 'the Lord our God.' [*Decretales Gregorii IX. Tit. 7. The Pope is called God, Decretum Gregorii XIII. Distinctio 96, Can. 7]*. It has a saviour of its own—the Church. It has a sacrifice of its own—the Mass. It has a mediator of its own—the Priesthood. It has a sanctifier of its own—the Sacrament. It has a justification of its own—that even of infused righteousness. It has a pardon of its own—the pardon of the Confessional; and it has in the heavens an infallible, all-prevailing advocate unknown to the Gospel—the 'Mother of God.' It thus presents to the world a spiritual and saving apparatus for the salvation of men, which neither sanctifies nor saves anyone. It looks like a church; it professes to have all that a church ought to have; and yet it is not a church. It is a grand deception; it is *'the all deceivableness of unrighteousness.'"*[9]

---

[9] Rev. Dr. J.A. Wylie: *The Papacy is the Antichrist*: Our Inheritance Ministries, 12 High Street, Polegate, East Sussex

Prophecy Lost

23. Isaiah 31:5

KJV	"As birds flying, so will the Lord of Hosts defend Jerusalem; defending also he will deliver it; **and passing over he will preserve it.**"
NIV	"Like birds hovering overhead, the LORD Almighty will shield Jerusalem; he will shield it and deliver it, he will **'pass over' it and will rescue it.**"
Good News	"Just **as a bird hovers over its nest** to protect its young, so I, the LORD Almighty, will protect Jerusalem and defend it."

Many Christians who hold to an historical view of Bible prophecy believe that this Scripture was actually fulfilled in December 1917. The deliverance of Jerusalem from the longstanding Moslem rule of the Ottoman Turks was accomplished, in answer to the faithful prayer of God's people, by the British forces under General Allenby, using aeroplanes for the first time in such a campaign.

The Modern Versions are at variance one with another. The NIV translation is similar to the KJV, but the Good News does not allow for such an interpretation at all: *"Just as a bird hovers over its nest to protect its young, so I, the LORD Almighty will protect Jerusalem and defend it."* The seriousness of the problem of different translations is perhaps illustrated here as clearly as it is anywhere— God's prophetic Word altered into something entirely different.

24. Isaiah 59:19

KJV	"So shall they fear the name of the LORD from the west, and his glory from the rising of the sun. **When the enemy shall come in like a flood, the Spirit of the LORD shall lift up a standard against him.**"
NIV	"From the west, men will fear the name of the LORD, and from the rising of the sun, they will revere his glory. **For he will come like a pent-up flood that the breath of the LORD drives along.**"

The second part of the Scripture is virtually unrecognisable in the NIV; this great word of prophecy is mutilated.

25. Daniel 12:4

KJV	"But thou, O Daniel, shut up the words, and seal the book, even to the time of the end: **many shall run to and fro, and knowledge shall be increased.**"
Good News	"He said to me, 'And now, Daniel, close the book and put a seal on it until the end of the world, **many people will waste their efforts trying to understand what is happening.**'"

The vivid portrayal of life as we now live it in the second half of the verse is obscured entirely in the Good News and other modern versions' mutilated renderings.

26. Daniel 9:26-27 (Daniel's 70th Week)

KJV	"And after threescore and two weeks shall Messiah be cut off, but not for himself: and the people of the prince that shall come shall destroy the city and the sanctuary; and the end thereof shall be with a flood, and unto the end of the war desolations are determined. And **he shall confirm the covenant with many for one week**: and in the midst of the week he shall cause the sacrifice and the oblation to cease, and for the overspreading of abominations he shall make it desolate, even until the consummation, and that determined shall be poured upon the desolate."
NIV	"After the sixty-two 'sevens,' the Anointed One will be cut off and will have nothing. The people of the ruler who will come will destroy the city and the sanctuary. The end will come like a flood: War will continue until the end, and desolations have been decreed. **He will confirm a covenant with many for one 'seven.'** In the middle of the 'seven' he will put an end to sacrifice and offering. And on a wing

	of the temple he will set up an abomination that causes desolation, until the end that is decreed is poured out on him."
Good News	"And at the end of that time God's chosen leader will be killed unjustly. The city and the Temple will be destroyed by the invading army of a powerful ruler. The end will come like a flood, bringing the war and destruction which God has prepared. **That ruler will have a firm agreement with many people for seven years**, and when half this time is past, he will put an end to sacrifices and offerings. The Awful Horror will be placed on the highest point of the Temple and will remain there until the one who put it there meets the end which God has prepared for him."

Careful comparison of Daniel's great words of prophecy in the *KJV*, *NIV*, and *Good News* versions demonstrates how the Protestant Historical view of these verses as predicting the sacrifice to end all sacrifices at Calvary, followed by the desolation of Jerusalem and the Temple in AD 70, is superseded now by the Futurist theory of Antichrist at the end of the church age. In the new translations, Antichrist, who has replaced Christ *"the Prince"* of the KJV rendering, will make and break a covenant with the Jews, first allowing them to offer sacrifices in a "rebuilt" temple and after three and a half years causing the sacrifice to cease. The "fulfilled" interpretation, which can only be received from the KJV translation, has the covenant confirmed and the sacrifice and the oblation ceased when Christ died after a ministry of three and a half years in the middle of the 70th week.[10]

Doctrine Lost

Apart from such enormous variations in the text and such radical changes in meaning, and apart from the loss of whole verses and even whole passages of Scripture, key words of much spiritual

---

[10] See Chapter 2, "Futurism Devised by the Jesuits - The Wiles of the Devil"; Subheading "The Seventy Weeks."

significance are changed or left out of the new editions. For example the word **"blood"** is omitted no less than thirty-four times in the New Testament by the **Good News Version.** As we have already noted, **"virgin"** is replaced, not translated, by "young woman" eleven times. **"Hell"** is another word that the new translators prefer to avoid, as do many of the new school of preachers. It is often replaced with **"Hades", "Sheol"** and **"world of the dead"**. The NIV changes it to **"grave"** in several instances. The word **"sin"**, another of the "buzz words" of the Bible, as one Charismatic preacher called it, has survived the purging of such terms in the new versions, although it has not fared so well in the pulpit, nor in everyday use in the nation.

27. Mark 2:17

KJV	"...I came not to call the righteous, **but sinners to repentance.**"
NIV	"...I have not come to call the righteous, **but sinners.**"
Good News	"...I have not come to call respectable people, **but outcasts.**"

The term "repentance" disappears several times from the New Testament in both the NIV and the Good News Version.

28. John 3:16

KJV	"For God so loved the world, that **he gave his only begotten Son**, that whosoever believeth in him should not perish, but have everlasting life."
NIV	"For God so loved the world that **he gave his one and only Son**, that whoever believes in him shall not perish but have eternal life."

Possibly the best known verse in the Bible teaches in the NIV that we are not sons and our God in heaven is not our father. The KJV tells us that God has only one begotten Son.

29. Matthew 5:22

KJV	"But I say unto you, That **whosoever is angry with his brother without a cause** shall be in danger of the judgment:…"
NIV	"But I tell you that **anyone who is angry with his brother** will be subject to judgment…"

According to this verse in the NIV, Jesus' conduct in Mark 3:5 would be subject to judgement.

30. Titus 3:10

KJV	"**A man that is an heretick** after the first and second admonition reject;"
NIV	"Warn **a divisive person** once, and then warn him a second time. After that, have nothing to do with him."
Good News	Give at least two warnings to **the person who causes divisions**, and then have nothing more to do with him."

The Scripture has been turned on its head. The "divisive" person that warns of error and heresy in the church (the "heresy-hunter") is liable to be the one that is excluded from fellowship and rejected. But Romans 16:17-18, *"Mark them which cause divisions and offences contrary to the doctrine you have learned; and avoid them,"* which is as clear in the NIV as the KJV demonstrates the poverty of the translation, *"divisive person."*

As American Bible teacher Dr. Charles Woodbridge once noted in a warning to the well-known evangelist Billy Graham: "If you persist in making common cause with those that deny the Word of God, and thus in minimizing the sharp line of distinction between those who are loyal and those who are disloyal to the Scriptures, it is my strong opinion that you will be known as the great divider of the church of Christ of the 20th century."[11]

---

[11] September, 1963, from "Dr. Billy Graham, the Champion of Compromise", <http://www.orlandobiblechurch.com/id27.html>accessed 2/11/06.

The loss of the term *heresy* in Scripture and from today's preaching has in a very real sense undermined and emasculated church history. The inference is that in the past, Christians were less enlightened, less tolerant and loving, and were diverted from the fullness of relationship with Christ by negative attitudes. This can be seen as part of the strategy of Satan for dividing the true church as well as seriously weakening the Word of God. Bishop Ryle's words summarise the issue very well.

> "Divisions and separations are most objectionable in religion. They weaken the cause of Christianity... But before we blame people for them, we must be careful that we lay the blame where it is deserved. False doctrine and heresy are even worse than schism. If people separate themselves from teaching which is positively false and unscriptural, they ought to be praised rather than reproved. In such cases separation is a virtue and not a sin ... The old saying never must be forgotten, 'He is the schismatic who causes the schism' ... Controversy in religion is a hateful thing ... But there is one thing which is even worse than controversy, and that is false doctrine, allowed, and permitted without protest or molestation."[12]

The term *reformation* has also been dropped from Hebrews 9:10 and with it the strong link with our Protestant heritage.

KJV	"Which stood only in meats and drinks, and divers washings, and carnal ordinances, imposed on **them until the time of reformation.**"
NIV	"They are only a matter of food and drink and various ceremonial washings—external regulations applying **until the time of the new order.**"

---

[12] Ryle: *Warning to the Churches,* London: Banner of Truth, 1967, pp. 109-110.

Good News	"...since they have to do only with food, drink, and various purification ceremonies. These are all outward rules, which apply **only until the time when God will establish the new order**."

The NIV and the Good News have replaced *reformation* with the term *new order*, which is entirely different and suggests departure from the past. It cannot be ruled out that in the near future we shall have a version called *The New Age Bible*.

Perhaps the foundations for such a bible are already being laid.

Isaiah 14:12-15

KJV	"How art thou fallen from heaven, **O Lucifer**, son of the morning! how art thou cut down to the ground, which didst weaken the nations! For thou hast said in thine heart, I will ascend into heaven, I will exalt my throne above the stars of God: I will sit also upon the mount of the congregation, in the sides of the north: I will ascend above the heights of the clouds; I will be like the most High. Yet thou shalt be brought down to hell, to the sides of the pit."
NIV	"How you have fallen from heaven, **O morning star**, son of the dawn! You have been cast down to the earth, you who once laid low the nations! You said in your heart, 'I will ascend to heaven; I will raise my throne above the stars of God;I will sit enthroned on the mount of assembly, on the utmost heights of the sacred mountain. I will ascend above the tops of the clouds; I will make myself like the Most High.' But you are brought down to the grave, to the depths of the pit."

The KJV makes it very clear that it is Lucifer whose self-exaltation caused his being thrown down into the pit. The NIV, on the other hand, is by no means as clear, as it uses the very same title that the Lord attributes to Himself in Revelation 22:16: *"I Jesus have sent mine angel to testify unto you these things in the churches. I am the root and the offspring of David, and the bright and morning star."*

Luke 11:2-4

KJV	"…When ye pray, say, **Our** Father **which art in heaven**, Hallowed be thy name. Thy kingdom come. **Thy will be done, as in heaven, so in earth.** Give us day by day our daily bread. And forgive us our sins; for we also forgive every one that is indebted to us. And lead us not into temptation; **but deliver us from evil.**"
NIV	"…'When you pray, say: "Father, hallowed be your name, your kingdom come. Give us each day our daily bread. Forgive us our sins, for we also forgive everyone who sins against us. And lead us not into temptation."

Again, the KJV is quite clear as to Whom we are praying—God, our Father in heaven, Whose will is done in heaven, Who alone can deliver us from evil. The Lord Jesus of the NIV only tells us that we are to pray to some indefinite father, and who that father is remains in the realm of our vain imaginings, making this prayer quite acceptable to those who prefer to honour the "whoever-one-wants-him-to-be" god of the New Age.

PART III
ARMINIANISM: A MAN-CENTRED GOSPEL

Chapter 11

The Origins of Arminianism

James (Jacob) Arminius (1560-1609) was a Dutch theologian who studied and taught the Gospel of the Lord Jesus Christ that had been rediscovered and proclaimed by the Reformation. Subsequently he changed his position and began to preach and teach a man-centred gospel. Calvin, Luther, Cranmer, Latimer, Zwingli, and Knox, among many other great preachers, taught the centrality of the grace of God and His gift of faith alone, for salvation in the Lord Jesus Christ. This Christ-centred gospel was, and is *"the power of God unto salvation to every one that believeth."*[1] In this section we set out to study the man-centred gospel that has become standard in many parts of what is still called "Evangelicalism." This man-centred message sees the receiving of the Gospel as deriving from a person's own faith. It assumes wrongly that salvation originates with the will of man by his choice or decision and it is finally to be positioned in the human heart. The Scriptures make clear that salvation originates with God, not to be within the human heart but to be "in Christ." For example, the Apostle Paul states in his own testimony *"...that I may win Christ and be found in him, not having mine own righteousness, which is of the law, but that which is through the faith of Christ, the righteousness which is of God by faith."*[2] How then did this man-centred salvation come into the Christian church? As we shall seek to show there has been a great falling away from the truths that were proclaimed at the time of the

---

[1] Romans 1:16
[2] Philippians 3:8-9

Reformation.[3] Many modern evangelicals, in sharing their gospel, publicly offer "invitations" such as, "Accept Jesus into your heart", "Invite Jesus into your life", or "Make a decision for Christ." Like Roman Catholicism, such a gospel looks for salvation in the human heart, and is thought to be brought about by man's own choice.

The author asks for the reader's patience in studying this third section of the book, in order to carefully take note of the record of history, the witness of Scripture and the testimony of post-Reformation servants of Christ who have warned of *"another gospel"* and *"another spirit."*[4] All that follows has been documented in order to demonstrate that much of what has come to be accepted as Christianity is misconceived. Totally missing in the modern man-centred message is the defining Biblical truth spelled out by the Apostle Paul, *"There is none righteous, no, not one: there is none that understands, there is none that seeks after God."*[5] In fact the Apostle makes clear to the would-be convert that there is absolutely nothing we have to offer to contribute to our salvation. God makes alive those *"who were dead in trespasses and sins."*[6] We shall show from the record of history that this man-centred Christianity has become what is now the official teaching of the Roman Catholic Church. The Second Vatican Council has taught that man is simply incapacitated or wounded by sin, and he can decide his own destiny in the sight of God.

> ". . . Nevertheless man has been **wounded by sin**. He finds by experience that his body is in revolt. His very dignity therefore requires that he should glorify God in his body, and not allow it to serve the evil inclinations of his heart. . . . When he is drawn to think about his real self he turns to those deep recesses of his being where God who probes the heart awaits him, and **where he himself decides his own destiny in the**

---

[3] This is fully documented in *Evangelicalism Divided* by Iain Murray (Banner of Truth Trust, 2000).
[4] 2 Corinthians 11:4
[5] Romans 3:10-11
[6] Ephesians 2:1

sight of God."[7]

Arminianism among evangelicals has been described as a half-way house to Roman Catholicism and has been responsible for much of the growth of the Ecumenical Movement. Man-centred "free-will" Christianity and Roman Catholicism are equally wedded to a wrong message. To understand this more fully we need the historical explanation of just how this whole system of thought arose. In this section we will use the eponymous term Arminianism to refer to that system which upholds a man-centred message.

An Historic Heresy

Dr. Lorraine Boettner, American author of two important books, *Roman Catholicism* and *The Reformed Doctrine of Predestination*, has given us an helpful observation to begin examining this difficult subject.

> "...Arminianism existed for centuries only as a heresy on the outskirts of true religion, and in fact it was not championed by an organized Christian church until the year 1784, at which time it was incorporated into the system of doctrine of the Methodist Church in England [by John Wesley]."[8]

We have shown earlier in this book[9] how in the sixteenth century Jesuit scholars were commissioned to undermine the *Received Text* and to re-interpret Bible prophecy in order to vindicate the Papacy from its widely held identification as the Antichrist.

However, shielding the Church of Rome from the sword of the Spirit would not be enough. The Reformation's newly rediscovered

---

[7] Vatican II Documents No. 64, *Gaudium et Spes*, 7 Dec 1965 in *Documents of Vatican II: The Conciliar and Post Conciliar Documents*, Austin P. Flannery, Ed. New Revised Edition, 2 Vols. (Grand Rapids, MI: Wm. B. Eerdmans Publishing Co., 1975, 1984) Vol. I, Sec. 14, p. 915
[8] Loraine Boettner: *The Reformed Doctrine of Predestination*
[9] See Chapter 2, "Futurism—Devised by the Jesuits—The Wiles of the Devil" and Chapter 3, "The Counter-Reformation—The Source of the Futurist View of Prophecy"

doctrines of grace, underlining the sovereignty of God and underpinning the eternal security of the believer, altogether at odds with the pretensions of the Pope, would need to be challenged and overturned. The Jesuits were commissioned to infiltrate the church and its institutions of learning.

The Pope's secret army of infiltrators was prophesied in the Scriptures, "*...false brethren unawares brought in, who came in privily to spy out our liberty which we have in Christ Jesus, that they might bring us into bondage:*"[10] The Apostle Peter also described them and what they would do.

> "*But there were false prophets also among the people, even as there shall be false teachers among you, who privily shall bring in damnable heresies, even denying the Lord that bought them, and bring on themselves swift destruction. And many shall follow their pernicious ways; by reason of whom the way of truth shall be evil spoken of.*"[11]

In his book *Arminianism: The Road Back to Rome*, Augustus Toplady, preacher, scholar, theologian, and hymn-writer ("Rock of Ages" and "A Debtor to Mercy Alone"), wrote that "as Arminianism came from Rome, so it leads thither again."[12] Also, he added the following:

> "...the Jesuits were moulded into a regular body, towards the middle of the sixteenth century; towards the close of the same century, Arminius began to infect the Protestant churches. It needs therefore no great penetration to discern from what source he drew his poison. His journey to Rome...
> ...was not for nothing. If, however, any are disposed to believe that Arminius imbibed his doctrines from the Socinians in Poland, with whom, it is certain, he was on terms of intimate friendship. I have no objection to splitting the difference; he

---

[10] Galatians 2:4
[11] 2 Peter 2:1-2
[12] Augustus Toplady: *Arminianism: The Road Back to Rome*, from *The Complete Works of Augustus Toplady*, Sprinkle Publications, [1794] 1987, pp. 54-55).

might import some of his tenets from the Racovian brethren, and yet be indebted, for others, to the disciples of Loyola."[13]

In England, in the seventeenth century, during the Arminian regime of William Laud, Archbishop of Canterbury from 1633 to 1645 and a persecutor of both Puritans and Covenanters, zealous Arminians were promoted to the best bishoprics. A famous letter written by a Jesuit to the Rector of Brussels and endorsed by Laud himself was found in the Archbishop's own study at Lambeth. A copy of this same letter was also found among the papers of a society of priests and Jesuits at Clerkenwell in 1627. The following is an extract from this notorious letter:

> "We have now many strings to our bow. We have planted *the sovereign drug Arminianism* which we hope will purge the Protestants from their heresy; and it flourisheth and beareth fruit in due season... ...I am at this time transported with joy to see how happily all instruments and means, as well great as smaller, co-operate with our purposes. But to return to the main fabric; OUR FOUNDATION IS ARMINIANISM."[14]

In his book *Justification by Faith Alone* Dr. Joel Beeke, Professor of Systematic Theology at the Puritan Reformed Seminary at Grand Rapids, exposing the error at the heart of the *free will* system, stated:

> "Arminianism errs in making part of the foundation of justification to rest on faith. By advocating conditional predestination and conditional faith in justification (God elects and saves those who believe), Arminianism is a cruel hoax. John Owen, the great Puritan divine, ridicules the Arminian condition of salvation by faith as an impossibility, saying it is 'as if a man should promise a blind man a thousand pounds upon condition that he will see.' Owen views the Christ of the Arminian as 'but a half-mediator' because He procures

---

[13] Ibid.
[14] S.G.U. Publication, No. 173, 142.

the end of salvation but not the means of it. Charles Spurgeon is more graphic. He likens Arminianism and Calvinism to two bridges. The Arminian bridge is wide and easy but does not bring its traveler safely to the opposite shore of the river. It stops short of eternal communion with God because something is left for the depraved will of the natural man to accomplish—exercising faith in Christ. The Calvinist bridge is narrow but spans the entire river, for Christ Jesus is the Alpha and the Omega for salvation and justification. Arminianism *looks* promising, but it cannot live up to its promises because it depends upon depraved humanity to act. In doing so, it deceives myriads of souls who think that they accept Christ by a simple act of their own will but do not bow under Christ's lordship. They imagine they have saving faith while their lives evidence that they remain spiritually dead. Calvinism *is* promising, for it places the entire weight of justification and salvation on the sufficiency of Christ and the operation of His Spirit who bestows and sustains saving faith.

"In the final analysis, if we base our justification on human faith, works, or anything else, the very foundations of justification crumble. For inevitably, the agonizing, perplexing, and hopeless questions of having enough of anything would surface: Is my faith strong enough? Are the fruits of grace in my life enough? Are my experiences deep enough, clear enough, persistent enough? Every inadequacy in my faith will shake the very foundations of my spiritual life. My best believing is always defective. I am too ungodly, even in my faith. Apart from Christ, the best of my best is '*as filthy rags.*' (Isaiah 64:6).

"Too many Christians despair because they cannot distinguish between the rock on which they stand and the faith by which they stand upon it. Faith is not our rock; Christ is our rock. We do not get faith by having faith in our faith or by looking to faith, but by looking to Christ. Looking to Christ is faith."[15]

---

[15] Joel Beeke, *Justification by Faith* (Grand Rapids, Michigan: Reformation Heritage Books)

The Founder of Arminianism, Its Articles, and the Synod of Dort

James Arminius (1560-1609) is generally regarded as the founder of the system of Arminianism. He was educated at the new Dutch University at Leyden and then at Geneva under the tutelage of Theodore Beza, Calvin's well respected follower and successor. Around 1591, after only a year at the Geneva Academy, he began to develop views that were to become diametrically opposed to the doctrines of free and sovereign grace that were taught at Geneva. He departed and continued his education elsewhere. He became a minister in Amsterdam and was later invited to become Professor of Divinity at the University of Leyden. It was from this point that he began propounding his theories with (guarded) vigour.

James (Jacob) Arminius[16]

As the doctrines of *free grace* were in the ascendancy at the time, his teachings on *free will* were bound to arouse controversy and bring him into conflict with the ecclesiastical authorities. This was a dangerous activity, as heresy could be a capital offence. Perhaps because of this Arminius was difficult to pin down. His

---

[16] Illustration of Arminius courtesy of Wesley Center Online: <http://wesley.nnu.edu/arminianism/arminius/>

teachings could be very ambiguous and sophistical. In 1605, for example, the Synod set nine simple questions for Arminius to answer in an attempt to clarify his position. He responded with nine opposite questions and employed scholarly and philosophical devices to avoid giving simple, straight answers. The first question was, "Which is first, Election, or Faith Truly Foreseen, so that God elected his people according to faith foreseen?" Arminius did not—perhaps dared not—give a straight answer. And so the controversy rumbled on even until after his death in 1609.

Eventually his followers, known as the *Remonstrants*, petitioned the Government of Holland with a five-point *Remonstrance*, which was a development of the core teachings of Arminius. It was systematised and published in January 1610 by Jan Uytenbogaert and Simon Episcopius, both former students of Arminius. They led forty-three fellow ministers in introducing their document *The Arminian Articles of Remonstrance* to the ecclesiastical authorities. Their objective was to bring about the convening of a synod, which would overthrow the Doctrines of Grace, which had been freely preached since the Reformation, and make the teachings of Arminius the official doctrine of the Reformed Churches in all of Europe. They were successful in the first part of their endeavour; a General Synod at Dordrecht (Dort) was called in 1618, and representatives attended it from all of the Reformed Churches in Europe, including those from England. The following is a summary of the five Remonstrance articles:

- **Free Will or Human Ability** - Arminius believed that the fall of man was not total, maintaining that there is enough virtue in man to enable him to choose to accept Jesus Christ unto salvation.
- **Conditional Election** - Arminius taught that election is based on the foreknowledge of God as to who would believe. Man's "act of faith" is the "condition" governing his being elected to eternal life, since God foresaw him exercising his "free will" in response to Jesus Christ.
- **Universal Atonement** - Arminius held that Christ died to save all men, but only in a potential fashion. Christ's death enabled God to pardon sinners, but only on condition that they believed.

- **Resistible Grace** - Arminius believed that since God wants all men to be saved, He sends the Holy Spirit to draw all men to Christ. But since man has absolute "free will", he is able to resist God's will for his life. Therefore God's will to save all men can be frustrated by the finite will of man. Arminius also taught that man exercises his own will first, and then is born again.
- **Falling from Grace** - If man cannot be saved by God unless it is man's will to be saved, then man cannot continue in salvation unless he continues to will to be saved.

In order to deal with these five articles of Arminianism, a conference was convened in 1618, which became known as the *Synod of Dort*. It was no convention of novices or of weaklings that met at Dort in 1618. Rev. J.A. McLeod, Principal of the Free Church of Scotland College, Edinburgh, described the Synod thus.

> "They had among their leaders and counselors some of the foremost divines of their day. And the conclusions at which they arrived in the avowal of their faith and in the condemnation of error were not hastily come to. They were the ripe decisions of a generation of theologians who were at home in their subject, expert in wielding their weapons and temperate and restrained in the terms in which they set forth their judgment. Coming as they did in point of time after the National Confessions and Catechisms of the Reformed Churches... ...except the documents of the Westminster Assembly, they with these documents of British origin are the culminating exhibition of our common Reformed Faith, when it was called upon to unfold its inmost genius and essence in self-defence against the revived Semi-Pelagianism of the early Arminians."[17]

These great theologians of the day sat for one hundred and fifty four sessions over a period of seven months, assessing the teachings of Arminius in the light of Scripture and concluding that they could

---

[17] John Macleod (1872-1948), Principal of the Free Church of Scotland College, Edinburgh. This address, "The Doctrine of the Sovereignty of God," was published in *The Evangelical Quarterly* (1941).

find no Biblical basis for his propositions. The Synod finally determined there was no reason to overturn the teaching of the Reformation. It reaffirmed the position that Arminius opposed. *The Articles of Dort* declared that God is entirely sovereign in salvation, "*...Salvation is of the LORD*"[18], and formulated five statements rebutting Arminian theology. In time these statements became known as The Five Points of Calvinism.

> "That Christ, which natural free-will can apprehend, is but a natural Christ of a man's own making, not the Father's Christ, nor Jesus the Son of the living God, to whom none can come without the Father's drawing, John 6:44."[19]

> "*...and as many as were ordained to eternal life believed.*"[20]

Thus, the teachings of Arminius and his cadre were unanimously rejected by the venerable divines assembled at the Synod of Dort. They were declared to be heresy. The positive response of the Assembly was the reaffirmation of the *Doctrines of Grace* as taught at the Reformation.

In order to refute the five points asserted by the Arminians, the Synod issued four *canons*, which were subsequently revised to five. These canons have come down to us today as the *Five Points of Calvinism* and are often remembered as "TULIP", an acronym that was devised to summarise the Canons of Dort in response to the heretical five-point scheme of the Arminian *Remonstrance*.

Total Depravity - This refers to the total inability of man to change his fallen state, 'dead in trespasses and sins'[21]. Because man is utterly dead, spiritually, he has not the capacity to do good

---

[18] Jonah 2:9
[19] Reverend Thomas Wilcox (1621-1687): Sermon entitled "Honey Out of the Rock - Psalm 81:16"
[20] Acts 13:48
[21] See Ephesians 2:1,5; Colossians 2:13; Psalms 80:18

or to exercise faith. Moreover, he does not have free will as it is "...in bondage under the elements of the world:"[22]

Unconditional Election - "Those of mankind who are predestinated unto life, God, before the foundation of the world was laid, according to His eternal and immutable purpose and the secret counsel and good pleasure of His will, hath chosen in Christ unto everlasting glory, out of His mere free grace and love without any other thing in the creature as a condition or cause moving Him thereunto."[23]

Limited Atonement or Particular Redemption - Christ died only for His sheep, for His church, for those numbered in the Elect, by name, from all Eternity.[24]

Irresistible Grace - Calvinists believe that the Lord possesses grace that cannot be resisted. The free will of man is so far removed from salvation that the elect are regenerated or made spiritually alive by God even before expressing faith in Jesus Christ for salvation. If God hath purposed from all Eternity to save His Elect, it follows that He must also provide the means for calling them into so glorious a Salvation. *"All that the Father giveth me shall come to me; and him that cometh to me I will in no wise cast out."*[25]

Perseverance of the Saints - The 1689 Baptist Confession again closely agrees with Dort. "Those whom God hath accepted in the beloved, effectually called and sanctified by His Spirit, and given the precious faith of His Elect unto, can neither totally nor finally fall from that state of grace, but shall certainly persevere therein to the end, and be eternally saved, seeing the gifts and

---

[22] Galatians 4:3; See also Romans 5:12; 2 Timothy 2:25

[23] This summary taken from the *Baptist Confession of Faith*, 1689. See also Romans 8:28-30; Ephesians 1:4-11; 1 Thessalonians 1:4-5; John 15:16; Romans 11:5; etc.

[24] See Ephesians 5:25; John 10:11

[25] John 6:37; See also John 6:44-45; Psalms 110:3; Galatians 1:15; 1 Peter 2:9, 5:10; Romans 8:20; Acts 16:14; Mark 3:13; Psalms 100:3; Psalms 65:4; Isaiah 27:12

calling of God are without repentance..."[26]

Pelagius and Semi-Pelagianism—the Forerunner of Arminianism

There is nothing new under the sun.[27] Essentially the Arminian controversy has been a re-run of a similar controversy which, more than a thousand years earlier, was waged between the British monk Pelagius and Augustine, Bishop of Hippo, as the early Church sought to formulate its theology.

Pelagius arrived in Rome at the dawn of the fifth century and spent most of his life in that city, studying, writing and teaching theology. He began asserting the self-governing ability of man before God. He denied original sin and the depraved state of mankind as well as the absolute requirement of God's Sovereign Grace in the salvation of His saints. Pelagius was condemned as a heretic by the Roman Church and the modified form of his heresy, *semi-Pelegianism,* was also condemned at the Council of Orange in 529. Semi-Pelagianism, the fore-runner of Arminianism, essentially teaches that humanity is tainted by sin, but not to the extent that we cannot cooperate with God's grace on our own—in essence, partial depravity as opposed to total depravity.[28]

However, the same Scriptures that refute Pelagianism also refute semi-Pelagianism. Romans 3:10-18 most definitely does not describe humanity as only being partially tainted by sin.[29] The Bible clearly

---

[26] See Romans 8:27-30; Philippians 1:6; John 6:39, 10:28; Romans 5:10, 8:1; etc.
[27] Ecclesiastes 1:9 *"The thing that hath been, it is that which shall be; and that which is done is that which shall be done: and there is no new thing under the sun."*
[28] "What Is Total Depravity?," <http://www.gotquestions.org/total-depravity.html> (accessed 16 September 2005)
[29] Romans 3:10-18 *"As it is written, There is none righteous, no, not one: There is none that understandeth, there is none that seeketh after God. They are all gone out of the way, they are together become unprofitable; there is none that doeth good, no, not one. Their throat is an open sepulchre; with their tongues they have used deceit; the poison of asps is under their lips: Whose mouth is full of cursing and bitterness: Their feet are swift to shed blood: Destruction and misery are in their ways: And the way of peace have they not known: There is no fear of God before their eyes."*

teaches that without God *drawing* a person, we are incapable of cooperating with God's grace. "*No man can come to me, except the Father which hath sent me draw him...*"[30] Nevertheless the semi-Pelagian view of man's ability to cooperate and to possess inherent or conferred righteousness is widely prevalent today.

As R.C. Sproul writes, "...the basic assumptions of this view persisted throughout church history to reappear in Medieval Catholicism, Renaissance Humanism, Socinianism, Arminianism, and modern Liberalism. The seminal thought of Pelagius survives today, not as a trace of tangential influence, but is pervasive in the modern church. Indeed the modern church is held captive by it."[31]

Pelagius, Augustine, and Luther's *The Bondage of the Will*

In AD 411, with the onset of Alaric's second raid on Rome, Pelagius fled the city with his pupil Coelestius, finding a safe haven in North Africa. In the purposes of God this brought him into the orbit of Augustine, although Pelagius soon moved on to Palestine. He left his protégé Coelestius behind at Carthage, but both men continued to promote the heresy of the autonomy of man and his free will over against the free grace and the Sovereignty of God. Pelagius was shocked by the prayer in Augustine's Confessions, "Grant what thou dost command, and command what thou wilt," which seemed to remove from man all freedom, and therefore all responsibility. Pelagius certainly thought that man needs God's grace, but by grace he meant man's power to choose the good, and God's revelation of that good in the Law, the Prophets, and, above all, in Christ. Each soul, he taught, comes into being in the same condition as Adam. There is no inherited guilt, no sin inherited from Adam by virtue of the Fall. The confrontation between Augustine and Pelagius about the will of man in his fallen condition was re-echoed eleven hundred years later in Erasmus' semi-Pelagian Diatribe[32] and Luther's answer in *The Bondage of the Will*. The able reformer, like Augustine, knew from Scripture that sinful man has a will, but his will is enslaved

---

[30] John 6:44
[31] R.C. Sproul, *Augustine and Pelagius* (Ligonier Ministries, 1996)
[32] *Diatribe seu collatio de libero* (*Discussion, or Colation, concerning Free-Will*), 1524.

and bent towards evil, and can do no good thing. For until man is converted and is renewed by the Holy Spirit, his will is captive to Satan and is "*taken captive by him at his* [Satan's] *will.*"[33]

The publisher's comments on *The Bondage of the Will* state that,

> "*The Bondage of the Will* is fundamental to an understanding of the primary doctrines of the Reformation. In these pages, Luther gives extensive treatment to what he saw as the heart of the gospel."[34]

J.I. Packer and O.R. Johnston add to this in the "Historical and Theological Introduction" to *The Bondage of the Will* by stating,

> "*The Bondage of the Will* is the greatest piece of writing that came from Luther's pen.
> "In... ...its vigour of language, its profound theological grasp,... ...and the grand sweep of its exposition, it stands unsurpassed among Luther's writings.
> "'Free will' was no academic question to Luther; the whole gospel of the grace of God, he held, was bound up with it, and stood or fell according to the way one decided it.
> "In particular, the denial of 'free-will' was to Luther the foundation of the Biblical doctrine of grace, and a hearty endorsement of that denial was the first step for anyone who would understand the gospel and come to faith in God. The man who has not yet practically and experimentally learned the bondage of his will in sin has not yet comprehended any part of the gospel;
> "'Justification by faith only' is a truth that needs interpretation. The principle of *sola fide* [by faith alone] is not rightly understood till it is seen as anchored in the broader principle of *sola gratia* [by grace alone]. ... .for to rely on oneself for faith is no different in principle from relying on oneself for works,..."[35]

---

[33] 2 Timothy 2:26
[34] *The Bondage of the Will*, Fleming H. Revell, 1957, Collation.

Yet another comment on this work of Luther's offers that, "Luther here refutes the Romish notion of 'free will' in man and upholds the absolute sovereignty of God in the salvation of sinners — as well as justification by faith alone. Luther clearly saw the issue of free will as the primary cause of his separation from Rome."[36]

The Bible teaches that faith itself is, and has to be, *a gift of God, by grace, and not of self.*[37]

Though the will is never forced, nor destined by any necessity of nature to perform evil, yet sinful man has lost all ability of will to perform any of the spiritual good which accompanies salvation. He is not able, by an act of the will, to repent and believe on the Lord Jesus Christ. He is not willing to be converted. Unless the Lord intervenes, man remains bound, for *"...men loved darkness rather than light, because their deeds were evil."*[38] A corrupt tree bears corrupt fruit. That is all it can do. The natural man is not able by his own strength to turn to God, or even dispose himself towards God, for *"No man can come unto me, except the Father which have sent me draw him:..."*[39] He is *"...dead in trespasses and sins;"*[40] He is at *"enmity against God."*[41] Grace or unmerited favour is essential, for man does not seek God. It is God who seeks him. It is instructive to note that all the sixteenth century Reformers were originally Augustinians, that is, they believed in the total depravity of man's nature and the absolute sovereignty of God's grace.

---

[35] J.I. Packer and O.R. Johnston: excerpts from "Historical and Theological Introduction" to *The Bondage of the Will* by Martin Luther, translated by Packer and Johnston, Grand Rapids, MI, Fleming H. Revell, division of Baker Book House Co., 1957, pp. 13-61.
[36] Reg Barrow: "FREE WILL vs. THE BIBLE" Still Waters Revival Books, <http://www.swrb.com/newslett/actualNLs/freewill.htm>, accessed April 9, 2006.
[37] Trinity Foundation: <http://trinity2.envescent.com/journal.php> See also Ephesians 2:8
[38] John 3:19
[39] John 6:44
[40] Ephesians 2:1
[41] Romans 8:7

Pelagius denied all of this and instead asserted the full ability and potential of the human will. He taught that man can eliminate sin from his life by the exercise of his will and can keep the commandments of God if he really wants to. He arrived at this conclusion by twisted logic that concluded, "God would not command man to do what cannot be done by man." Thus Pelagius, in considering the will, ignored, or rather played down, the consequence of Adam's fall. The Scriptures show us that man was created able, but lost his ability through his apostasy. But Pelagius insisted that no obligation could ever be placed outside man's limitless capacity for good. He established the definitive Pelagian view that if God commands anything we must be able to obey. God has no right to command if we are unable to obey!

In July AD 415, at the Synod of Jerusalem, Pelagius was condemned *in absentia*. In December of the same year, at the Synod of Lydda (Diospolis), he appeared, but managed to escape condemnation by what B.B.Warfield has described as follows:

"... only by a course of the most ingenious disingenuousness ... and of leading the Synod to believe that he was anathematizing the very doctrines that he himself was proclaiming. ... Pelagius obtained his acquittal by a lying condemnation or a tricky interpretation of his own teachings. In the words of Augustine, 'Heresy was not acquitted, but the man who denied the heresy',[42] and he would have himself been anathematized if he had not anathematized the heresy."[43]

As with Arminius, in Pelagius we see a man purporting to contend for truth who brims with equivocation. He exploited his escape from condemnation to the maximum, falsely claiming an endorsement for his heresies. But he was soon to be undone. A

---

[42] St. Augustine's Anti-Pelagian Works, cited in *The Nicene & Post Nicene Fathers*, Vol. 5. pp.14-27

[43] B.B. Warfield, *Select Library of the Nicene and Post-Nicene Fathers of the Christian Church* (New York: Charles Scribner's Sons, 1905), 13-71.

two-pronged attack by Augustine[44] and Jerome[45]—a powerful combination—led to Pelagius's condemnation by two African councils in 416, a decision upheld by Pope Innocent I, who in 417 excommunicated Pelagius and Celestius. Though Innocent's successor, Zosimus, at first overturned this verdict and action, he was shaken by such a storm from the African bishops that he not only changed his mind, but also wrote a letter requiring Western bishops to endorse the condemnation. On May 1, 418, the teachings of Pelagius were declared to be anathema. His supporters deserted him in droves to save their own skins, although his heretical teachings on *free will* continued "underground." After this nothing more is heard of Pelagius. One source has him dead by 420, another report says he lived for at least another twenty years. Despite his formal discrediting, his teachings kept resurfacing for more than a century, until they were firmly repudiated at the Council of Orange in 529.

The Conclusion to the Canons of the Council of Orange begins with a clear and comprehensive statement that states,

> "And thus according to the passages of holy scripture quoted above or the interpretations of the ancient Fathers we must, under the blessing of God, preach and believe as follows. The sin of the first man has so impaired and weakened free will that no one thereafter can either love God as he ought or believe in God or do good for God's sake, unless the grace of divine mercy has preceded him. We therefore believe that the glorious faith which was given to Abel the righteous, and Noah, and Abraham, and Isaac, and Jacob, and to all the saints of old, and which the Apostle Paul commends in extolling them (Heb. 11), was not given through natural goodness as it was before to Adam, but was bestowed by the the grace of God. And we know and also believe that even after the coming of our Lord this grace is not to be found in the free will of all who desire to be baptized, but is bestowed

---

[44] "AUGUSTINE OF HIPPO (354–430)," <http://www.tlogical.net/bioaugustine.htm>
[45] "JEROME (C. 345–C. 419)," <http://www.tlogical.net/biojerome.htm>

by the kindness of Christ, as has already been frequently stated and as the Apostle Paul declares, *'For it has been granted to you that for the sake of Christ you should not only believe in him but also suffer for his sake.'* (Phil. 1:29) And again, *'He who began a good work in you will bring it to completion at the day of Jesus Christ.'* (Phil. 1:6). And again, *'For by grace you have been saved through faith; and it is not your own doing, it is the gift of God.'* (Eph. 2:8). And as the Apostle says of himself, *'I have obtained mercy to be faithful.'* (1 Cor. 7:25, cf. 1 Tim. 1:13). He did not say, 'because I was faithful', but 'to be faithful.' And again, *'What have you that you did not receive?'* (1 Cor. 4:7). And again, *'Every good endowment and every perfect gift is from above, coming down from the Father of lights.'* (Jas. 1:17). And again, *'No one can receive anything except what is given him from heaven.'* (John 3:27). There are innumerable passages of holy scripture which can be quoted to prove the case for grace, but they have been omitted for the sake of brevity, because further examples will not really be of use where few are deemed sufficient."[46]

Truth is ever hammered out on the anvil of error, and in the purposes of God, this controversy was the vehicle used to define the doctrines of *Free and Sovereign Grace*. Cometh the hour, cometh the man, and the servant of God in this watershed in the development of Christian Theology was Augustine of Hippo. For more than a millennium his teachings on the Sovereignty of God and His gift of Free Grace were held dear by true believers until the controversy was revived by Arminius and his followers in the seventeenth century. Like all of Adam's fallen race, the regenerate Augustine was most certainly prone to error. But at the same time the Lord endowed him with an insight into the workings of His Sovereign Grace that has not been surpassed. Augustine's influence was enormous. B.B.

---

[46] The Canons of the Council of Orange, (529 AD) <http://www.reformed.org/documents/index.html?mainframe=http://www.reformed.org/documents/canons_of_orange.html> (Accessed 25 February 2006)

Warfield described the Reformation as "the triumph of Augustine's doctrine of grace over his doctrine of the Church." R.C. Sproul has written that "the Reformation witnessed the ultimate triumph of Augustine's doctrines of grace over the legacy of the Pelagian view of man."[47] It was Augustine who was the bulwark chosen by God to stem the tide of error, which has ebbed and flowed over the centuries through the teachings of Pelagius.

Augustine was the first of the "Church Fathers" to codify the Doctrines of Grace and to confront and refute the impostures of human *free will* in salvation. His recorded preaching and writings against Pelagius are so voluminous that we cannot begin to explore them here. It suffices to say that his wisdom was acknowledged even by Arminius and that he was the man principally responsible under God for the fact that the false teachings of Pelagius are widely recognised as such today.

What is mystifying, humanly speaking, is that, notwithstanding the above, the heresy of *free will* in salvation has repeatedly resurfaced, albeit in modified guises, and that the doctrines of Free and Sovereign Grace have been assailed at diverse times despite Augustine's masterful expositions of these cardinal doctrines and his systematising of them into a whole Body of Divinity.

---

[47] Dr. R.C. Sproul, *Augustine and Pelagius*

Chapter 12

Catholicism and Arminianism in England and France During the Sixteenth and Seventeenth and Eighteenth Centuries

The sixteenth-century Council of Trent was convened on December 13, 1545, ostensibly to discuss the reformation of the Roman Catholic Church. This was merely a subterfuge or, in up-to-date language, "spin." In reality, the purpose was to exonerate the Church from its widespread identification as the Antichrist of Scripture and to attack and condemn the doctrines of the Reformation, particularly the doctrines of Free and Sovereign Grace. It declared these to be "anathema." Unlike the other Councils and Synods we have considered in this section, the decrees of this "ecumenical council" have no validity whatsoever for saints of God, for Trent was an instrument of the Papacy to counter the Reformation. It was set up "hot on the heels" of the Roman Church's Inquisition, which was instituted by Pope Paul III in 1542 to combat Protestantism.

Looking again at Trent, its decrees, and dogmas, we can demonstrate to Arminians that they can find their cherished semi-Pelagian views on *free will* enshrined in the decrees of this notorious council. Whilst Trent officially condemned the teachings of Pelagius, it succeeded in tacitly restating them, employing the "ingenious disingenuousness" and theological double talk which has been the hallmark of the Jesuit Order. The same equivocation and prevarication displayed by Pelagius and Arminius were to be found in abundance in this Council.

From start to finish it was characterised by corruption, bribery, deceit, and duplicity. Even its claim to be called "Ecumenical Council" was misleading. The Jesuits had seen to it that it was packed with placemen and cronies (closely resembling the First Vatican Council in 1870, which voted through Papal infallibility). The vast majority of bishops in attendance were Italians, many of them from a diocese especially created by the Pope so that they would represent his views and ensure that he would get his way, which of course he did.[1]

The canons of the Council of Trent are still binding on all Catholics to this day and are part of the *Dogma* of the Church of Rome. They oppose the core beliefs of the Reformation on free grace and justification and stress that salvation is impossible without adherence to these canons. They proclaim the Arminian view, *free will* being exalted over the Sovereign Grace of God. It is perhaps worth taking note of the irony that many who subscribe to these Tridentine views assert that "Calvinism" has its roots in Romanism, when their own *Arminian* soteriology was so firmly affirmed at this notorious council of the ancient enemy of the saints of God.

We make reference to Trent for another reason. It proved to be a watershed in the rapid ascendancy of Arminianism to its place of prominence in the church of our day. We shall see how both Roman Catholic monarchs and Anglo-Catholic Arminian prelates took the Canons of Trent as a licence to disenfranchise, persecute, torture, and murder the true saints of God after the manner of the Papal Inquisition.

The Council of Trent

The infamous Council of Trent had been in session for some eight years when Mary Tudor ascended the Throne of England in 1553. In the words of Wetzel, "Bloody Queen Mary made England Catholic again."[2] The year after her coronation she married Philip II of Spain and very quickly the Catholic persecution of Protestants began, decreed by the Council of Trent and carried out by the Inquisition.

---

[1] William Cunningham: *Historical Theology*, Vol. 1, p. 483 ff.
[2] "A Chronology Of Biblical Christianity" by R.C. Wetzel, *Reformation History Library*, CD-ROM (Rio, WI: Ages Digital Library), 154.

"In reference to the Calvinistic doctrines—the doctrines of free and sovereign grace held by the Reformers in England, Toplady observes, 'Queen Mary and her Spanish husband well knew that Calvinism is the very life and soul of the Reformation; and that Popery would never flourish till the Calvinistic doctrines were eradicated.' Her efforts to destroy by sword and faggot those who upheld the Truth earned for her the unenviable appellation of 'Bloody Mary.' The charge on which many of them were burnt at the stake was that they held to the doctrine of predestination and rejected the Arminian and Popish doctrine of free-will."[3]

Yet, as J.C. Ryle reminded us late in the nineteenth century,

"A very popular history of our English Queens hardly mentions the martyrdoms of Queen Mary's days! Yet Mary was not called 'Bloody Mary' without reason, and scores of Protestants were burned in her reign. It is... as certain that the Romish Church burned our Reformers as it is that William the Conqueror won the Battle of Hastings."[4]

Mary Tudor so detested *free grace* that "... life alone was wanting to her to have completely overthrown the Reformation in England and to have placed again the kingdom beneath the Romish yoke."[5] During the short reign of "Bloody Mary," John Rogers (translator of the Matthew Bible), Bishops Hugh Latimer and Nicholas Ridley, Archbishop Thomas Cranmer, and two hundred eighty-one other men and women were martyred.

In the seventeenth century, during the reigns of the four Stuart Kings—James I, Charles I, Charles II and James II—Arminianism grew to become the prevalent faith of the Church of England and made considerable progress in Scotland, too.

James I, although himself a Calvinist in soteriology, with a robustly Calvinist archbishop of Canterbury, George Abbot, favoured

---

[3] "Arminianism," from the tract, "Another Gospel," by William MacLean.
[4] Bishop J.C. Ryle: *Light From Old Times,* p.16.
[5] *History of the Westminster Assembly*, p.27.

"High Churchmen" who accepted his doctrine of "the divine right of kings." They tended to be Arminian in sympathy.

William Laud, who later became archbishop of Canterbury under Charles I, was one of them. Led by Laud, and greatly disliking Puritans, "...Charles promoted many Arminians as Prelates. ... Absolute personal predestination had come to be thought of as a distinctly Puritan assertion, and, when, after 1660 the Restoration set the pendulum swinging against all that Puritanism had stood for, Calvinism had the status of an oddity maintained by nonconformists. Anglican theologians with few exceptions were Arminian in type, as indeed they are still."[6]

In the twenty years from Laud's being made a bishop in 1621 until his imprisonment in the Tower of London in 1640, he wreaked, almost single-handedly, more havoc and destruction on our nation and on the cause of God's Truth than any other individual professing Christian in our history. Even from 1602, while he was still at university, "Laud became a marked man and known as a very lukewarm Protestant, if not a friend of Popery, and an open enemy of the pure Gospel of Christ... ...In 1622, before he had been a Bishop for a year, ... [he] ...ordered, that no one, under the degree of a Bishop or a Dean, shall 'preach on such deep points as predestination, or election, or the universal efficacy, resistibility, or irresistibility of God's grace.'"[7]

In 1623, when Charles I ascended the throne and married Henrietta, a zealous Papist, Laud, by now Bishop of London, encouraged them to oppress the Puritans and their true gospel of *free grace*. "It really came to this, that men said you might lie or swear or get drunk, and little notice would be taken; but to be a Puritan or a Nonconformist, was to commit the unpardonable sin."[8] In 1633, by means of political manipulation and Jesuitical intrigue, Laud became Archbishop of Canterbury. He had assumed for his party and himself unquestionable powers (in the style of the Papacy), which undermined even the authority of the King. "Laud obtained an undivided ascendancy over Charles I, prohibited doctrinal controversy respecting *Arminian* tenets, and commanded the suppression of afternoon lectures, which

---

[6] J.I. Packer: *Arminianism*
[7] Bishop J.C. Ryle *Light From Old Times*, p.266 - 276.
[8] *Ibid*, p.278.

were generally conducted by Puritan divines.[9]

The character of Laud may be seen in relation to his part in the trial, sentencing, imprisonment, and torturing by the notorious Star Chamber of Dr. Alexander Leighton in London. Leighton, a courageous and plainspoken Scotsman, declared that both king and Anglican state-church were "under the laws from the Scripture." Later he described Arminianism as "The Pope's Benjamin, the last and greatest monster of the man of sin; the elixir of Anti-Christianism; the mystery of the mystery of iniquity; the Pope's cabinet; the very quintessence of equivocation." [10]

"A sketch of Leighton's history is given in the preface to a letter which Samuel Rutherford wrote to him while in prison. The sketch says that Leighton, because of his zeal for Presbyterian (Calvinistic) principles and against the innovations of Laud, was arrested in 1629 and kept in an abominable cell sixteen weeks before his trial by the Star Chamber. Because of his severe distress that had brought skin and hair almost wholly off his body, he could not attend his trial. The Star Chamber condemned the afflicted and aged divine to be degraded as a minister, to have one of his ears cut off and one side of his nose slit, to be branded on the face with a red-hot iron, to stand in the pillory, to be whipped at a post, to pay a fine of £1000, and to suffer imprisonment until the fine was paid. When this inhuman sentence was pronounced, Laud took off his hat, and holding up his hands, gave thanks to God who had given the Church victory over her enemies! The sentence was executed without mercy, and Leighton lay in prison till upwards of ten years. When liberated he could hardly walk, see, or hear. He died in 1649.

"Three other brave Puritans—Burton, Bastwick and Prynne—each of whom spoke openly of his own resolution to follow the Bible only, suffered similar cruelties. Henry Burton (1578-1648) was one of the Puritan divines whose fate was

---

[9] William Maxwell Hetherington, *History Of The Westminster Assembly,* p.63.
[10] Christopher Ness: *An Antidote Against Arminianism* (published in 1700)

intimately bound up with that of Laud. On April 23, 1625, shortly after Charles I acceded to the throne, Burton wrote to the King complaining that both Laud and Richard Neile (Archbishop of York) harboured Catholic sympathies. This threw him out of favour with all concerned, and was the first step in a chain of events which led to Burton's imprisonment, together with William Prynne (1600-1669), who confronted Laud's Arminianism, and John Bastwick (1593-1654). All three men were condemned in 1636 to have their ears chopped off and to be imprisoned for life, together with sundry fines and other penalties. Prynne's ears were only partially lopped, but he suffered the additional indignity of being branded on the cheeks with the letters "S.L" ("seditious libeler"), and great numbers were reduced to entire destitution, because they dared to write against Laud's popish ceremonies." [11]

The most godly men were ruthlessly persecuted, many having to flee the country and take refuge in Europe and the American colonies. The patience of a largely God-fearing nation finally was exhausted, and the people rebelled. This precipitated the English Civil War.

In the events preceding this national disaster, Laud was impeached on November 3, 1640. A few days earlier, the Earl of Strafford who was Lord Lieutenant of Ireland and a Papist was also impeached. It was discovered that the two had been in league for twelve years. Papers seized demonstrated that these men were indeed administrators of the "Sovereign Drug Arminianism" and were prepared to go to any lengths in pursuit of their goals. Though Laud and Strafford were incarcerated in the Tower, their confederates continued to plot to capture London and Parliament itself. This plot was revealed to the Commons on May 2, 1641, by Mr. John Pym. The conspirators absconded and the usual mendacity of the captive Arminians began. However, in the same year, "Arminianism was officially condemned by the House of Commons."[12]

---

[11] *History Of The Westminster Assembly*, p.65
[12] Wetzel, p.164.

On June 12, 1643, Parliament issued an order for an assembly of Puritan divines, chaired by William Twisse, to meet at Westminster to redefine the creed and doctrine of the Church of England. This Westminster Assembly completed its work in 1646 and "affirmed a strong Calvinistic position and disavowed the errors of Arminianism, Roman Catholicism and sectarianism."[13]

Of Laud and his confederates, the evangelical Bishop J.C. Ryle stated, "Had half the zeal he displayed in snubbing Calvinists, persecuting Puritans, promoting Arminians, and making advances towards Rome been shown by...[Anglican divines]...in propagating Evangelical religion, it would have been a great blessing to the Church of England."[14] To which we add, to all the Church in England. But God was and is Sovereign in all of human history.

After the Civil War (1642-1651), the monarchy was restored, and Charles II, son of Charles I and his French Queen Henrietta Maria, ascended the throne of England. Like his father, Charles II was married to a Roman Catholic, Catherine of Braganza. The Jesuit and Arminian influence was restored to the Court of the Monarch.

James II, brother of Charles II, succeeded him and attempted to re-establish the Church of Rome in England. He promoted Catholics to high office and put seven leading bishops on trial for refusing to allow his declarations to be read out in all the churches. His actions stirred up longstanding public fears of a return of Popery.

The Protestant opposition, represented by seven prominent noblemen, was emboldened to invite William of Orange to assume the crown and his wife, James' elder daughter, to become Queen Mary II. Thus, by the grace of God, began the Glorious (and bloodless) Revolution of 1688 in England and Scotland. The Bill of Rights was enacted the following year, restoring Parliament's proper powers and securing the Protestant Throne and the Reformed religion established by Law.

Persecutions in France

At that same time, in the late seventeenth century, the experience of Christians in France was very different. *The Revocation of the Edict*

---

[13] Ibid.
[14] *Light From Old Times*, p.278.

of Nantes in 1685 led to the martyrdom of many members of the French Reformed Church. As the nineteenth-century American historian John Dowling records, "King Louis XIV of France, a bigoted papist, at the persuasions of La Chaise, his Jesuit confessor, publicly revoked that protecting edict, and thus let loose the floodgates of popish cruelty upon the defenceless protestants .... In the cruelties that followed, the policy of Rome appeared to be changed. She had tried, in innumerable instances, the effect of persecution unto death, and the results of the St Bartholomew's Massacre had shown that it was not effectual in eradicating the heresy. Now her plan was by torture, annoyance, and inductions of various kinds suggested by a brutal ingenuity, 'to wear out the saints of the Most High.'"[15]

Engravings of Papal Medals struck in the sixteenth, seventeenth, and eighteenth centuries by triumphant "Vicars of Christ" illustrate the malevolent spirit masquerading as the "Holy Spirit" which persecuted the French Protestant Huguenots.

Special commemorative medal struck by Pope Gregory XIII (1572-85)[16]

---

[15] John W. Dowling: *The History of Romanism* 1847

[16] The St. Bartholomew's Day Massacre on August 24th of 1572—The horrendous slaughter of men, women, and children of over 100,000 people including over 50,000 in Paris alone. The reason: religious intolerance of the French Protestants involved in the Reformation. What did Pope Gregory XIII – the Vicar of Christ on Earth – think about such merciless killing? He praised Catherine de Medici (the instigator) and commissioned a medal to be cast in honor of the event, with the inscription "Slaughter [*strages*] of the Huguenots." <www.reformation.org/bart.html>

"When news of the St Bartholomew's Day Massacre reached the Vatican there was jubilation! Cannons roared—bells rung—and a special commemorative medal was struck—*to honor the occasion!* The Pope commissioned Italian artist Vasari to paint a mural of the Massacre—which *still* hangs in the Vatican!"[17]

Henry IV adopted the Roman Catholic faith, but issued the Edict of Nantes (1598), which both recognised Catholicism as the official religion and gave the Huguenots certain rights, such as freedom of worship. Under Louis XIV, the clergy regained its influence, and the Huguenots were again persecuted. A medal was struck to commemorate the massacre of the Huguenots in the Cevennes, one of the persecutions directed by Louis XIV against Protestants during this period. This wave of persecutions eventually led finally to the total revocation of the Edict of Nantes in 1685, which destroyed the civil and religious liberties of the Huguenots.

This medal, executed in Rome by the Italian medallist Giovanni Hamerani (1673), commemorated the massacre of the Huguenots in the Cevennes, one of the persecutions directed by Louis XIV against the Protestants during this period. It appears to celebrate rather than criticise this massacre, with Religion guiding the slaughter.[18]

---

[17] "The Saint Bartholomew's Day Massacre" <http://www.reformation.org/bart.html>, accessed 4/12/06
[18] "LOUIS XIV: MASSACRE OF THE HUGUENOTS IN THE CEVENNES" HAMERANI, Giovanni: France, 1673, Bronze, Obv: Equestrian Portrait of Louis XIV "LVD. XIV. D. G. FR. ET. NAV. REX." Rev: Warrior, watched over by Religion, stomps on Gorgon "QVIS CONTRA. NOS. (Who Is Against Us)"; Signed: IO. HAMERANVS FECIT, found on web page: <http://www.historicalartmedals.com

These engravings of Popish medals, triumphantly glorying in massacre and slaughter, reveal that Antichrist spirit which deserves the thoughtful (and prayerful) attention of all who profess faith in Christ; especially in this age where "evangelicals" are seeking reunification with the Church of Rome. The discerning reader will note that the acclaimed victory of the Antichrist Papacy was over Calvinism or the doctrines of Free & Sovereign Grace. So-called Arminian Protestants have never been a threat to the Papacy. She has no cause to fear her own spiritual offspring. When a Pope strikes a medal celebrating "Arminianism Overthrown," we might have reason to believe that the Leopard has changed its spots; but that shall never happen. The *"house divided against itself shall not stand."*[19]

Whitefield and Wesley

The eighteenth-century Evangelical revival in England, "the Great Awakening," was led by George Whitefield, a Calvinist, and by John Wesley, an Arminian. Although they were able to cooperate with each other publicly in apparent harmony, controversy and doctrinal conflict were inevitable for they were not preaching the same gospel. In 1739, Whitefield invited Wesley to share with him the spectacular open-air ministry that he had established in Bristol, London, and in Gloucester and, in 1739, asked him to take charge of it while he was in America. On his return from evangelising New England, Whitefield returned to Bristol and discovered that all was not well. In his splendid biography of Whitefield, Arnold Dallimore records the great evangelist's reaction to what he found:

> "'Sad tares have been sown here,' he wrote. 'It will require some time to pluck them up. The doctrines of the gospel are sadly run down, and most monstrous errors propagated.'"[20]

---

[19] Matthew 12:25
[20] Arnold Dallimore, *George Whitefield* (Banner of Truth, 1980), 66.

George Whitefield[21]

By *sad tares* and *monstrous errors* Whitefield was referring not only to the Wesleys' "dressing up the doctrine of Election in such horrible colours," but also the "Perfection" teaching which had become particularly prevalent at Bristol. During his former ministry in England, Whitefield had taken it for granted that by *Perfection* Wesley did not mean anything more than a high state of Christian maturity. But, while in America, he had learnt that Wesley was teaching his hearers that they could actually come into a condition of entire sinlessness. Whitefield heard people assert that they had

---

[21] Illustration of George Whitefield courtesy of Havel's House of History < http://www.havelshouseofhistory.com Autographs%20of%20Religious%20Leaders%20WET-WHI.htm>

reached this condition, and one of Wesley's close friends in Bristol, Edward Nowers, was particularly zealous in this assertion. Whitefield wrote:

> "Brother N[owers] tells me that, for three months past, he has not sinned in thought, word or deed. He says he is not only free from the *power* but from the very in-being of sin. He now asserts it is *impossible* for *him* to sin."[22]

The following year Whitefield wrote Wesley a letter as a response to his sermon entitled "Free Grace." The letter, dated December 24, 1740, included the following extracts:

> "From some time before and especially since my last departure from England, both in public and private, by preaching and printing, you have been propagating the doctrine of *universal redemption*. And when I remember how Paul reproved Peter for his dissimulation, I fear I have been sinfully silent for too long. O then be not angry with me, dear and honoured Sir, if now I deliver my soul, by telling you, that I think in this you greatly err. ... ... I shall only make a few remarks upon your sermon, entitled 'Free Grace.'... ... Honoured Sir, how could it enter into your heart, to chase a text to disprove the doctrine of election, out of the 8th of Romans, where this doctrine is so plainly asserted. ... ... Indeed, honoured Sir, it is plain beyond all contradiction, that St Paul, through the whole 8th of the Romans, is speaking of the privileges of those only who are really in Christ. And let any unprejudiced person read what goes before, and what follows your text, and he must confess 'all' only signified those that are in Christ. ... ... Had anyone a mind to prove the doctrine of *election* as well as of *final perseverance*, he *could* hardly wish for a text more fit for his purpose, than that which you have chosen to disprove it. After the first paragraph, I scarce know whether you mentioned it so much as once, through your whole sermon. But your discourse, in my opinion, is as little to the purpose as your text,

---

[22] Ibid.

and instead of warping, does more and more confirm me in the belief of the doctrine of God's *eternal election.* I shall not mention how illogically you have proceeded. ...

"Without the belief of the doctrine of election, and the immutability of the free love of God, I cannot see how it is possible that any should have a comfortable assurance of God's eternal salvation. ... ... If I must speak freely, I believe your fighting so strenuously against the doctrine of election, and pleading so vehemently for a sinless perfection, are among the reasons or culpable causes why you are kept out of the liberties of the gospel, and from that full assurance of faith that they enjoy, who have experimentally tasted and daily feed upon God's electing, everlasting love. ... ... The doctrine of universal redemption, as you set it forth, is really the highest reproach upon the dignity of the Son of God and the merit of His blood. "Consider whether it be not rather blasphemy to say as you do, 'Christ not only died for those that are saved, but also those that perish.'"[23]

A misleading, hagiographic image of John Wesley has filtered down to us, which is widespread in today's Evangelical circles. Harold Vinson Synan, an Arminian and Pentecostal historian, has given this appraisal of Wesley and the age in which he lived.

"In arriving at his mature theological convictions, Wesley borrowed from many sources. His doctrines were distilled primarily from the *Anglo-Catholic* tradition in which he was educated, rather than from the continental Reformed Protestant tradition. Methodism, with its *strong Arminian* base, was in essence a reaction against the uncompromising Calvinism, which had dominated English social, religious, and political life during much of the 17th century. If the Calvinists taught that only the elect could be saved, the Methodist taught that anyone could find salvation. If the Calvinist could never be

---

[23] Ibid., 553.

certain that he was in the elect circle, [a misrepresentation][24] the Methodist could know from a crisis experience of conversion that he was saved. From the beginning, Methodist theology placed great emphasis on this conscious religious experience. This empirical evidence of salvation is what Wesley and his followers have since offered to the world".[25]

John Wesley[26]

---

[24] Author's note
[25] H.V. Synan: *The Holiness-Pentecostal Movement in the United States* (Grand Rapids, MI: William B. Eerdmans Publishing Company, 1971), p. 14.
[26] Illustration of John Wesley courtesy of Swordsearcher <http://www.swordsearcher.com/christian-authors/john-wesley.html>

Synan's sympathetic appraisal portrays Arminianism in a favourable light, but, as a Canadian publication of fifty years ago continues to warn us, "Let us not think that the malignant spirit of persecution that moved the Arminians—led by Scottish Bishop Thomas Sydserff, Archbishop Laud, and others—died at the end of the Covenanting Struggles of long ago. The Arminians of today hold precisely the same false doctrines, and are just as relentlessly opposed to the absolute sovereignty of God and to unconditional election as were the Arminians of old."[27]

---

[27] *The Contender* - Nova Scotia, April 1955

Chapter 13

"New Revivalism"
Charles Finney, D.L.Moody, and a Man-Centred Gospel

"Revivals changed into revivalism as subjective experience was emphasised above objective truth."[1]

In the first half of the nineteenth century, the Holiness Movement swept through both America and Europe. This new revivalism was a victory of pragmatism over the authority of scripture. It was a further erosion of earlier Calvinistic beliefs, especially the doctrines of election and predestination. The so-called "Second Great Awakening," which sprang out of the Holiness Movement in the late 1820s and the1830s, was, as author Michael Bunker has suggested, "really just a Jesuitical backlash against the staunch Grace doctrine focus of the real Great Awakening."[2]

> "Reacting against the pervasive Calvinism of the Great Awakening, the successors of that great movement of God's Spirit turned from God to humans (to a man-centered gospel) from the preaching of objective content, namely Christ and Him crucified, to the emphasis on getting a person to 'make a decision.'"[3]

---

[1] Alan Morrison, Diakrisis Ministries: <http://www.diakrisis.org>
[2] Michael Bunker: *Swarms of Locusts - The Jesuit Attack on the Faith*, P.O. Box 216, Smyer, Texas 79367, p.80.
[3] Ibid.

Charles Finney

Charles Grandison Finney (1792-1875) was the man who created the "decisionism" concept in evangelism, where a person is led through an "altar call" and is pressured to "decide for Christ." There are no "altar calls" and there is no "decisionism" to be found in the New Testament. The Bible merely declares that after the preaching of the true Gospel, "many believed."[4]

In his day, Finney was extremely influential. He still is. He has been described as "the icon of modern evangelicalism." Moral Majority leader Jerry Falwell said that Finney "was one of my heroes and a hero to many evangelicals, including Billy Graham."

Charles Finney[5]

Finney ministered in the wake of the "Second Awakening" and began conducting revivals in upstate New York. One of his most popular sermons was "Sinners Bound to Change Their Own Hearts." This was the theological understanding from which he developed his new methods. One result of Finney's revivalism was the division of Presbyterians in Philadelphia and New York into Arminian and

---

[4] Michael Horton: "The Disturbing Legacy of Charles Finney," *Modern Reformation Magazine*, Jan/Feb 1995.
[5] Picture courtesy of Wikipedia
<http://en.wikipedia.org/wiki/Image:Use_finney_charles.jpg>

Calvinistic factions. His "New Measures" brought about a whole new era of Christian evangelism. They included the "anxious seat" and "mourner's bench," which led to the "invitation" or "altar call", the now common practice of calling sinners to come to the front to receive Christ. He instituted emotional tactics that led to fainting and weeping, and other "excitements," as Finney and his followers called them. A sermon preached by Pennsylvania Pastor Fred Zaspel, focusing upon the impact of Finney and his new revivalism, provides a solemn warning about what is happening in the Arminian-dominated church today.

"He could work a crowd to fever pitch and to fanaticism ('excitements') of various forms—faintings, shakings, weepings and so on; and all for good reason! Decisions for Christ were made! Sinners made profession of faith! ... ... This is the foundation of Finneyism, which lives today. Revival can be brought to town in a briefcase. It is not a supernatural work of God; it is simply the right use of the constituted means. And this is the fountain of his 'new measures' which are so well known to us today. But again it does work. It gets results. It gets people to make 'decisions.' And so how could it possibly be wrong? Should we allow some tradition and prescribed ideals to interfere with success? Finney himself writes with considerable embarrassment shortly after these 'Western revivals' were over. The results, it turned out, were not what they appeared. Few contacts 'stuck.' The area where Finney had been and where such excitement had been generated was now 'burnt ground'— unable to be burned by the gospel again. People were turned off like never before. Their 'decisions' were spurious, and now they were more hostile to the gospel than they had been before.

"This then is the fountainhead of much modern Christianity. Today's 'church growth' seminars insist that theology gets in the way of seeing sinners saved. Instruction is given in 'the art of appeal' and 'the effective altar call' and 'how to get decisions' and 'the use of story in preaching', sad stories, emotional manipulation, seventeen stanzas of the invitation hymn. In all this we reflect our debt to Charles Finney. In some circles it is the 'barking' and screaming and roaring and laughing, the gibberish of tongues, and other rather strange things that work. All this is the outgrowth of Finney, whose theology of manipulation 'got results'. With him, a new era of Christian evangelism was born which lives strong today."[6]

As Michael Horton wrote of the revivalist in Modern Reformation,

"Finney believed that human beings were capable of choosing whether they would be corrupt by nature or redeemed— referring to original sin as an 'anti-scriptural and nonsensical dogma.' In clear terms Finney denied the notion that human beings possess a sinful nature... ... Not only did the revivalist abandon the doctrine of justification, making him a renegade against evangelical Christianity; he repudiated doctrines such as original sin and the substitutionary atonement, that have been embraced by Roman Catholics and Protestants alike. Therefore Finney is not merely an Arminian, but a Pelagian. He is not only an enemy of evangelical Protestantism, but of historic Christianity of the broadest sort."[7]

Let us just pause here. We do know that "there is no new thing under the sun."[8] Here we are back again to the denial of original sin and the Sovereign grace of God, the exaltation of the free will of man amounting to the rejection of the entire Reformation view of Christianity. That "Sovereign Drug Arminianism" can be seen to have become the potent and all pervasive potion coursing through the veins of the professing churches, seemingly with no antidote short of another Reformation.

J.H. Merle d'Aubigne, theologian and preacher, 'the People's Historian' (1794-1872) stated in his History of the Reformation in England:

---

[6] Pastor Fred G. Zaspel: *Human Ingenuity aand Gospel preaching:* Cornerstone Church, Skippack, PA , July 2002

[7] Dr Michael Horton: The Disturbing Legacy of Charles Finney, Jan/Feb 1995

[8] Ecclesiastes 1:9

"To believe in the power of man in the work of regeneration is the great heresy of Rome, and from that error has come the ruin of the Church. Conversion proceeds from the grace of God alone, and the system which ascribes it partly to man and partly to God is worse than Pelagianism."[9]

Dwight Lyman Moody

Whilst Finney was Pelagian in his teachings, D.L. Moody, the American Evangelist, was the great apostle of the Arminian gospel in the nineteenth century. In 1873-74 he and Ira D. Sankey (the gospel singer and hymn writer) conducted a major evangelistic campaign in Scotland, in the course of which thousands professed to have believed in Christ. They held campaigns throughout all of Britain. Although most were impressed with the many thousands of "conversions"—there were many "Reverend" gentlemen who sat quietly at Moody's feet to be lectured by the great Revivalist—there were a small few that opposed what was going on. One who did was James Kidwell Popham (1847-1937), a pastor in Brighton in England who expressed his concern passionately:

"Disclaiming the bigotry, I am bound to say I am opposed to the religious movement of which Messrs. Moody and Sankey are the leaders. I am opposed to it because I fail to see what Mr. Moody so confidently asserted at Birmingham—that the present work is God's. Every religious movement must be judged more by its doctrines than by what we usually see paraded—results. The teachings of its leaders must be brought to God's word, and tested by it. *'To the law and to the testimony; if they speak not according to this word, it is because there is no light in them.'*[10] ... ...It is truly awful to see the dishonour done to Christ by the preaching and singing of these 'evangelists.' Where are the scripture evidences that Christ is knocking, and 'has knocked many times already,' at the heart of every person to whom Messrs.

---

[9] J. H. Merle d'Aubigne: *The Reformation in England* (London, 1962), Vol. 1, p. 98.
[10] Isaiah 8:20

Moody and Sankey may speak or sing? If He desires to dwell in this or that particular heart, what shall hinder? ... ...Assuming that it is the will of God that every creature should be saved, which is not true, men have made the conversion of sinners an art, and have resorted to all sorts of unscriptural methods to compass their end. 'Sadly forgetful' of him who said '*I kill and I make alive,*'[11] they are 'madly bold' in their efforts to wrest God's special work out of His hands. We have the new doctrine of Regeneration by faith, singing theology, sudden conversions, the enquiry room, sensational advertisements such as 'February for Jesus, Liverpool for Jesus, body and soul for Jesus, etc.' And when these new appliances have completed the task allotted them, we have an exhibition of the work done! ... ...The parable of the sower is *not* applicable to this religious movement, since Mr. Moody has *no* good seed to sow. To be sure he reads the Word of God, but then he endeavours to expound it, and this exposition is nothing less than a fouling of the pure waters of truth." (Ezekiel 34:19)[12]

Later, describing Moody and Sankey's evangelism, Popham wrote, "By the galvanising apparatus these men are using, they succeed in evoking 'mere emotion,' and this is called conversion, and these galvanised, but dead souls, are then called Christians. Oh, horrible profanity! A shocking caricature of a true Christian of God's living army." (Ez. 37:10).

The concerns of Pastor Popham were shared by the Reverend Dr. John Kennedy of Dingwall, a well-respected evangelical leader in Scotland at the time of the campaign. He felt that the preaching made light of sin and wrote a tract, "Hyper-Evangelism, Another Gospel, Though a Mighty Power," which listed his objections to Moody's movement.
- That no pains were taken to present the character and claims of God as Lawgiver and Judge, and no indication given of a desire to

---

[11] Deuteronomy 32:39
[12] J.K.Popham, "Moody and Sankey's Errors Versus the Scriptures of Truth," <www.truegospel.net>

bring souls in self-condemnation to "accept the punishment of their iniquity."
- That it ignored the sovereignty and power of God in the dispensation of His grace.
- That it afforded no help to discover, in the light of the doctrine of the cross, how God is glorified in the salvation of the sinner that believes in Jesus.
- That it offers no precaution against tendencies towards Antinomianism on the part of those who professed to believe.

Warnings given about the "great" revivals of the eighteenth and nineteenth centuries equally apply today. One such warning was given by American theologian Robert Lewis Dabney at the end of the nineteenth century.

> "American Protestantism is characterized by a peculiar evil which I may describe by the term 'spurious revivalism.' The common mischief resulting from all its forms is the over-hasty reception into the communion of the churches of multitudes of persons whom time proves to have experienced no spiritual change. In most cases, these mischievous accessions are brought about by sensational human expedients. It is an unpopular thing for a minister of the gospel to bear this witness. But it is true. And my regard for that account which I must soon render at a more awful bar than that of arrogant public opinion demands its utterance."[13]

Another more recent warning has been given by The Trinity Foundation.

> "There was too little discrimination between true and false religious feeling. There was too much encouragement given to outcries, faintings, and bodily agitations as probable evidence

---

[13] R.L. Dabney, "The Modern Invitation System Examined," 1892, from "Revival in the Church – Do We Need It?"
<http://www.rapidnet.com/~jbeard/bdm/Psychology/revival.htm>
Biblical Discernment Ministries, accessed 3/19/06.

of the presence and power of God. There was, in many, too much reliance on impulses, visions, and the pretended power of discerning spirits. There was a great deal of censoriousness and of sinful disregard of ecclesiastical order. The disastrous effects of these evils, the rapid spread of false religion, the dishonour and decline of true piety, the prevalence of erroneous doctrines, the division of congregations, the alienation of Christians, and the long period of subsequent deadness in the church stand up as a solemn warning to Christians, and especially to Christian ministers in all times to come."[14]

Charles Spurgeon, fighting the downgrade controversy, expressed his concern too.

"A very great portion of modern revivalism has been more a curse than a blessing, because it has led thousands to a kind of peace before they have known their misery; restoring the prodigal to the Father's house, and never making him say, 'Father, I have sinned.' How can he be healed who is not sick, or he be satisfied with the bread of life who is not hungry? The old-fashioned sense of sin is despised. ... Every thing in this age is shallow. ... The consequence is that men leap into religion, and then leap out again. Unhumbled they came to the church, unhumbled they remained in it, and unhumbled they go from it."[15]

Those who encourage visions, dreams, faintings, slaying in the "spirit" and bodily agitations are, in effect, advocating a return to Roman Catholic mysticism. Revival can be characterised by mysticism, and it was carried directly into Protestant thinking through the revivals of John Wesley in eighteenth-century England. Wesley was very well versed in the writings of Roman Catholicism's mystics. He was not reticent in speaking of them fondly and was instrumental in publishing a great number of them. Although Wesley identified

---

[14] *The Trinity Foundation: Review,* July/August 1991, <http://trinityfoundation.org>
[15] C.H. Spurgeon, Metropolitan Tabernacle, (1882).

the Papacy as the Antichrist of scripture, this adopted mysticism stayed with him all his life. It is to be observed today in revivalism.

"The emphasis on visions and dreams, special extra-Biblical revelations, and the guidance of the Spirit through these revelations all belong to the tradition of mysticism. Indeed there is a striking resemblance between revivalism and the modern Charismatic movement. Yet, mysticism is contrary to the Scriptures — it is a theology of feelings, emotions, and imagination with scant regard for doctrine. Of course we would not include all revivalists in this. George Whitefield and Jonathan Edwards are notable exceptions. However, in most instances revivalism pays little attention to doctrine, and at worst, is an enemy of the truth."[16]

---

[16] <www.rapidnet.com/-jbeard/bdm/Psychology/revival/htm>

Chapter 14

The Pentecostal and Charismatic Movements

John Wesley's Arminian teachings had inspired the founders of The Holiness Movement, who introduced into the Christian community the idea that "sinless perfection" or "entire sanctification" can be achieved in this life through a second work of grace or a "second blessing." In time this would become identified with "The Baptism of the Holy Spirit" and the speaking with tongues of Pentecostalism and the Charismatic Movement. In his book *The Holiness - Pentecostal Movement in the United States* (see footnote p124), pentecostal historian Vinson Synan's description of the arrival of the "first wave" of Pentecostalism (preceding the Charismatic second and the current signs and wonders' "third wave") is instructive:

"Although the Pentecostal Movement began in the United States, itself a significant fact, its theological and intellectual origins were British. The basic premises of the movement's theology were constructed by John Wesley in the Eighteenth century. As a product of Methodism, the Holiness-Pentecostal movement traces its lineage through the Wesleys to Anglicanism and thence to Roman Catholicism."

"This theological heritage places the Pentecostals outside the Calvinistic, Reformed tradition which culminated in the Baptist and Presbyterian movements in the United States. The basic Pentecostal theological position might be described as Arminian, perfectionistic, premillenial and charismatic."[1]

---

[1] Michael Bunker: *Swarms of Locusts*, Writers Club Press, P.O. Box 216, Smyer, TX 79367

Evan Roberts and the Welsh Revival

At the beginning of the twentieth century, once again there was much talk of "revival". Historian R.C. Wetzel notes that in 1904, "Evan Roberts began the Welsh Revival."[2] This comment seems perceptive, for it is unlikely that this year long aberration was begun by GOD, marked as it was with a "de-emphasis on preaching, ... interruptions by worshippers, stress on the baptism of the spirit, and Spirit guidance... (and) ...Lay preachers such as Evan Roberts at center-stage..."[3] This appears to have been a thoroughly Arminian event.

Its historical significance lies in the fact that it was the precursor to, and has been linked with, the "Pentecostal Revival" which began at Azusa Street in Los Angeles in 1906 and is said by many to be continuing today. The *Dictionary of Pentecostal and Charismatic Movements* records that "in 1904-05 reports came to Los Angeles of a substantial revival that was taking place in Wales, largely associated with the work of Evan Roberts. In Chicago, 'Holiness' publisher, S.B. Shaw was the author of *The Great Revival in Wales* (1905), which was widely read in the Los Angeles area in 1905 and 1906. People who read the book began to establish cottage prayer meetings where they sought God for a similar revival among the churches of Los Angeles."[4]

Therefore it is clear that the name of Evan Roberts is closely connected with both the Welsh revival and with later happenings at Los Angeles. A quote from the preface written for Frank Bartleman's book, *What Really Happened at Azusa Street*, seems to be both ironical and self-contradictory:

"To the praise and honor of God, the Azusa Street Revival brought glory to *no man*. As testimony to this, no man's name is connected with it. However, it can be safely said that no more faithful witness to its events could be found than *Frank*

---

[2] R.C. Wetzel: *A Chronology of Biblical Christianity,* pp. 210, 211.
[3] *Dictionary of Pentecostal & Charismatic Movements*, p.881: Regency Reference Library, Grand Rapids, Michigan.
[4] Ibid., p. 31

Bartleman."[5]

In fact, it can be argued that Azusa Street was not, as Pentecostals now insist, a spontaneous "revival", nor a sovereign work of the Holy Spirit, but was initiated by Evan Roberts in Wales via his correspondence with Frank Bartleman in Los Angeles.

Welsh "Revival" Spreads to North America

Frank Bartleman is described as "the primary chronicler of Pentecostal origins in Los Angeles."[6] In the preface to his book, originally entitled *How Pentecostals Came to Los Angeles*, it is stated, "pamphlets telling of the visitation of the Spirit of God in Wales in 1904 provided the spark for the great revival in Los Angeles in 1906. During 1905, as Frank Bartleman corresponded with Evan Roberts in Wales and they agreed in prayer, as he and others spread the message of the Welsh revival ... the spark became a spreading flame that burst forth into a world-wide conflagration of Pentecostal Revival in the Church of Jesus Christ."[7]

The various manifestations and excesses of the *Toronto Blessing* and its offspring, the *Pensacola Outpouring* (or *Laughing Revival*) in the 1990s are nothing new. The same characteristics and phenomena were to be found at Azusa Street and were experienced during the *Latter Rain* movement of 1948. In all of them the experiences or "blessings" were passed on from person to person. Just as more recently people have travelled to Toronto or Pensacola to obtain the "Blessing", in like manner an earlier generation travelled to Los Angeles to seek revival and the outpouring or "Baptism of the Holy Spirit" with "the gift of tongues."

All of these movements have one common denominator—they are all Arminian. They all preached and continue to preach a "gospel" that is unlikely to save. We know that the Sovereign God can save in any situation in which He is truly sought. We also know from the Apostle Paul that "*whether in pretence, or in truth Christ*

---

[5] Frank Bartleman: *What Really Happened at Azusa Street*, Preface.
[6] *Dictionary of Pentecostal and Charismatic Movements*, p.50.
[7] Derek Owers: *The Charismatic Movement* Bible Theology Ministries, P.O. Box 415, Swansea SA5 8YH

is preached"[8] there can be cause for rejoicing. However, we remember *"that in the latter times some shall depart from the faith, giving heed to seducing spirits and doctrines of devils."*[9]

Scripture teaches us to expect apostasy, not revival. Church history demonstrates this over and over again. This has perhaps never been more true than it is today. For we are now in a time of great apostasy. Counterfeit Christianity is again in the ascendancy, with the foundations of the true faith very much under attack. *"Another gospel"* is being preached with *"another Jesus"*, and *"another spirit"*[10] and with *"all deceivableness of unrighteousness"*.[11] *"And for this cause God shall send them strong delusion, that they should believe a lie; That they all might be damned who believed not the truth, but had pleasure in unrighteousness."*[12]

This is a solemn matter. It is Almighty God Himself who sends delusion upon those who *"received not the love of the truth."*[13] To those whom he has chosen, He says, *"But we are bound to give thanks alway to God for you, brethren beloved of the Lord, because God hath from the beginning chosen you to salvation* and *belief of the truth."*[14] God's people will not ultimately be ensnared by apostate movements, which masquerade as "revival", nor will they succumb to *"The Sovereign Drug Arminianism."*

There is a misconception among the great majority of Charismatic and Evangelical churches in our day. It is the belief that the Charismatic Movement is a genuine work of the Spirit of God. But just as Pentecostalism was man-manufactured, so too was the Charismatic Movement, although both surely have very many genuine believers who belong to Christ but are caught up in the deception.

Vatican II and the Charismatic Movement

What should deeply concern all lovers of Truth is the fact that from

---

[8] Philippians 1:18
[9] 1 Timothy 4:1
[10] 2 Corinthians 11:4
[11] See Chapter 10, "Bible Verse Comparisons"; Comparison Number 22.
[12] 2 Thessalonians 2:11-12
[13] 2 Thessalonians 2:10
[14] 2 Thessalonians 2:13

its beginnings in the early 1960s the Charismatic Movement had the full backing of the Vatican. In 1965, *The Second Vatican Council* officially opened the way for Charismatic "renewal" within the Catholic Church. It was also decreed that "the Church should become a full and active participant in the ecumenical movement."[15]

In a previous book *All Roads Lead to Rome,* this writer described in more detail the early history of the Charismatic Movement and the involvement of the Roman Catholic Church. Cardinal Augustin Bea (Jesuit personal Confessor to former Pope Pius XII and President of the *Secretariat for Promoting Christian Unity*) spoke to the Council of the need for the Church to "strive to revitalise its own inner life, so that it can be manifested to our separated brethren, an ever clearer image according to the gospel."

> "The 'separated brethren' had been 'heretics' for many hundreds of years before the Council was convened. Suddenly, with 'this new movement of the Holy Spirit' they were 'welcomed back into the fold.' David Du Plessis, the Pentecostal leader known as 'Mr. Pentecost', was invited to attend the third session of Vatican II as Cardinal Bea's personal guest. In 1967, two years after the Council officially opened the way for renewal, the first Charismatic 'Baptism in the Spirit' experiences of Catholics occurred at Duquesne and Notre Dame Universities. The Church of Rome officially adopted its own renewal movement – the only denomination to do so."[16]

Remembering Our History

We do well to remember our history. We need to be aware that Vatican II reaffirmed the decrees and anathemas of the Council of Trent in the very same year, 1965, as it welcomed back the "separated brethren." As we have already seen, in order to counter the Reformation, Trent had asserted *free will* and denounced the

---

[15] *Dictionary of Pentecostal & Charismatic Movements*, p. 111.
[16] Michael de Semlyen: *All Roads Lead to Rome – The Ecumenical Movement*: Dorchester House Publications, p.24.

149

Doctrines of Grace as "accursed."[17] Important to remember too is the excerpt from the Jesuit letter found in Archbishop Laud's study in 1627:

> "We have now many strings to our bow. We have planted *the sovereign drug Arminianism* which we hope will purge the Protestants from their heresy; and it flourisheth and beareth fruit in due season...I am at this time transported with joy to see how happily all instruments and means, as well great as smaller, co-operate with our purposes. But to return to the main fabric; OUR FOUNDATION IS ARMINIANISM."

The calculating Papacy must have determined that the most effective method of undermining and destroying the gospel of the "heretics" was to replace it with the new revivalist gospel of so many of the "separated brethren." The hidden agenda of Vatican II was to undermine Calvinism and to promote Arminian ecumenism among the Protestant churches. Jesuit Cardinal Augustin Bea was the man chosen to play the key role.

The Charismatic Renewal Movement is viewed by many as the daughter of Pentecostalism; but it is also the product of Popery, the implacable enemy of the true Gospel and of the saints of the Most High God. The Pope of Rome, the Cardinals, and the Jesuits must be delighted that their centuries-old strategy has proved to be so successful. They may struggle to believe their own good fortune that they have lived to witness "Protestant" evangelicals zealously promoting their Arminian doctrines "...with '*all power and signs and lying wonders*' by '... *even him, whose coming is after the working of Satan.*"[18]

They must thank their God as the "heretics" beat a path back to unity with the "Mother Church" and as Charismatic leaders queue up to meet with the Roman Pontiff and to join their flocks in "worship" with tongues-speaking Catholics. But, they do not recognise in

---

[17] See Chapter 12, "Catholicism and Arminianism in England and France During the Sixteenth and Seventeenth Centuries"; Subheading "The Council of Trent."
[18] 2 Thessalonians 2:9

themselves the fulfilment of the words the Lord Jesus spoke to His disciples: '... *there shall arise false Christs; and false prophets, and shall show great signs and wonders; insomuch that, if it were possible, they shall deceive the very elect.*"[19]

We ask the question, "What is it that unites supposedly Protestant evangelicals with Roman Catholics whose allegiance is to the avowed enemy of the Protestant Reformation?" Apart from widespread ignorance and neglect of Church History, we suggest a twofold answer—shared "spiritual" experiences and Arminianism.

The main burden of this book has been today's neglect of history by both church and nation and the costly consequences of such disregard. History is the repository of experience and knowledge, of lessons learnt and unlearnt. It can be seen as the outworking of the Holy Spirit in the life of the invisible church, the elect of the Lord Jesus Christ. Few believers today know that historic evangelicalism has long shared a common heritage in the "solas" of the sixteenth-century Protestant Reformation. The Reformation "solas" affirmed: Scripture alone (*Sola Scriptura*), Christ alone (*Solus Christus*), Grace alone (*Sola Gratia*), Faith alone (*Sola Fide*), and to God be the Glory alone (*Soli Deo Gloria*). In short, the "solas" were the rallying cry of the reformers.

---

[19] Matthew 24:24

Chapter 15

The Abandoning of the Protestant Reformed Religion

Apparently careless of all that has gone before, leading evangelicals have chosen to ignore the lessons of the past and the testimonies of the saints and martyrs of Jesus. Seduced by the wiles of the devil in compromising their once sound doctrine, they have bowed to the "modernising" pressures of the world, abandoning their Protestant identity, embracing ecumenism and accepting individual Roman Catholics as brothers and sisters in Christ. The first and second *National Evangelical Anglican Conferences* that met at Keele and Nottingham in England in 1967 and 1977, respectively, launched and furthered the new policy of Anglicans towards the fast growing ecumenical movement. There was a new desire on the part of the new evangelicals to be united with ritualistic Anglicans, essentially Roman Catholics in belief and practice; and also to liberals who believed in a fallible Bible. But, as the Prophet Amos enquired: *"Can two walk together, except they be agreed?"*[1]

Well-respected English evangelicals such as John Stott and J.I. Packer, whose writings have been held in high esteem by conservatives for many years, endorsed the statements from these Conferences, and in so doing set aside Gospel truth in favour of accepting fellow Anglicans as true brothers and sisters in Christ.

John Stott, author of *Basic Christianity*, who chaired the first "NEAC" at Keele, gave that Conference a warning that "evangelicals had acquired a reputation for narrow partisanship and obstructionism and that they needed to repent and change." He made clear that the

---

[1] Amos 3:3

Conference was accepting not only Anglo-Catholics and liberals as fellow Christians but Roman Catholics too:

"All who confess the Lord Jesus as God and Saviour, according to the Scriptures, and therefore seek together their common calling to the glory of one God, Father, Son and Holy Spirit, have a right to be treated as Christians; and it is on this basis that we wish to talk with them."

Dr. Jim Packer, author of *Knowing God*, who just a few years before in 1961 had described the doctrine of justification by faith alone, *sola fide*, as "...like Atlas, it bears a world on its shoulders, the entire evangelical knowledge of saving grace," changed his position in the early 1960s on this defining doctrine and signed up to Keele. Much later, in 1994, he demonstrated his revised, new evangelical view by also signing *Evangelicals and Catholics Together*, the document that has rocked American evangelicalism. In an article "Why I Signed It", Professor Packer refers to *Sola Fide* as "small print." He asked the question: "May ECT realistically claim, as in effect it does, that its evangelical and Catholic drafters agree on the gospel of salvation?"..."Answer - Yes and No." "No", Professor Packer says, "with respect to the small print." Thus Sola Fide, a burning issue for Reformation martyrs, and for Professor Packer an issue that once bore a world on its shoulders, is relegated to "small print."

Evangelicals and Catholics Together

What many Christians believe to have been the most significant event in almost five hundred years of church history took place on March 29, 1994. On that day twenty leading evangelicals and twenty leading Roman Catholics signed the joint declaration, *Evangelicals and Catholics Together: The Christian Mission in the Third Millennium*. Ten years later, on May 30, 2004, *The New York Times* reported on this alliance between Catholics and Evangelicals that is redefining Christianity in America.

"In 1960, the last time a Roman Catholic ran for president on the Democratic ticket, evangelical Protestant leaders warned their flocks that electing John F. Kennedy would be like handing the Oval Office to the Antichrist ... ... Forty-four years later Evangelicals and conservative Catholics have forged an alliance that is reshaping American politics and culture ... ... Exactly 10 years ago, a group of Evangelical and Catholic leaders and scholars released a document called *Evangelicals and Catholics Together.* It was the result of a dialogue started by the Rev. Richard John Neuhaus, a Catholic priest in New York who edits the journal *First Things,* and Charles Colson. The two men convened a group of prominent theologians and religious leaders. The Evangelical side included the late Bill Bright, founder of Campus Crusade for Christ, the religious broadcaster Pat Robertson, and theologians like James I. Packer. The Catholic side included the late Cardinal John O'Connor of New York and the theologian Avery Dulles, now a cardinal. Their manifesto was primarily theological, but it included overt political pledges to work together on issues like abortion, government aid for religious schools, and strengthening the 'traditional family,' in part a reaction to the growing gay rights movement. The document shook the Evangelical world ... ... By 2000, Mr. Colson and James Dobson, the broadcaster who founded *Focus on the Family,* were invited to the Vatican. ... ...Evangelical institutions like Wheaton College in Illinois and Gordon College in Massachusetts began inviting Catholics to speak on campus".[2]

The Evangelical and Catholics Together document, which overturns the Reformation and does devastating damage to the cause of Christ, was actually begun as a specific task in September 1992. Larry Lewis of the Southern Baptist Convention, Jesse Miranda of Assemblies of God, John White of the Geneva College of the National Association of Evangelicals, and others, including two Jesuits, Avery Dulles and Juan Diaz-Vilar, joined Colson and Neuhaus in the writing process. All of this was under the watchful eye of Jesuit Cardinal Idris Cassidy, the Head of Rome's *Pontifical Council*

---

[2] *The New York Times* May 30, 2004.

for Promoting Christian Unity, said by Neuhaus to have given "very active support throughout the process." The document urges "Catholics and Evangelicals...to stop aggressive proselytisation of each other's flocks," which is code for, "Evangelicals must not preach the True Gospel to Catholics." It further states, "Leading Catholics and Evangelicals are asking their flocks for a remarkable leap of faith: to finally accept each other as Christians."

As former Roman Catholic priest and author, Richard Bennett laments in his excellent book *Catholicism: East of Eden*,

> "The devastating effect of the New Evangelical compromise with the Gospel is to put a stop to the evangelising of Roman Catholics across the world. If this compromise of the true Gospel of Jesus Christ is accepted, then Bible-believing churches will refrain from evangelising Catholics. The impact on the true church in third world Catholic countries of Central and South America, in Africa, as well as in Spain, Portugal and the Philippines, is already apparent. If this anti-evangelical trend continues unchecked it will become ruinous to the spiritual welfare of millions of souls. But this is exactly the policy the ECT signatories promote when they state, '…it is neither theologically legitimate nor a prudent use of resources for one Christian community to proselytise among active adherents of another Christian community.' Since when has it been theologically illegitimate to expose error and heresy?"[3]

Hence, the Counter Reformation objectives of the Council of Trent have almost been accomplished. The distinctive doctrines of the Reformation, which separated Evangelicals from the Arminianism of Popery, are set at nought by our own "Protestant" leaders.

True and False Ecumenism

True ecumenical unity is clearly defined in the Scriptures. In the words of the Apostle Paul, *"There is one body, and one Spirit, even as ye are called in one hope of your calling; One Lord, one*

---

[3] Richard Bennett: *Catholicism: East of Eden – Insights for the 21st Century*, Berean Beacon Press, p.292.

faith, one baptism, One God and Father of all, who is above all, and through all, and in you all."[4] Thus followers of Christ who place their faith solely in the one triune God and His written Word, as did the Lord and the Apostles after Him (*Sola Scriptura*), are one in body, in Spirit, and in truth. They are saved before the all-Holy God by grace alone (*Sola Gratia*), through faith alone (*Sola Fide*), and in Christ alone (*Solo Christo*), and all glory and praise is to God alone (*Soli Deo Gloria*). Through the centuries, these five biblical principles or "solas" have helped the persecuted church hold fast to the simplicity of the Gospel. True ecumenism is fellowship or working together in adherence to these "solas" which maintain the foundation of true unity in the Lord. To the degree to which these key basic biblical standards are embraced, true unity will be evident.

On the other hand, false ecumenism, typically institutionalised, joins together professing Christian groups in common causes and activities, with one or more of the parties involved unconverted. While purporting to confess the Lord Jesus Christ according to the Scriptures, for the most part the five biblical principles, the "solas" that display the basis of true unity in the Lord are compromised. The extent to which these principles are not upheld usually indicates the degree of submission of the particular church or organisation to Rome.

The *World Council of Churches* is such an institution. Those organisations participating within it have no agreement on any of the five principles demonstrating the foundation of true unity solely in the Lord Jesus Christ. Likewise the Pope and his Church, in apostasy from the true Gospel, are without any of the five biblical standards. Counterfeiting the body of the Lord Jesus Christ, they are intent on finding successful ways to bind all to the visible, active and attractive pontifical throne.

Let us recall the Jesuit statement in the notorious letter found in Archbishop Laud's study: "Our foundation is Arminianism."[5] What was written in the letter has proven to be prophetic: "It flourisheth and beareth fruit in due season" and "we hope (it) will purge the Protestants from their heresy". Yes, it does flourish in our day; and

---
[4] Ephesians 4: 4-6
[5] See Chapter 11, "The Origins of Arminianism"; "An Historic Heresy."

the majority of Protestants have been purged from their faith of *Free and Sovereign Grace*. This faith, the one and only true Gospel which the Papacy set out to overturn with its Counter-Reformation launched at the Council of Trent (1545-1563), is often now derided even by professing Protestants as "Hyper-Calvinism". The Jesuits and Arminians would seem to have succeeded beyond their wildest dreams.

And the prophet saith: *"When the enemy shall come in like a flood, the **Spirit of the LORD** shall lift up a standard against him."*[6] Friends, this is a solemn matter. The end result of Arminianism is this: *"There is a generation that are pure in their own eyes, and yet is not washed from their filthiness."*[7] Is it not to the Arminian that the LORD saith: *"He feedeth on ashes; a deceived heart hath turned him aside, that he cannot deliver his soul nor say, is there not a lie in my right hand?"*[8] Woe Arminians! *"...because with lies you have made the heart of the righteous sad, whom I have not made sad."*[9]

From his pulpit at the Metropolitan Tabernacle C. H. Spurgeon was forthright in his declarations of the doctrines that he believed comprised the revealed truth of God:

> "It is no novelty, then, that I am preaching; no new doctrine. I love to proclaim these strong old doctrines, which are called by nickname Calvinism, but which are surely and verily the revealed truth of God as it is in Christ Jesus. By this truth I make a pilgrimage into the past, and as I go, I see father after father, confessor after confessor, martyr after martyr, standing up to shake hands with me. Were I a Pelagian, or a believer in the doctrine of free-will, I should have to walk for centuries all alone. Here and there an heretic of no very honourable character might rise up and call me brother. But taking these things to be the standard of my faith, I see the land of the ancients peopled with my brethren—I behold multitudes who confess the same as I do, and acknowledge that this is the

---

[6] Isaiah 59:19
[7] Proverbs 30:12
[8] Isaiah 44:20
[9] Ezekiel 13:22

religion of God's own church."[10]

To lay aside the regeneration of the divine Person of the Holy Spirit and to replace this by faith and confidence in a man-centred message is fatal. In such teaching instead of a divine Person being the sole efficient cause of being "born again", an individual's thoughts and affections remain on himself. This is religion substituting for a real relationship with the living God. Indeed, sinful man likes to have it so; he wishes to have all aspects of life under his own control. In this respect, Catholicism and Arminianism serve him well, they both appeal to his pride. The great problem with all of this is the inner emptiness and unregenerated lifestyle that goes with such teachings.

Contrasting with this, the real Christian hope is that the Spirit of God will beget a man to new life in Christ. Those who are begotten to a new and spiritual life are quickened to a new and lively hope. In the words of the Apostle Peter, *"Blessed be the God and Father of our Lord Jesus Christ, which according to his abundant mercy hath begotten us again unto a lively hope by the resurrection of Jesus Christ from the dead."*[11]

Where there is true faith and love of the Lord, there is in the midst of all things *"a joy unspeakable and full of glory."*[12] In Arminianism however, this foundation of deep inner fellowship with the Lord is missing. The belief that salvation begins by Christ first coming into the sinful heart of a man is unscriptural. The dead and ungodly person can be made acceptable to God only by being *"in Christ"*, as the New Testament makes very clear: *"To the praise of the glory of his grace, wherein he hath made us accepted in the beloved."*[13] Compared to this, Arminianism is soul damning. It assumes that the human heart is a fit place for Christ to dwell and it takes for granted that the human person initiates salvation. We often hear appeals or invitations such as: "accept Jesus into your heart, as He Himself asks you in His Word;" and *'behold, I stand at the door, and knock: if any man hear My voice, and open the door, I*

---

[10] C. H. Spurgeon: Sermon "Election", delivered on 2 September 1855, at New Park Street Chapel, Southwark.
[11] I Peter 1:3
[12] 1 Peter 1:8
[13] Ephesians 1:6

will come in to him, and will sup with him, and he with me.'"[14] The misuse of this text to imply that salvation does in fact begin in the human heart is a serious deception. The invitation expressed in Revelation 3:20-21 is given after the Lord had rebuked the Laodiceans with a list of reprehensible sins, and then commanded them to repent, *"... I rebuke and chasten: be zealous therefore, and repent."*[15] Fellowship with the Lord is **not without repentance and faith**. The misuse of this text without this vital foundation is destructive to all Christian living. A person's only hope lies outside himself and in Christ Jesus by His worth and power. Christ Jesus Himself proclaimed the spiritual deadness and wickedness of the human heart: ... *"that which cometh out of the man, that defileth the man. For from within, out of the heart of men, proceed evil thoughts, adulteries, fornications, murders, thefts, covetousness, wickedness, deceit, lasciviousness, an evil eye, blasphemy, pride, foolishness: all these evil things come from within, and defile the man."*[16] In the Scripture, salvation is seen consistently to be in Christ.

God's holiness is the distinguishing factor among all of His essential characteristics. We need to be in right standing before the All Holy Sovereign God on the terms He prescribes. God's Word determines that one cannot be right before God and remain true to Arminian teaching. As we have seen, it contradicts and opposes the truth of the Bible on the defining matter of how any person enters into a relationship with Him. You may cling to such teachings and traditions to your own eternal peril, or you may do what so many men and women have done before you.[17] Turn to the Sovereign God in faith alone for the salvation that He alone gives, by the conviction of the Holy Spirit, based on Christ's death and resurrection for His own elect, and believe on Him alone, *"to the praise of the glory of his grace."*[18]

---

[14] Revelation 3:20-21
[15] Revelation 3:19
[16] Mark 7:20-23
[17] See Epilogue, Section E, "How Understanding the Doctrine of Election Changed My Life", for the personal testimony of one such person.
[18] Ephesians 1:6

We quote Spurgeon again and let him have the final word on this crucial matter:

> "And I have my own private opinion, that there is no such thing as preaching Christ and him crucified, unless you preach what now-a-days is called Calvinism. I have my own ideas, and those I always state boldly. It is a nickname to call it Calvinism. Calvinism is the gospel, and nothing else. I do not believe we can preach the gospel, ... unless we preach the sovereignty of God in his dispensation of grace; nor unless we exalt the electing, unchangeable, eternal, immutable, conquering love of Jehovah; nor, I think, can we preach the gospel, unless we base it upon the peculiar redemption which Christ made for his elect and chosen people; nor can I comprehend a gospel which lets saints fall away after they are called ... after having believed."[19]

"Thus saith the LORD, Stand ye in the ways, and see, and ask for the old paths, where is the good way, and walk therein, and ye shall find rest for your souls. But they said, We will not walk therein."[20]

---

[19] C. H. Spurgeon: Sermon "Christ Crucified", delivered on 11 February 1855, at Exeter Hall, Strand.
[20] Jeremiah 6:16

Epilogue

A. "Notes from a former Charismatic to Christians in the Charismatic Movement"

"God forbid that I should glory save in the cross of our Lord Jesus Christ, by whom the world is crucified unto me, and I unto the world.[1]

Calvary and Pentecost – the Balance Lost

Gradually, and without many appearing to notice it, the balance has been shifted away from Calvary and the accompanying crushing antagonism of false religion endured by our Lord and by His disciples ever since; and onto Pentecost and the work of the Holy Spirit.[2] This makes for a gospel based primarily on happenings and feelings and on receiving from God rather than giving to Him. We are called to serve and suffer, not to reign and prosper. *"For unto you it is given in the behalf of Christ, not only to believe on Him, but also to suffer for His sake:"*[3]

This shift of emphasis from Calvary to Pentecost, accompanied by the weakening of the Word and disregard for doctrine, has opened the floodgates to error and heresy on a scale not seen before, perhaps at any time in the whole history of the church. In a remarkably subtle way it has undermined the centrality of the death of Christ and His once and for all sacrifice and atonement for sin.

Turning to Ourselves

Personal testimonies of conversion and much new reading matter tend to be self-orientated and experiential rather than centred on sin, repentance, and the call to the cross. The great seduction is to turn us from heaven to earth, from the true God to the altar of self, from denial to esteem of self, from God's truth to Satan's lie. This ties in closely with the New Age teaching which has invaded the church with its message of man's self-sufficiency drawn from Eastern

---
[1] Galatians 6:14
[2] Directly contradicting the Lord Jesus' words that *"But when the Comforter is come, whom I will send unto you from the Father, even the Spirit of truth, which proceedeth from the Father,* **he shall testify of me***:"* John 15:26
[3] Philippians 1:29

religions.

Thus is the door opened for "the experiencing of the real presence" and other forms of extra-Scriptural activity to emerge. Many conservative evangelicals feel that this has been the legacy of the Charismatic Movement and are accordingly hostile to it and everything about it.

The Holy Spirit and His gifts tend to occupy centre stage, and Charismatic Christians glory much in miracles and healings, signs and wonders. But, *"God forbid that I should glory, save in the cross of our Lord Jesus Christ... ."*[4] God gives His gifts as He chooses to give them, but there is also the massive counterfeit which claims to be renewal rather than heresy, and leads into so much error. The error so often relates to proportion. 'Without proper proportion, a medicine becomes a poison', and faith becomes folly. The Scriptures are added to in countless prophetic messages and "words from the Lord" which are not to be found in the Bible, not in any version. "But," protests the Charismatic enthusiast, "the God that I worship is a big God; he wouldn't limit himself to the contents of just one book." He certainly doesn't, but very understandably, He has limited us. *"Ye shall not add unto the word which I command you, neither shall ye diminish ought from it, that ye may keep the commandments of the Lord your God which I command you."*[5]

The Bible can easily become a kind of "lucky dip" with Scripture used to confirm preconceived ideas and desires as well as to promote favoured theories and schools of thought. Clear guidance is not forthcoming from leadership, as so many preachers are afraid of offending their congregations or prejudicing their reputations.

The New Heresies

The Word of God is used in a selective and irresponsible fashion to justify "naming and claiming" and "positive confession", as well as the exercising of "dominion" over our circumstances through the "word of faith". Just how the interpretation of a single Scripture apparently unsupported in the rest of the Bible can form the basis for an entire movement or system of belief is difficult to understand. Yet

---

[4] Galatians 6:14.
[5] Deuteronomy 4:2

this happens again and again as Christians who feel themselves enlightened by the renewal have gradually abandoned the old paths for the new. Examples of such derivative verses are Genesis 1:28[6], the basis for "the Dominion mandate"; Isaiah 53:5[7], the authority for universal healing; Romans 8:19[8], the "Manifest Sons of God" movement; Acts 3:20-21[9], restoration of the kingdom by the church; and John 14:13[10], "naming and claiming" and "prosperity". In support of these formularised expressions of faith, Psalm 105:15 is often cited, *"touch not mine anointed, and do my prophets no harm"*, meaning don't criticise anything taught by any recognised Christian ministry. This verse may have already come to mind for those readers who are unhappy with what is argued in this booklet.

Apart from the cults, which most Christians realise deny the divinity of Christ and His atonement, a plethora of heresies has been imported from the United States, where the mixture of moral majority and Kingdom Now theology, "televangelism", and right-wing politics has proved irresistible to so many sincere Christians. Among them and under the appealing veneer, it is not difficult to glimpse the familiar old heresies of Arianism and Gnosticism in new guise.

Constructing the Kingdom, Marketing the Gospel

The reclaiming and restoring of Christ's kingdom, "strategic evangelisation", and the Biblical reconstruction or Christianization of society are all on the agenda. Business groupings, many of them

---

[6] Genesis 1:28 And *God blessed them, and God said unto them, Be fruitful, and multiply, and replenish the earth, and subdue it: and have dominion over the fish of the sea, and over the fowl of the air, and over every living thing that moveth upon the earth.*

[7] Isaiah 53:5 But *he was wounded for our transgressions, he was bruised for our iniquities: the chastisement of our peace was upon him; and with his stripes we are healed.*

[8] Romans 8:19 For *the earnest expectation of the creature waiteth for the manifestation of the sons of God.*

[9] Acts 3:20-21 And *he shall send Jesus Christ, which before was preached unto you: Whom the heaven must receive until the times of restitution of all things, which God hath spoken by the mouth of all his holy prophets since the world began.*

[10] John 14:13 And *whatsoever ye shall ask in my name, that will I do, that the Father may be glorified in the Son.*

multi-national, are being set up to reorganise, equip, share skills, prosper, and pray for businesses according to "kingdom principles". In the United States experiments are being conducted for whole communities to be organised or "reconstructed" in this way. Before His scourging, Jesus told Pilate, *"My kingdom is not of this world; if my kingdom were of this world, then would my servants fight."*[11] The Charismatic church is taken up with "doing a new thing".[12] Growth, strategy, planning, organisation, claiming territory, setting targets and goals, liberation theology, and the social gospel are all part of it. But how do we reconcile all of this with the Bible's instructions to *"walk in the old paths where is the good way"* and to *"remember the former things of old"*?[13]

Praise marches and other ecumenical gatherings, which set out to claim the ground, the place, the town or country in the name of Jesus, have been part of the strategy for church growth as well as for inter-church unity. Many believers who have taken part in them question whether these marches really have Biblical warrant or whether they are just "a good idea." Songs like "We'll Take This Land for Jesus" inspire the marchers, and Scriptures out of the Old Testament, relating to gaining territory and marching around the city walls are often quoted, but it is hard to see how it can be squared with the teaching of the New Testament. In fact it doesn't seem to accord with the message of the Gospel at all. The great commission is the assignment of the church **to call believers out** of the kingdoms of this world **not to take back** the kingdoms of this world for Christ.

The wider strategy of claiming "half of the world for Christ" by AD 2000 and all the other projects for the Decade of Evangelism made an unscriptural presumption. In their zeal for mission, they placed so much emphasis on the decade ahead that they undermined the preparedness of the church for our blessed hope, the imminent return of The Lord Jesus Christ. There is a tremendous need for revival today, and all of us should long for and pray for this and for a

---

[11] John 18:36
[12] This idea comes from the reading, out of context, of Isaiah 43:19, which states, *"Behold, I will do a new thing; now it shall spring forth; shall ye not know it? I will even make a way in the wilderness, and rivers in the desert."*
[13] Isaiah 46:9

great harvest of souls. But no revival was ever founded on our own efforts or on a planned campaign. It can only be a sovereign work of God.

Counting Heads: Tares among the Wheat

Is the practice of numbering people any more acceptable today than when King David did it? David afterwards confessed to God, *"I have sinned greatly in what I have done."*[14] Statistics relating to "commitments" or conversions at crusades for projecting church growth or "marketing" the Gospel are gravely misused. It must ever be stressed that **only the Lord knows His own.** The inevitable result of a head-counting mentality is the undiscerning inclusion of tares among wheat in the Body of Christ. Some pastors justify this by pointing out that there is to be no separation until the time of the harvest. But the Lord's teaching on the parable of the wheat and the tares makes very clear that this parable refers to **the world** and not to the church.[15] The Body of Christ is not supposed to have tares[16] that resemble the wheat within the Body.

The modern church is thought to be filled with Christians who have stopped at conversion. They are seen as saved but not submitted—born again, but not "baptized in the Spirit". They are said to have decided for Christ, but are not yet ready to be in obedience to Him and all of His Word. Of course we cannot know or judge, but such are unconverted sympathisers. They call Him Lord, but they do not know Him. Without question the Gospel preached in awakening power will cause men to search the Scriptures, to hunger and thirst after righteousness and not to rest until they **know** that they have that blessed assurance that they are born of God. A pastor who insists that those who claim simply to love Jesus and affirm His Lordship are assuredly brothers in Christ is irresponsible before God. This "easy-believism" denies the Christ of the Bible who was nailed to the cross by false religion. *"And why call ye me,*

---

[14] 2 Samuel 24:10
[15] Matthew 13:38 says, *"The field is the world; the good seed are the children of the kingdom; but the tares are the children of the wicked one;"*
[16] And certainly not "weeds", the translation used by most modern Bible versions, which when growing alongside, do not remotely resemble wheat.

Lord, Lord, and do not the things which I say?" asks Jesus in Luke 6:46. We are called to obedience to the Scripture, to answering temptations as He did with "it is written, we shall live by every word of God";[17] to demonstrating love for Him by keeping His commandments;[18] to affirming that His Word is truth;[19] and to contending earnestly for it.[20]

The Importance of Doctrine

"Doctrine is the immune system of the church which is infected with spiritual aids. Diseases and afflictions, heresies and false teaching are rife. The patient is very sick." People have become so taken with "experiences" and "relationships" that they have tended to relegate the doctrine of the Word of God to a secondary position. There is a widely held belief that as long as you claim to "love Jesus" then you must be "one in the Spirit." The problem that the Scripture poses is that it reveals "another Jesus", "another Spirit", and "another Gospel". We must ever seek to discern the Spirit, as we are warned that "Satan disguises himself as an angel of light."[21] Of course, experience and relationships are important, but they must flow from a correct understanding of doctrine, rather than provide the principles upon which we form our beliefs.

In today's climate, doctrine is out of fashion. Relativism rules, contributing to what Spurgeon called "the downgrade" of truth. *"What is truth?"* Pilate asked Jesus.[22] The certainty that used to be has been squeezed out by the world in the church with its liberal and "higher critical" approach to all things.

"This Bible version says this and that version says that." The definitive and final word is no more; and thus the manifestations of

---

[17] Luke 4:4 *"And Jesus answered him, saying, It is written, That man shall not live by bread alone, but by every word of God."*
[18] John 14:15 *"If ye love me, keep my commandments."*
[19] John 17:17 *"Sanctify them through thy truth: thy word is truth."*
[20] Jude 3 *"Beloved, when I gave all diligence to write unto you of the common salvation, it was needful for me to write unto you, and exhort you that ye should earnestly contend for the faith which was once delivered unto the saints."*
[21] 2 Corinthians 11:4f *"And no marvel; for Satan himself is transformed into an angel of light."*
[22] John 18:38

God's power—the phenomena—become the focus of faith. Crucial matters of doctrine that cause offence to some are suppressed or by-passed. Paul warned Timothy that *"the time will come when they will not endure sound doctrine; but after their own lusts shall they heap unto themselves teachers, having itching ears."*[23] That time has come. Few Christian ministries are now being established with clear Statements of Faith; nor are congregations across the denominations today familiar with their own Articles, Confessions, and Creeds, as every assembly of Christians once was.

As the inter-Church process gathers momentum, few Christians are willing to face up to the question of ecumenical unity, searching the Scriptures as the Bereans did. Liberalism (or "has God said?"[24]) among Church leaders and theologians has prepared the ground for this kind of unity, as the modern critical approach to the Scriptures questions the certainties and undermines the very foundations of faith. Although this is probably the single most important issue in the church today, it is rarely discussed and debated among the wider congregation, and little attempt is made to educate people about what is involved. Even churches that style themselves as reformed manage to avoid facing up to things. It is seen as so very much easier, and more loving, to find a formula, work out a compromise and concentrate on other things. But the issue will not go away. For the issue is that of the Gospel itself, of *sola fide* and *sola Scriptura* (faith alone and Scripture alone), of Christ and only Christ. The alternative to this is idolatry. There is no middle ground, no neutral position, no fence to sit on. No ambiguity, half-truth, or compromise is acceptable to God. As the prophet Elijah said to the people before the great victory at Mount Carmel: *"'How long halt ye between two opinions? If the Lord be God, follow him: if Baal, then follow him'. And the people answered him not a word."*[25]

"And they shall turn away their ears from the truth, and shall be turned unto fables."[26]

---

[23] 2 Timothy 4:3
[24] Genesis 3:1 *"Now the serpent was more subtil than any beast of the field which the LORD God had made. And he said unto the woman, Yea, hath God said, Ye shall not eat of every tree of the garden?"*
[25] 1 Kings 18:21
[26] 2 Timothy 4:4

The Narrow Way

> ... *"narrow is the way that leadeth unto life, and few there be that find it."*[27]

The Scriptures are full of warnings and admonitions to keep us all on the narrow path. We are intended to guide one another accordingly; and by Scripture to reprove, correct and instruct in righteousness[28], *"that we henceforth be no more children tossed to and fro,and carried about with every wind of doctrine, by the sleight of men, and cunning craftiness,whereby they lie in wait to deceive"*.[29] This is not "negative"; this is life as we are expected to find it and live it; it is the pilgrim's progress through our sinful world.

Un-Christian Practices

Nor are followers of Christ being given clear direction relating to un-Christian practices. It is encouraging that several denominations have now begun to tackle Freemasonry. However, few churches are prepared to deal properly with homosexuality or with Alternative Medicine including homeopathy and hypnotism. The issues of abortion and the sanctity of life are avoided from the pulpit. Many liberal "evangelicals" now favour abortions in principle, and an Archbishop of York was the leading advocate in the House of Lords in favour of experimentation on human embryos. Few Christians in the public arena will openly oppose abortion altogether and stand firm on the magnificent Scriptures that so clearly emphasise our human identity before conception, according to God's providence. *"Thine eyes did see my substance, yet being unperfect; and in thy book all my members were written, which in continuance were fashioned, when as yet there were none of them."*[30] The vote in The Commons, on the night of Monday, 23 May 1990, with a huge majority in favour of experimentation on embryos, was both monumental and shocking. One evangelical described it as "the

---

[27] Matthew 7:14
[28] 2 Timothy 3:16
[29] Ephesians 4:14
[30] Psalm 139:16

greatest rebellion of man against God since the Garden of Eden." Graduating from the license we have awarded ourselves to **terminate** life, we have now chosen to play God to the extent that henceforward we shall actually **select** life.

The Word of Faith

The frequent preaching of John 14:13, *"whatever you ask that will I do"*, and Matthew 21:22, *"whatsoever ye shall ask in prayer, believing, ye shall receive"*, so easily can become an abuse of Scripture. Over emphasis may lead directly to "positive confession" and faith in faith as a power that we can direct. But *"Thy will be done"*, not mine, is the Lord's prayer. "Faith never knows where it is being led," said Oswald Chambers, "but it loves and knows the One Who is leading."[31] "Faith in faith" within a church can also undermine individual freedoms and the proper functioning of the Body of Christ. For example, churches' expansion programmes are funded by "faith", just as are "televangelist" ministries in the United States. The claim is that "if the faith isn't properly exercised, God cannot or will not act."

The prophetic leading of those few privileged "apostles" or "prophets", who are the new elite who hear the Lord's voice or who "see pictures" or have had a special experience, very often determines the direction of the church and its resources. Disagreement may be seen as hostile, even as an attack on the "level of faith" exercised by the fellowship.

The "Toronto Blessing", which came out of the Word of Faith movement, was (and is) believed to be such a special experience. To obtain it, a pilgrimage to Toronto was (and is) necessary, reminiscent of a mystical experience sought at Lourdes or Fatima. Many evangelical churches imported this very mixed blessing which proved to be divisive and disruptive.

God Must Heal

If someone isn't healed, under Word of Faith, there has been a failure in the exercise of faith. The alarming insistence on healing and the selection of Scripture to oblige God to heal, which seems to borrow from Christian Science, plays a major part in many tragedies

---

[31] Oswald Chambers: *My Utmost for His Highest*, March 19

and causes carnage in the Body of Christ. God is sovereign. He heals when He heals and provides us wonderfully with the faith to pray, believing we will receive even when sometimes we don't. To insist on formulae for health constructed somehow from the Scriptures is to cling to our earthly substance instead of our Christian hope. It also creates casualties. Guilt and failure of faith, which can be devastating, are laid on those Christians who have lost loved ones. Charismatic believers are encouraged, if not conditioned, to stand fast on a "word of faith", an isolated portion of Scripture that they feel certain the Lord has given them, which relates to their personal well-being. They may continue to "positively confess" or hold fast to this promise of health or prosperity, while their declining circumstances clearly demonstrate there is no possible reason for doing so. In this way sick dependants have been allowed to die without medical help and capable able-bodied businessmen have drifted into bankruptcy. To the outsider faith has become folly.

 The "prosperity schools" and "word of faith" ministries have much to answer for in this regard, as have church leaders who fail to speak out clearly against such practices. The shepherds must guide the sheep. Christ's teaching calls for His disciples to bear hardship and persecution and accept the path of affliction and of suffering and to carry our cross. The New Testament and the history of the church reveal that God's servants spent little or no time concerning themselves with their earthly bodies, nor with their worldly possessions. Instead they were carried forward by their hope of heaven and their desire to share the Gospel and contend for the faith. Those men and women did not place their faith in their circumstances, in prosperity, or earthly reward; or in visions, miracles, or prophecies and isolated words from Scripture. They placed their faith in Him, *"the King eternal, immortal, invisible, only wise God."*[32] They simply took Christ at His Word, which directs all of us to, *"take no thought, what ye shall eat, or what ye shall drink; nor yet for your body, what ye shall put on ... But seek ye first the kingdom of God, and His righteousness; and all these things shall be added unto you."*[33]

---

[32] 1 Timothy 1:17
[33] Matthew 6:25, 33

Faith in God or Faith in Man?

The totality of Christ's saving work on the cross; the fact that we did nothing, nor can do anything to contribute to our own salvation, and that our faith itself is a gift from Him;[34] the wonderful doctrine of justification by faith alone—all of this is under attack from many directions. The focus of faith has shifted away from preaching and from the Word onto the sacraments, onto gifts and signs and wonders, or onto both. In the United States *Charismatic Bible Ministries*, a major organisation founded and supported by many of the best known American Charismatic leaders, has had as its motto, "Unity and love through signs and wonders". This is very far from *sola Scriptura* and "faith and faith alone."

Evangelism – Commitment and Compromise

Unquestionably the Lord has much used Billy Graham's gift of evangelism in the past. But for many years the Billy Graham Organisation's crusades, very much part of the ecumenical movement, were "re-dedicating" thousands of Roman Catholics alongside the many others who had gone forward in response to the invitation that is made. Many thousands of men and women, stirred by the Scriptures and responding to what they thought to be the call of God through the famous evangelist, have been sent back to Roman Catholic places of worship, having been "re-dedicated" to that faith, according to the organisers. Here is the demonstration that "Commitment to Christ" and obedience to His Word are not the same thing. Few would want to cast doubt on the sincerity of those who go forward to answer the call on such an occasion. However, only God knows whom He has called to discipleship. In his book, *You Call Me Lord,* John MacArthur sums up the problem very clearly.

> "Listen to the typical presentation nowadays. You will hear sinners entreated with words like, 'accept Jesus as personal Saviour', 'ask Jesus into your heart', 'invite Jesus into your life', or 'make a decision for Christ'. It may surprise you to learn that none of these is based on biblical terminology. They

---
[34] Ephesians 2:8

are the products of a diluted gospel. It is not the Gospel according to Jesus Christ. The Gospel that the Lord Jesus proclaimed was a call to discipleship, a call to follow Him in submissive obedience, not just a plea to make a decision or pray a prayer."[35]

The Lord Jesus taught that the cost of following Him is high, and that we should weigh it carefully before embarking on the journey.[36] The way is narrow and few find it.[37] He also makes it clear that there are those who call Him Lord, who perform signs and wonders, and who do wonderful works in His name, who are not destined to enter the kingdom of heaven.[38]

Looking to Men rather than Christ

"Cursed be the man who trusteth in man, and maketh flesh his arm, and whose heart departeth from the Lord." Jeremiah 17:5.

One of the most serious problems in the church is that men are looking to men, and not to Christ. Many of today's Christians are so impressed with the reputation of well-known preachers and evangelists and dazzled by their style, that they are inclined to drop their guard and abandon discernment. For example, when the teaching is given by one who may have a PhD in theology, an eloquent preaching style, an air of humility, and a considerable reputation, it can all too often be enough to convince most of today's Christians that the message comes from God. It very often does not. Gatherings organised around celebrities have the apparent merit of attracting large numbers. At such performances the message tends to be a weak one and references to the gospel come across almost inevitably as part of the entertainment, with Christ receiving the strong endorsement of the celebrity. The impact of such an occasion is to send everyone away happy, but one wonders whether many or

---

[35] John MacArthur Jr.: *You Call Me Lord*: Marshall Pickering 1988.
[36] Luke 14:28 *"For which of you, intending to build a tower, sitteth not down first, and counteth the cost, whether he have sufficient to finish it?"*
[37] Matthew 7:14 *"Because strait is the gate, and narrow is the way, which leadeth unto life, and few there be that find it."*
[38] Matthew 7:21-23

indeed any at such gatherings are challenged or troubled by the conviction of sin.

Nowhere in the Scriptures is the Gospel preached as an extension to other activities, organised to bring in the target audience. Such events, which include pop concerts and joyful celebratory services on TV, are readily justified in public relations terms as creating a positive witness or image for Christianity. It is recognised that no one is likely to be confronted with gospel truths that might cause offence, but it is felt that making church more attractive, loving, and welcoming is a worthy objective. But does the Creator of the universe, the jealous God of the Old Testament, really need the help of popular culture or the fame of men to reach His elect? The great danger in this form of evangelism is that it causes us to look to men and to compromise with the world. The popularity of the celebrity with Christians and non-Christians alike is seldom impaired and often enhanced on such occasions, and this gives us a guide. *"Woe unto you when all men speak well of you! For so did their fathers to the false prophets."*[39]

Whatever happened to our Christian hope, our treasure in heaven? What became of the longing for his coming, the eager expectation for the day of the Lord? Where is the sense of the holiness of the Lord—the reverend fear and awe of the Almighty God, the creator and judge of the world? Where is the fervent prayer, the love of truth, the jealousy for purity in doctrine and the hatred of idolatry? What has happened to the urgent concern for the souls of more than a thousand million religious Anglicans, Orthodox, and Catholics in the world today without assurance of salvation, in bondage to the sacraments and to a system of works and ritual? Where is a heart of compassion for those who seek truth but are imprisoned by such deception? Where is the cry for the cleansing of the church and for deep repentance because we have failed them, our own kinsmen, by pretending not to see? Where are the preachers today who do not persistently avoid the clear message of Revelation 17? Where are the watchmen who sound the alarm? Why do they, who hear the sound of the trumpet, not take warning?[40]

---

[39] Luke 6:26
[40] Ezekiel 33:3ff

In the confused climate, perhaps the primary cause for failure in the church is the conspicuous absence of leaders who lead. There are many leaders who follow, many who look across one at another and lead by being led, by following the prevailing wind of change in the church. But few are the shepherds who guide the sheep onto and along the narrow path. Where are the men and women of courage to stand against the tide, men of boldness to preach the gospel of obedience and sacrifice, of integrity to stress the cost of discipleship and of humility who know the certainty of knowing that they do not know? Where are the Christian leaders scorning popularity who are ready to lay down their reputations and lose their lives? Where, too, are the pastors, responsible before God, determined to guide their flocks into green pastures regardless of the price that might be paid; shepherds who warn, as Paul did, of grievous wolves, of false brethren, and of the existence and prevalence of another gospel and a different spirit? Where are the leaders who know, as Matthew Henry has reminded us, that "evil abounds when good men stay silent"? Where are the men of faith like the reformers of old, like Whitfield, Spurgeon and Ryle, fearless and constant, holding fast with their followers to that liberty in which Christ had made them free? "Controversy in religion," as Bishop Ryle reminded the church, "is a hateful thing."

> "It is hard enough to fight the devil, the world and the flesh, without private differences in our own camp. But there is one thing which is even worse than controversy, and that is false doctrine tolerated, allowed, and permitted without protest or molestation. It was controversy that won the battle of Protestant Reformation. If the views that some men hold were correct, it is plain we never ought to have had any Reformation at all! For the sake of peace, we ought to have gone on worshipping the Virgin, and bowing down to images and relics to this very day!"[41]

The Apostle Paul was the most divisive and controversial character portrayed in the entire book of Acts. Because of this, he

---

[41] Bishop J.C. Ryle: sermon entitled, "Warning #6 to the Church - The Fallibility of Ministers"

was beaten with rods, stoned and left as dead, chained and left in a dungeon, dragged before magistrates, and barely escaped assassination. Yet so pronounced in him were his convictions that it came to a point when the unbelieving Jews in Thessalonika declared: *"These that have turned the world upside down are come hither also."*[42]

> "God pity those pastors and Christian leaders whose main objective is the growth of their organisations and whose main concern lest their 'boats be rocked.' They may escape involvement in controversy, but they will not escape the judgement seat of Christ."[43]

Were Ryle and other great men of faith alive today they would scarcely recognise the popular and comfortable Christianity which "celebrates" at every opportunity and merely seeks the world's approval instead of confronting its sin and need for the Saviour. They would be horrified by the accommodation with false religion, knowing that this must undermine and eventually destroy the foundation of our lives. *"If the foundations be destroyed what can the righteous do?"*[44] They would deplore the weak and equivocal leadership, which accommodates so much false doctrine and causes confusion for those who try to follow.

In an address to the British Evangelical Council in 1969, one among them, and truly a prophetic voice in his generation and beyond, expressed their likely reaction very powerfully, with a message as important today as then. Citing the Scripture in 1 Corinthians 14:8, *"For if the trumpet gives an uncertain sound who shall prepare himself to the battle?"* Dr. Martyn Lloyd-Jones made clear that he believed that the enemy are not just present but rampant in the camp. "Sound the alarm," he thundered, "Sound the alarm."

---

[42] Acts 17:6
[43] Ian Paisley: "Bishop J.C. Ryle First Anglican Bishop of Liverpool" <http://www.ianpaisley.org/article.asp?ArtKey=ryle>
[44] Psalm 11:3

B. Papal Rome and the EU
Richard Bennett and Michael de Semlyen

Papal Rome is widely respected and admired by the world. She is seen as well organized, successful and influential, as well as dignified and authoritative. The aura of uncritical acclaim around the person of successive popes is unique to the Church of Rome. No other global institution has it. Her pronouncements on moral issues carry great weight. So well regarded is the Papacy today that the acceptance of her extends even to Evangelicals, most of whom have ceased to question her doctrine.

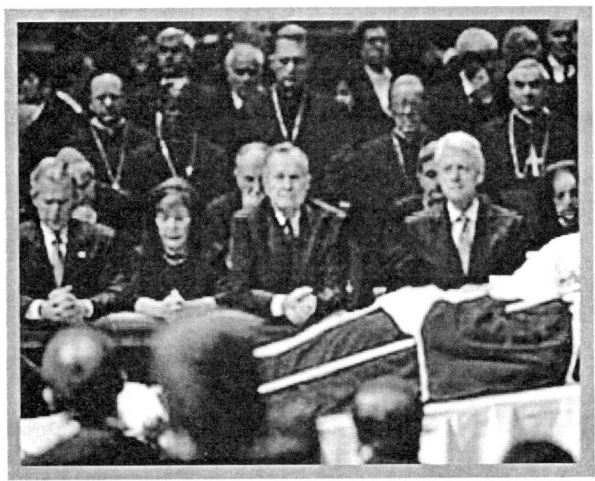

US President George W. Bush, First Lady Laura Bush, and former US Presidents George Bush and Bill Clinton before the Catafalque of Pope John Paul II at his funeral on April 4, 2005.[1]
"...*With whom the kings of the earth have committed fornication*..."[2]

Why then should we take a position contrary to this avalanche of present-day approval? We do so because we are commanded by the

---

[1] Photo from the Christian Today web page:
<http://www.christiantoday.com/news/church/last.mourners.queue.to.see.pope.john.paul.ii.before.funeral/461.htm>
[2] Revelation 17:2

Lord God to proclaim His truth and His warnings. For all is not at all as it seems. We believe that the late great British preacher Dr. Martyn Lloyd-Jones was correct when he proclaimed that "the Roman Catholic Church is a counterfeit and a sham; it represents prostitution of the worst and most diabolical kind...It binds the souls of its people absolutely, just as Communism and Nazism did, and it is itself a totalitarian system."[3]

Papal Pronouncements on Europe

On August 31, 2003, Pope John Paul II entrusted the future of the new Europe to the Virgin Mary. In the words of the Catholic news agency Zenit,

> "He placed Europe in Mary's hands, so that it would 'become a symphony of nations committed to building together the civilization of love and peace.' Last Sunday, the Holy Father urged that the final draft of the European Constitution should recognize explicitly the Christian roots of the continent, as they constitute a 'guarantee of a future.'"[4]

The official teaching of Rome makes clear that this statement concerning "the Christian roots of the continent" is a facade. When the Pope or his Church use the term "Christian" they mean "Roman Catholic". A recent official decree of Rome condemns "the tendency to read and to interpret Sacred Scripture outside the Tradition and Magisterium of the Church."[5] Rome officially proclaims that the Christian Church of Christ **is** the Catholic Church. In her decree she states,

> "Therefore, there exists a single Church of Christ, which subsists in the Catholic Church, governed by the Successor of

---

[3] *Roman Catholicism* by Dr. D.M. Lloyd Jones, Bible League Quarterly (20 Thistlebarrow Road, Salisbury SP1 3RT, England) Oct-Dec 1981
[4] Date: 2003-08-31 Code: ZE03083104 <http://www.zenit.org/english/ 9/3/03>
[5] DOMINUS IESUS September 5th 2000 Para 4 <http://www.vatican.va/roman_curia/congregations/cfaith/documents/rc_con_cfaith_doc_20000806_dominus-iesus_en.html>

Peter and by the Bishops in communion with him."[6]

Just as the Nazis declared non-Aryans to be non-humans, so now the Church of Rome declares other churches to be non-churches. Her official words are,

"...the ecclesial communities which have not preserved the valid Episcopate and the genuine and integral substance of the Eucharistic mystery, are not Churches in the proper sense..."[7]

In the same document, Dominus Iesus (September 5th 2000), footnote 51 refers to a decree, which states,

"We declare, say, define, and proclaim to every human creature that they by necessity for salvation are entirely subject to the Roman Pontiff."[8]

The mind of Rome is thus expressed in her official decrees. Once the Protestant nations are committed to the emerging European superstate and its Constitution, the Vatican's plan to once again "Christianize" the European Union will be implemented. As described by the London *Sunday Telegraph*, "The Pope is calmly preparing to assume the mantle which he solemnly believes to be his Divine Right - that of new Holy Roman Emperor, reigning from the Urals to the Atlantic."[9]

The Vatican as a "Unique Contribution" to the EU

The EU already has most of the attributes needed for nationhood. It has a passport, a flag, a single currency and an anthem. It has also drawn up in its proposed constitution the further characteristics of nationhood such as a president, international ambassadors and a foreign secretary. The Vatican carefully gives soul to all of this by claiming that this is "a unique contribution to the building up of a

---

[6] Ibid., Para. 17
[7] Ibid., Para. 17
[8] Henry Denzinger, *The Sources of Catholic Dogma*, Tr. by Roy J Deferrari from *Enchiridion Symbolorum*, 13th ed (B. Herder Book Co., 1957), #469.
[9] *Sunday Telegraph*, July 21st 1991

Europe open to the world". The Pope in his *Ecclesia in Europa* states,

> "One and universal, yet present in the multiplicity of the Particular Churches, the Catholic Church can offer a unique contribution to the building up of a Europe open to the world. The Catholic Church in fact provides a model of essential unity in a diversity of cultural expressions, a consciousness of membership in a universal community which is rooted in but not confined to local communities, and a sense of what unites beyond all that divides."[10]
>
> "The Particular Churches in Europe are not simple agencies or private organizations. Rather, they carry out their work with a specific institutional dimension that merits **legal recognition, in full respect for just systems of civil legislation.**"[11]

"Particular Churches in Europe" is simply a pretense. The Vatican views itself as **the** Particular Church, and officially states,

> "The Catholic faithful are required to profess that there is an historical continuity—rooted in the apostolic succession—between the Church founded by Christ and the Catholic Church."[12]

From the decrees published it is clear that, apart from the Church of Rome establishing herself as the "unique contribution to the building up of a Europe open to the world", she claims for herself "legal recognition" in accord with her own "civil legislation". This has been the basis of the Vatican's political manipulation over the centuries. While Rome carefully prepares her own legal place, she will tolerate no rivals - "the ecclesial communities which have not

---

[10] *Eccelsia in Europa*, Para. 116, <www.vatican.va/holy_father/john_paul_ii/apost_exhortations/documents/hf_jpii_exh_20030628_ecclesia-in-europa_en.html> 9/23/03

[11] Ibid., Para. 20, 7/15/03 Bolding in any quotation indicates emphasis added in this paper unless otherwise noted.

[12] DOMINUS IESUS, Para. 16

preserved the valid Episcopate are not Churches in the proper sense."[13] Most certainly they are not to be included as part of the "unique contribution to the building up of a Europe open to the world"!

As author Adrian Hilton has warned in a recent article in *The Spectator*, "the issue of European religious union is one that has been concealed even deeper than the plans for political union, but the ratchet towards a Catholic Europe is just as real. The former Pope's demand that 'God' be featured in the emerging European constitution has been echoed by many leading Catholic politicians and bishops. While on the surface such a reference may offend only Europe's atheist and humanist contingent, it must be observed that when the Vatican refers to God, she sees herself as God's infallible vice-regent upon earth, the leading organ of divine expression; indeed, according to its publication *Dominus Iesus* [5 September 2000], as the only mediator in the salvation of God's elect, insisting that all other Churches, including the Church of England, 'are not Churches in the proper sense'."[14]

The Real Meaning of the Pope's Message to Europe

The *Ecclesia in Europa* pronouncement is one of the cleverest made by former Pope John Paul II. It is a masterpiece that purportedly proclaims the Christian message, while in fact it teaches the rites and rituals of the Papacy. For example the concept of the "Gospel of hope" is mentioned forty times in the dissertation. The message however is not one of hope; rather it is an adept counterfeit. For example Paragraph 74 begins by stating, "A prominent place needs to be given to the celebration of the sacraments, as actions of Christ and of the Church ordered to the worship of God, to the sanctification of people and to the building up of the ecclesial community." The Pope thus presents his physical, symbolic sacraments as the efficacious cause of salvation. In place of the direct obedience to Christ Jesus demanded in the Gospel of faith, the sacraments are purported to be "actions of Christ". This is where the

---

[13] Ibid., Para 17
[14] Adrian Hilton, "Render unto the Pope", *The Spectator*, 30 August, 2003, <http://www.spectator.co.uk

Vatican's pretense of "hope" lies. Such sacraments are declared necessary for salvation in the official teaching of Rome,

> "The Church affirms that for believers the sacraments of the New Covenant are necessary for salvation. 'Sacramental grace' is the grace of the Holy Spirit, given by Christ and proper to each sacrament."[15]

By setting aside the direct work of God in Christ Jesus, the sacraments of Rome are an attempt to steal from Christ His Priesthood and an attempt to rob Him of His power as Mediator. The Roman Church attempts to rob God the Holy Spirit of His peculiar work as the Sanctifier, by attributing His power of giving grace to its own rituals. Thus it attempts to rob God the Father of His prerogatives of justifying and forgiving sinners. This is the reality behind the concept of the "Gospel of hope" that permeates the Pope's message to Europe. Throughout the centuries, Rome has substituted her sacraments for the Gospel in a consistently degrading insult to the grace of God. Shameful to God and damning to men is the Pope's memorandum to Europe.

We are at a seminal moment in history, as the Holy Roman Empire re-emerges as a European Superstate. Throughout her history the Papacy has remained self-governing and invincible to every restraining force other than that of the power of God in the Gospel. Bible believers need to be aware of the times in which we live, we need to study the history of the EU in order to see the outworking of the guile of Rome.

A Short History of the EU

After the destruction, ruin and enormous human cost of the Second World War, statesmen and politicians resolved to ensure that it would never happen again. In 1946 Sir Winston Churchill suggested in a famous speech at Zurich in Switzerland that, "we must build a kind of United States of Europe". This was not, as Euro-enthusiasts have often insisted, a commitment for Britain to participate in the

---

[15] Catechism of the Catholic Church (Liguori, MO: Liguori Publications, 1994) Para. 1129

European project. Churchill envisaged a Western Europe of free independent sovereign nations, not an undemocratic federal Superstate. Together the nations would reach for a destiny of unprecedented co-operation and harmony.

In 1950 the Schuman Plan proposed the supra-national pooling of the German and French coal and steel industries in order to lay the basis of European economic unity. The partial merger of the economies of the two traditional enemies would ensure continuing peace between them. French Foreign Minister Robert Schuman and German Chancellor Konrad Adenauer signed the agreement, *The Treaty of Paris,* as co-founders of the Franco-German Coal and Steel Confederation. Like their colleagues Jean Monnet and Paul Henri Spaak, they were both devout Roman Catholics who shared the vision of successive post-war Popes for a re-Catholicized and united Europe. Adenauer and Schuman, along with Alcide de Gasperi, all three "founding fathers", are in the process of being made into "Saints" by the Vatican as a reward for founding the new Europe "on Roman Catholic principles".

The European Economic Community (The EEC), established in 1957 by *The Treaty of Rome* brought in Italy, Holland, Belgium and Luxemburg to join France and Germany, removing trade barriers between member states and unifying their economic policies. It made clear to those with sufficient stamina to read the Treaty's lengthy and turgid document that the aim of the project was always to achieve political unity in economic disguise, "an ever closer union".[16]

In 1962 the Common Agricultural policy was introduced with a single European market and price fixing, which has consistently favored French farmers. *The Northwest Technocrat* commented on the developing design of the European project at that time, "Fascism in Europe is about to be reborn in respectable business attire, and the Treaty of Rome will be finally implemented to its fullest extent. The dream of a Holy Roman Empire returning to power to dominate and direct the so-called forces of Christian mankind of the Western world is not dead, but still stalks through the antechambers of every national capital of continental Western Europe, in the determination of the leaders in the Common Market to restore the Holy Roman

---

[16] Vid *Treaty of Rome*, Articles 164-188

Empire with all that that means!"[17]

Nearly thirty years later, the London-based *Sunday Telegraph* was to express the same concern in a major article headed "Now, a Holy European Empire?" It stated,

> "The Vatican notoriously thinks in centuries. In Pope John Paul II we have the most political pope of modern times. It is in the movement towards federalism of the Common Market, with the coming membership of Eastern European countries, as well as in the turmoil of the Soviet Union, that the Pope may see the greatest possibility for an increase in Catholic political power since the fall of Napoleon or since the Counter-Reformation. The Common Market itself started under the inspiration of Catholic politicians – such as Adenauer of Germany, Paul Henri Spaak, Jean Monnet and Robert Schuman....The EC Social Charter and the socialism of Jacques Delors (President of the European Commission) are imbued with Catholic social doctrine. If European federalism triumphs, the EC will indeed be an empire. It will lack an emperor: but it will have the Pope. It is difficult not to think that Wojtyla realises this."[18]

In 1967 Prime Minister Harold Wilson announced that Britain would apply to join the European Community (the Common Market). The British people voted to do so in a referendum in the belief that they were joining a closer trading relationship, a kind of club, rather than being bound into an evolving Superstate. Unfortunately no more people had read *The Treaty of Rome* in the 1960s than had read *Mein Kampf* in the 1930s. Politicians and opinion formers, who should have known better, accepted assurances that no loss of sovereignty was involved in acceding to the EEC.

In 1973, Prime Minister Edward Heath, who definitely did know better, committed Britain into membership of the EEC. Ireland and Denmark joined the same year. In 1979, the European Parliament

---

[17] *The Northwest Technocrat*, 1962
[18] Sunday Telegraph, 25 August 1991

was established in Strasbourg with its first direct elections. The word "economic" was carefully dropped from the name of the project that was now to be described as the *European Community* (EC). Greece joined the EC in 1981, which was the year of the *Single European Act* - enacting the gradual transfer of executive, legislative and judicial powers from member States to EC "instrumentalities". Spain and Portugal signed up to the EC in 1986, making a total of twelve member states. In 1990, East Germany joined as part of a united Germany.

In February 1992, *The Maastricht Treaty*, or Treaty of European Union, was signed at Maastricht in Holland by the foreign and finance ministers of the member states. Its objective was to bind the twelve nations into cooperation or "ever closer union" on a range of issues other than economic and trading. To this end the EC was renamed *The European Union*. The Maastricht Treaty established economic and monetary union, which would lead ultimately to all member states sharing a single currency. The religious dimension, although not apparent, was the key to what was being formed. Among European leaders who were most influential in furthering the Maastricht agenda were Jacques Delors and Dutch Prime Minister Ruud Lubbers (both Jesuit educated) as well as devout Catholics German Chancellor Kohl and Prime Minister Felipe Gonzales of Spain. These four leaders were all products of the Roman Catholic Social Movement, which believes that "there is no nobler task than the unifying of our continent" and views the idea of a united Europe as essentially a Catholic concept.

The Amsterdam Treaty followed and was signed in 1997 as a further notch of the ratchet of "ever-closer union", meaning in fact, ever diminishing sovereignty, following the principle of *acquis communautaire* (which asserts "**that what has been acquired cannot be taken away**"). The Amsterdam Treaty gave more powers to the unelected Commission and particularly to its unelected President as the initiator, administrator, mediator, negotiator and guardian of the Treaties. *The Treaty of Nice*, signed by Prime Minister Tony Blair in December 2000, was the last in the series of treaties, which have progressively drained the UK of its sovereignty. At Nice there was finally and irrevocably established the EU as a sovereign federal state. A new European criminal code, *Corpus Juris*, will replace the classic, longstanding British criminal code. Vital elements such as Trial by Jury and Habeas Corpus are missing from this new code.[19]

EU Supreme Power

Even before the Treaty of Nice came into force, the EU Constitutional Convention, presided over by former French President Valery Giscard d'Estaing, produced its first draft of a constitution for Europe in October 2002. On 13 June 2003 a final version of the draft *Treaty Establishing a Constitution for Europe*, was produced. Quoting from the London *Daily Telegraph*,

"To the strains of Beethoven's Ode to Joy, the Convention on the Future of Europe proclaimed agreement yesterday on a written constitution for a vast European Union of 450 million citizens bringing together East and West. Valery Giscard d'Estaing, the chair of the 105-strong body, held up a text...'We have sown a seed and I am sure that seed will grow and bring fruit. Europe's voice will be heard and respected on the international stage. Instead of a half-formed Europe, we have a Europe with a legal identity, with a single currency, common justice, a Europe which is about to have its own defence.' There was no vote. M Giscard, famed for his autocratic style during 16 months of stormy debates, simply discerned consensus among the MPs, MEPs, and national envoys. Few were willing to spoil the party by crying foul.... The Constitution gives the EU full 'legal personality' and determines that EU law will have primacy over the law of member states. It prohibits Westminster from legislating in most areas of national life - agriculture, justice, energy, social policy, economic cohesion, transport, the environment, and aspects of public health – unless Brussels chooses to waive its power."[20]

---

[19] See Frederick Forsyth *"The Abolition of Habeas Corpus"* and Lord Stoddart on Corpus Juris, <http://www.bullen.demon.co.uk> 11/18/03
[20] Ambrose Evans-Prtichard, "Few willing to spoil the party for Giscard" in <www.telegraph.co.uk/news/main.jhtml?xml=/news/2003/06/14/weu14.xml> 6/17/03

"If the new constitution is accepted, the EU will no longer be a treaty organization in which member states agree to lend power to Brussels, for certain purposes, on the understanding that they can take it back again. Rather, the EU will itself have become the fount of power, with the ability to sign international treaties in its own right. It will have its own President, foreign minister and foreign policy; its own parliament, supreme court, flag, anthem and currency. It will have become a sovereign state, in fact a federal superstate. The member states whose constitutions will be subject to this higher constitution, will cease to be sovereign. The new order will be irreversible. M Giscard made clear that the national veto is to be abolished in 50 new areas, including immigration and asylum."[21]

Under the new Constitution's rules, no nation would be allowed to secede from the EU except by a two-thirds majority vote of member states in agreement with the secession.

The Same Spirit - of Domination

The EU would acquire competence in "all areas of foreign policy, including the progressive framing of a common defence policy"; though major decisions must be unanimous. The European Court, which acquires vast powers, would ensure that member states "actively and unreservedly support the EU's common foreign and security policy". Article 8 of the draft Constitution, which also imposes "an obligation of loyal cooperation vis-à-vis the Union" of member states, reinforces the supremacy of EU law over the laws of member states.[22] An EU attorney-general would be able to prosecute "cross-border crime", a catch-all term that would allow

---

[21] Ambrose Evans-Pritchard worldwatchdaily.org/index.cfm/ fuseaction/home.sa/ a/9699 7/7/03 See also
Noel Malcolm *Daily Telegraph* 28/7/03 'A Federal Constitution with the Heart of a Manifesto'
http://www.telegraph.co.uk/opinion/
[22] www.euroscep.dircon.co.uk/corpus4.htm 11/18/03

Brussels the supreme jurisdiction throughout the EU. The Constitution, as drafted, lacked any serious democratic dimension and was clearly designed to strengthen the EU power structure for the benefit of the European elite. Doubtless the intention was to force it through with the minimum of real democratic scrutiny until it was stalled - probably only temporarily - by its rejection by referenda of the French and Dutch people.

This spirit of absolute autocracy that is to govern the EU is frighteningly akin to the spirit that rules in the Vatican, "The First See is judged by no one."[23] Rome's stamp upon the pages of history has ever been "no accountability". Its laws also state, "It is solely the right of the Roman Pontiff himself to judge, in cases mentioned in its Canon (1405), those who hold the highest civil office in a state."[24] **The same spirit of despotism in both systems loudly proclaims supreme caution.**

"The Abandoning of a Thousand years of History"

The Treaty that established the new Constitution, which was due to be agreed by the Intergovernmental conference in 2004 was far more extensive than any previous treaty. Derek Heathcote-Amory, the Conservative Party representative at the Constitutional Convention, rightly described it as "bigger than the treaties of Maastricht, Amsterdam and Nice rolled together." The implications of such huge changes, "the abandoning of a thousand years of history", have not been really understood by the majority of the British people. Little by little, treaty by treaty, first the EEC, then the EC, then the EU; people have become used to Europe and bored with it; and with so many scare stories about Brussels, so-called dangers threatening their independence and sovereignty, so many eurosceptics "crying wolf". It has all being going on as long as they

---

[23] *Code of Canon Law*, Latin-English ed., New English Tr. (Wash. DC: Canon Law Society of America, 1983) Can. 1404 All canons are taken from this source unless otherwise stated.
[24] Canon 1405, Sec.1 Can. 1401:1 states, "By proper and exclusive right the Church adjudicates: 1. cases which regard spiritual matters or those connected to spiritual matters."

can remember – and, after all, Britain does have the fourth largest economy in the world, and in the main they have prospered. The problem is that the wolf is now at the door!

Many of those who cherish Britain's independence and who do not want to give away that for which two world wars were fought to retain, realize this. If the continuing moves to establish the Constitution for Europe were to be ratified by the UK parliament, it would be the first time that the United Kingdom has adopted or acceded to a wholly written constitution. How could the UK adopt such a constitution, having never had one before? The answer would seem to be straightforward. The people must give their consent.

The EU's Power Symbols

The EU Parliament's main base is Strasbourg in France. The city symbolises the dream of Franco-German integration that was at the heart of the Holy Roman Empire of Charlemagne. In December 2000, the European Union opened its new Parliament building there. It is patterned after Dutch artist Pieter Breugel's famous painting of the Tower of Babel. Breugel's painting portrays the Tower unfinished, as does the new EU building, which is built to appear unfinished in close resemblance to the painting. Outside the Parliament building is a statue of the goddess, Europa, riding a Bull. Inside, the dome displays a colossal painting of the Woman riding the Beast. The woman riding the beast symbol also appears on some of the "two-euro" coins that have been minted.

The same imagery has appeared on EU postage stamps, including the British one issued in 1984 to commemorate the second elections for the European Parliament. The EU's conscious use of such symbolism creates the impression that it wishes to bring to mind Europe's desire to rule using all the power it has at its disposal. In Scripture, the Woman riding the Beast is revealed in Revelation 17. The identification with the Church of Rome has long been apparent to Bible believers. This interpretation of Bible prophecy did much to empower the Reformation. Only Papal Rome is a city which is sited on seven hills, a religious system, whose Prelates "are arrayed in purple and scarlet color", a civil state *"with whom the kings of the earth have committed fornication"*[25], historically, with hands that are crimson with the blood of Bible believers, that has been *"drunken with the blood of the saints, and with the blood of the martyrs of Jesus."*[26] Papal Rome is the only worldwide religious system that calls itself and its virgin goddess "Mother".

History Also Unveils What is Now Happening

A brief review of European history helps with this identification of the Papacy with Scripture. After the collapse of the Roman Empire in the fifth century, the Papacy continually sought to establish the same dominance, as had the Caesars (in fact successive Popes used the same name—*Pontifex Maximus*). They did so by weaving together both temporal and spiritual jurisdictions and blasphemously assumed to themselves the office of "the Vicar of Christ". In that spurious role, in the course of a few centuries, they were able to subjugate the kings of Europe who became their vice regents.[27] Thus century-by-century the "Mother Church" succeeded in extending her power, usurping that of civil governments. Under the guise of religion she planted her own hierarchical system of government, with its exhaustive financial requirements, in each of Europe's kingdoms. The blending of things civil and sacred was the Vatican's hard to resist method of operation in those dark ages. Unhappily this is still so today, and will be so again, once power and control have been consolidated in the new "United States of Europe". *"Semper eadem"*, Rome never changes.

The duplicity of the Papacy's perpetual mixing of political and spiritual powers could surely not be better portrayed than in God's Word in Revelation 17. The Apostle John beheld the ten-horned beast, representing the Roman Empire, carrying a woman dressed in purple and scarlet, decked with gold, precious stones and pearls. She is a harlot, and the mother of harlots and abominations, the paramour of kings, the pitiless persecutor intoxicated with the blood of the saints and of the martyrs of Christ Jesus. The angel told John, *"The seven*

---

[25] Revelation 17:2
[26] Revelation 17:6
[27] For fuller treatment, see J. A. Wylie, *The History of Protestantism* (Rapidan, VA 22733: Hartland Publications, 2002) Orig. publ. 1878. Four vols, particularly Vol. I, Ch. 3 "Development of the Papacy from the Time of Constantine to Hildebrand".

heads are seven mountains, on which the woman sitteth."[28] To explain this singular fact and to avoid guesswork, he adds, "*the woman which thou sawest is that great city, which reigneth over the kings of the earth.*"[29] The city is indisputably Rome. The name upon the harlot's brow is "mystery". The city cannot be pagan Rome, about which there was no mystery. In contrast, Papal Rome was mysterious and continues to be elusive. Babylon, in the book of Revelation, is a city and an harlot. Jerusalem, in the same book, is a city and a bride. Babylon is the deceptive lover of earthly kings; Jerusalem the chaste bride of the King of Kings. The contrast is between Church and Church, the faithful Church and the Apostate Church.

The Flag – Another EU Spiritual Symbol

The flag of the European Union, blue with a design of twelve stars in a circle derives from the twelve stars that, in Catholic tradition, are the halo around the head of the Virgin Mary.[30] The stars stem from the belief that twelve is the symbol of perfection and of what is unchangeable. The political purposes behind all of these symbols are much debated; the Biblical significance, however, is revealing.[31] According to the European Union publication *Europe's Star Choice:* "The flag has its roots in Romanism, takes its symbolism from Romanism, and represents the Roman Catholic ideal." The design, with its halo of stars, was inspired by many pictures of the Virgin Mary, the most prominent of which is on the *Council of Europe* stained glass window in Strasbourg Cathedral.

The EU's "single market", "social chapter" and "subsidiarity" are concepts of Roman Catholic social teaching, originating with Pope Pius XI in the 1930s, and adopted by Hitler's Vatican-backed Third

---

[28] Revelation 17:9
[29] Revelation 17:18
[30] For further detail, see Adrian Hilton, *The Principality and Power of Europe: Britain and the emerging Holy European Empire* (Dorchester House Publications, P.O. Box 67, Rickmansworth, Herts, WD3 5SJ, England) p. 55.
[31] Documentation on these EU symbols are found on the following WebPages: <www.pointsoftruth.com/beastarises.html> 7/7/03; <http://fp.thebeers.f9.co.uk/europe.htm> 7/7/03; <http://groups.yahoo.com/group/PatriotSaints/message/270> 7/7/03; <www.ianpaisley.org/article.asp?ArtKey=eu4> 7/7/03

Reich. Nazi Finance Minister Walther Funk, styled as the architect of Hitler's "New Europe", issued a compendium of papers in 1942, which contained detailed plans for a Europe bearing close resemblance to the Europe now emerging. Funk's papers described: "The European Economic Community", "The Common European Currency", "Harmonisation of European Rates of Exchange", A Common Labour Policy and a European Regional Principle. The last has now become known as the Europe of Regions Policy—England is to be replaced by seven regions, which with Scotland, Wales and Northern Ireland will total ten regions in all. Together they are to replace the United Kingdom!

The Third Reich to be followed by the EU

The Third Reich, like the EU, was an attempt to revive the Roman Empire. The higher strategy of the Vatican and the acquiescence of the Catholic Central Party had brought Hitler to power. Instrumental in this strategy were Reich Chancellor Franz von Papen and Papal Nuncio Monsignor Pacelli, the future Pope Pius XII. Von Papen goes down in history as the man who obtained Hitler his two-thirds majority, signed the law which made him Head of State, and was also responsible for the enormously important Concordat with the Church of Rome in 1933. He declared, "...the Third Reich is the first power in the world to put into practice the lofty principles of the Papacy."[32] Incredibly, given his responsibility for Nazi atrocities, he was acquitted at Nuremberg and later became Papal Chamberlain to Pope John XXIII. Pacelli, as Pope Pius XII, became notorious for his silence with regard to the Holocaust and the other appalling crimes committed by the Fascists in Europe. The Vatican's attempts to canonise him have proved highly controversial.

The Nazi leadership was mainly Roman Catholic. Hitler and Himmler were greatly influenced by the Jesuits, as was Mussolini whose Father Confessor was a Jesuit. Hitler said of Himmler, "..in Himmler I see our Ignatius de Loyola."[33] Joseph Goebbels was also

---

[32] Robert d'Harcourt, "Franz von Papen l'homme à tout faire..." (*L'Aube,* 3 Oct. 1946) in *The Vatican Against Europe* by Edmond Paris, Tr. from French by A. Robson, First English Ed 1961 (184 Fleet Street, London, EC4: The Wickliffe Press, 1961) p. 271.

Jesuit-educated, as was Walter Schellenberg, who led the SD or Sicherheitsdienst, the Security Service of the SS, and before being sentenced to death at Nuremberg for crimes against humanity, stated that, "...the SS organisation has been constituted by Himmler according to the principles of the Jesuit Order. Their regulations and the spiritual exercises prescribed by Ignatius of Loyola were the model Himmler tried to copy exactly."[34]

The lesson and warning of history is that undemocratic regimes whose leaders owe allegiance to the Pope or practise "the lofty principles of the Papacy" pose a threat to individual liberty, and carry out religious persecution. For example, the Inquisition was alive and well in the Balkans in the 1940s. "Convert or die" was the choice on offer to 900,000 Orthodox Serbs in the new state of Croatia, run by Nazi puppet Anton Pavelich and Roman Catholic Primate, Archbishop Alois Stepinac. Two hundred thousand were "converted"; seven hundred thousand, who preferred to die, were tortured, shot, burned, or buried alive. This appalling persecution, carried out mainly by Ustashi priests and friars "for the triumph of Christ and Croatia", included many of the worst atrocities of the War; certainly the mutilations were horrific, the savagery terrible.[35]

Few people know what took place in Croatia during the Second World War—news of it has been simply suppressed. Nor do they understand what happened in the Balkans in the 1990s. The re-establishing of Croatia as an independent state, during the disintegration of Yugoslavia in the 1990s, is instructive. The European Union, led by Germany ignored the protest of Britain and many other nations in pressing for this to happen. The Vatican was the first to recognise the reborn Croatia. Writing in September 1991 in the *Sunday Telegraph* historian Andrew Roberts expressed surprise that:

"...almost the entire Western media have chosen to champion the Croats. ... how are the Serbs expected to react to the decision to adopt the Ustashi's chequered symbol as the

---

[33] Libres Propos, Flammarion, Paris 1952
[34] Edmond Paris, *The Vatican Against Europe* (London: Wycliffe Press, 1961)
[35] *The Vatican's Holocaust* (Springfield, MO: Ozark Books, 1986)

Croatian national flag? In Krajina it takes longer than the attention span of today's CNN broadcaster to forget the way Franciscan friars participated in the slaughter of Serbs in Croatian Bosnia. Orthodox Serbs were promised protection if they converted to Catholicism and were then killed, after they entered the churches, as the priests looked on."[36]

None of this is surprising if we know the history of Roman Catholicism. "From the birth of Popery in 600, to the present time, it has been estimated by careful and credible historians, that more than FIFTY MILLIONS of the human family have been slaughtered for 'the crime' of heresy by popish persecutors, an average of more than forty thousand religious murders for every year of the existence of Popery."[37] The Scripture speaks prophetically of her lust for power and blood; history has recorded many of the gruesome details.

The Papacy has been predominant throughout the whole history of Europe. It has left its mark and record on most of the major nations. In times past it has proven itself to be totally dominant in its control of Kings and Princes. The whole history of the Western world over fourteen centuries has been plagued by the intrigues and machinations of the Church of Rome in unceasing pursuit of her global designs. In the words of the historian J.A. Wylie,

"...as regards the influence of Popery on government, it were easy to demonstrate, that the Papacy delayed the advent of

---

[36] *Sunday Telegraph*, 15 September 1991

[37] "No computation can reach the numbers who have been put to death, in different ways, on account of their maintaining the profession of the Gospel, and opposing the corruptions of the Church of Rome. A MILLION poor Waldenses perished in France; NINE HUNDRED THOUSAND orthodox Christians were slain in less than thirty years after the institution of the order of the Jesuits. The Duke of Alva boasted of having put to death in the Netherlands, THIRTY-SIX THOUSAND by the hand of the common executioner during the space of a few years. The Inquisition destroyed, by various tortures, ONE HUNDRED AND FIFTY THOUSAND within thirty years. These are a few specimens, and but a few, of those which history has recorded; but the total amount will never be known till the earth shall disclose her blood, and no more cover her slain" John Dowling, *History of Rome* in *Scott's Church History*, Book 8

representative and constitutional government for thirteen centuries. Superstition is the mother of despotism; Christianity is the parent of liberty. There is no truth which the past history of the world more abundantly establishes than this. It was through Christianity that the democratic element first came into the world... **The papal government is the very antipodes of constitutional government: it centres all power in one man: it does so on the ground of divine right; and is therefore essentially and eternally antagonistic to the constitutional element.** Its long dominancy in Europe formed the grand barrier to the progress of the popular element in society, and to the erection of constitutional government in the world."[38]

Our Hope and Prayer for Europe

Once again we have come to a defining moment in history. Once more the Vatican is engaged in placing its hallmark and its rituals on the face of Europe to further its familiar agenda. It does so in a number of different ways directed from the highest levels of command in the Vatican. Firstly, it operates directly through its civil ambassadors in each European nation. According to the Catholic Almanac "Papal representatives 'receive from the Roman Pontiff the charge of representing him in a fixed way in the various nations or regions of the world.'"[39] Secondly, the Roman Church also deals directly and legally with individual nations through its many legal concordats. Less directly it operates through its representation and influence in most of the governmental agencies of Europe. This involvement, especially in the area of finance and business, is documented in her Almanac under the heading of "Governmental Organisations". These include the United Nations, the Council of Europe, the Organisation of American States, the International Organisation for the Unification of Private Law, and the International

---

[38] J.A. Wylie, *The Papacy*, Book III. Chapter III, "Influence of Popery on Government" http://www.wayoflife.org/papacy/03-03.htm> 9/25/03

[39] *Our Sunday Visitor's Catholic Almanac* 1998 (Huntington, IN: Our Sunday Visitor, Inc., 1997) p.168

Council on Grain, among others. Rome has her observers and delegates in all of these many listed organisations.[40] Finally, she operates through her own people in Europe whose allegiance is first and foremost to the Roman Catholic Church. Many of her people have access to positions in the ruling structure of their nation. As Roman Catholics, they are enjoined by the Vatican to use both influence and position to bring that nation into line with papal policy on any particular issue.

We need to pray that Europe will not be taken back to the state that it was in, spiritually and politically, during the Middle Ages. inwardly and spiritually feeble. By her laws and ceremonies, her Bishops, Priests and laity are obliged to accept the system that recognises the Pope as the universal "Sovereign Father" while denying the true Father and the Son. From its traditions, history, and crises, it is evident that it is an institution lacking the Gospel of grace in Christ, one that walks in darkness and in the shadow of death.

In contrast, the true Christian faith may outwardly look small and weak; but inwardly, and in essence, it is the strongest power on earth. That same power liberated most of Europe at the time of the Reformation. It is the power that is in Christ Jesus the Lord, and inseparable from Him. In the words of the Apostle Peter, *"Blessed be the God and Father of our Lord Jesus Christ, which according to his abundant mercy hath begotten us again unto a lively hope by the resurrection of Jesus Christ from the dead."*[41] The reason for our confidence is our relationship to the risen Saviour the Lord Jesus Christ. He is Lord, the universal King and Sovereign, the Priest and Saviour. Christ Jesus our Lord is a Prophet, anointed with the Spirit and furnished with all gifts necessary for the instruction, guidance, and salvation of His people through His written Word, the Holy Scriptures. He and His Gospel of grace are our hope for the future of Europe. Our inheritance is reserved in heaven, on earth however we *"are kept by the power of God through faith..."*[42]

We remember that the greatest power of God has often been

---

[40] *The Catholic Almanac* 1998, p.171
[41] I Peter 1:3
[42] I Peter 1:5

experienced in times of the greatest declension, such as the time of the eighteenth-century Revival and that of the Reformation itself. *"The people that walked in darkness have seen a great light: they that dwell in the land of the shadow of death, upon them hath the light shined."*[43] God in His sovereignty and in His divine timing can bring a people to the Bible, to His truth of salvation by grace alone, through faith alone, in Christ alone. When He pleases He is able with one word of His grace, to renew Europe by an act of His power, and make His enemies the footstool of Christ. We pray that He will give us the faith of the Reformers and of all those in the history of Europe who have given their lives for Biblical Truth. For the European Union we pray the words of the prophet of the Lord, *"Turn thou us unto thee, O LORD, and we shall be turned; renew our days as of old."*[44] God can send forth His Spirit when He pleases. He did so at the time of the Reformation; we pray that He will do so again now! We remember the words of John Owen at another tuning point of history. He spoke of his own nation, England, at a time of social disintegration yet looking for revival. We now need that same faith and confidence for Britain and for the future of all the EU,

> "When God will do this I know not: but I believe God can do this: He is able to do it—able to renew all his churches, by sending out supplies of the Spirit, whose fullness is with Him, to recover them in the due and appointed time. And more; I believe truly, that when God hath accomplished some ends upon us, and hath stained the glory of all flesh, He will renew the power and glory of religion among us again, even in this nation."[45]

Watch and Pray—Sound an Alarm in Zion

The Church of Rome is one of the major players in the "creeping totalitarianism" of the New World Order. Her designs on the EU are

---

[43] Isaiah 9:2
[44] Lamentations 5:21
[45] John Owen, *The Works of John Owen* (Johnstone & Hunter, 1850-53; Reprinted by The Banner of Truth Trust, Edinburgh EH12 6EL, 1976) Vol. 9, p 514

a major part of the unfolding global strategy. We need to watch and pray as the "Fourth Reich" emerges out of its embryo. A watchman of old was expected to guard against robbers and disturbers of the peace. We are all commanded to be watchmen, *"to watch and pray"*. There has been a dreadful apathy that has afflicted the household of God, an indifference to the clear threat to our ancient liberties and Protestant identity from both the EU and the Church of Rome. As watchmen of the Lord today we are to guard against false teachers and false religion. We are to watch and discern the actions and words of the one who would seek to supplant the Gospel with apostasy and tyranny. Our task under God is to sound an alarm, *"Blow ye the trumpet in Zion, and sound an alarm in my holy mountain: let all the inhabitants of the land tremble: for the day of the LORD cometh, for it is nigh at hand."*[46] Now even more than in the days of old the commands of the Lord are to be obeyed, *"Son of man, I have made thee a watchman unto the house of Israel: therefore hear the word at my mouth, and give them warning from me."*[47] As we make our stand, so also we pray expecting to see the power of God at work in Europe, *"…they that wait upon the LORD shall renew their strength; they shall mount up with wings as eagles; they shall run, and not be weary; and they shall walk, and not faint."*[48] We owe the liberty that we yet enjoy to Jesus Christ the Lord. By His faithfulness and perfect sacrifice He has satisfied the demands of the broken law of the All Holy God. It is He, the Son of God, who has made us free. *"If the Son therefore shall make you free, ye shall be free indeed."*[49]

There is genuine unity of all true believers throughout the world. There is but one faith. All true believers are converted by the same Holy Spirit, and receive the same work of grace, which places them in the Beloved. In Christ Jesus we are spiritually one and called to stand fast in this liberty, and stand firm in His truth. *"Stand fast therefore in the liberty wherewith Christ hath made us free, and be not entangled again with the yoke of bondage."*[50]

---

[46] Joel 2:1
[47] Ezekiel 3:17
[48] Isaiah 40:31
[49] John 8:36
[50] Galatians 5:1

C. The Foundations Under Attack
The Roots of Apostasy

(Address given by the author to the United Protestant Council on November 1, 1997)

The apostasy that we have witnessed in the twentieth century; the compromise on essentials and the attack on the fundamentals actually have their roots in the nineteenth century. That century provided Great Britain with unprecedented prosperity, political power and global influence as well as the "feel good factor." At the same time, prominent committed Christians such as Livingstone, Wilberforce and Shaftesbury brought the gospel to the lost and social reform to the deprived and excluded. Victorian values, to which we look back with such nostalgia today, were derived from the Scriptures and brought many blessings and earned much respect abroad. On the face of it, all seemed to be well with the church too, but appearances were deceiving. Malign spiritual forces were at large, principalities and powers, spiritual wickedness in high places conspiring to undermine the very foundations of the faith.

During the course of that benign and well-intentioned century the Protestant Reformed religion established by law, which for centuries had stood firm, yielded ground to its sworn enemy—and came under sustained attack on several fronts. The Catholic Emancipation Act was enacted in 1829 and the Jesuits allowed to return to England. Within four years the Romanising movement within the Church of England had been launched at Oxford. As we shall see, Anglo-Catholicism was set to play a crucial role in the attack on the foundations of the Reformed faith and in the strategy of the Counter-Reformation.

That strategy was laid out unmistakably by Cardinal Manning speaking to a gathering of Jesuit leaders in 1870—the very year that Papal Infallibility was instituted.

> "Great is the prize for which you strive. Surely a soldier's eye and a soldier's heart would choose by intuition this field of England. None ampler or nobler could be found. It is a head of Protestantism; the center of its movements and the stronghold of its power. Weakened in England it is paralyzed everywhere.

Conquered in England it is conquered throughout the world. Once overthrown here, all else is a war of detail. All the roads of the world meet in one point, and this point reached, all the world is open to the Church's will."

As at the time of the Reformation the Word of God itself came under sustained attack. The Futurist interpretation of Bible prophecy propagated unsuccessfully by the Jesuits at the time of the Reformation had been repackaged and disseminated into the church through the flood of tracts of the newly formed Brethren movement and the Anglo-Catholic Tractarians. This new understanding of Daniel, 2 Thessalonians and Revelation laid the foundation of a false theology of Antichrist—the spurious Scriptural basis for the modem ecumenical movement. A new Bible was required; and was duly produced by Anglo-Catholic scholars, Professors Westcott and Hort. Their Revised Version of the Bible was based on corrupted manuscripts rejected by the Reformation, but it became the father of almost all modem versions. Its translation of the prophetic passages related to Antichrist lent itself to the new futurist theology. Protestant author and former Secretary of the Protestant Truth Society, Albert Close wrote in 1916: "The Jesuits have enticed our theological professors and the Plymouth brethren to fire high over the head of the great Antichrist; one in the past the Praeterist, the other in the future the Futurist Antichrist. Between these two schools the whole Christian ministry has been mixed up, and is practically sitting on the fence. Few ministers now preach Daniel or Revelation." Of course that remains the case today.

Given the impact in the theological colleges and the wider church of the new Higher Criticism in the climate of Darwinism and advancing humanism it is not surprising that the new understanding of Bible prophecy spread as quickly as it did. The Scofield Reference Bible appeared in the 1920s and was greatly influential especially among Pentecostals. Full of scholarly footnotes, it incorporated Futurist theology into its Dispensationalist scheme in such a way that few were able to distinguish it all from the inspired Scriptures. Dispensational Futurism has subsequently spread widely in evangelical circles especially among Charismatics and is now accepted by the majority of Christians as the new orthodoxy. This has seriously weakened the spiritual armoury of the church. With the Antichrist yet to appear and the Papacy vindicated from its accusers, the authority of Scripture was enhanced among those who sought reconciliation with Rome. The Counter-Reformation, so hostile and confrontational towards heretics in the past had emerged with a new face and a new strategy, and an ecumenical Bible. In 1910 at the *Edinburgh World Missionary Conference* the modem ecumenical movement was born.

Antichrist was no longer the Roman Papacy, except to a diminishing remnant, but a political world ruler who would appear at the end of the age. A few generations would pass and Christians raised on or drawn to the new Bible versions and the new eschatology would be ready to abandon and even repent of the Reformation separated position regarding Rome (this is also the Constitutional position). The new climate in which tolerance and unity is preferred to truth ensured this would happen. The "ancient landmark" could be removed within the Church of England. It was, at Keele, in 1967.

The First National Evangelical Conference met at Keele in April 1967 with 1000 clergy and laity taking part. It has been described as having marked a turning point in Anglican evangelicalism in the twentieth century. And now thirty years after Keele, the majority of evangelicals who are still in the Church of England look back with considerable satisfaction at what they see as the great achievements of the Keele Conference. They believe it was at Keele that at last the unity, which they had longed for and prayed for, became a reality. Those who were regarded as conservative evangelicals repented of their withdrawal and their sectarian attitudes and began to engage with the wider church and the world.

The conference had been primed to deal with the new policy of Anglican evangelicals towards ecumenism. The ecumenical movement had gained wide acceptance within the Church of England and beyond, and careful preparations had been made for the Keele Conference to successfully launch the "new evangelicalism" which was to unite evangelicals with their Anglo-Catholic and liberal brethren.

Dr Michael Ramsay, the Anglo-Catholic Archbishop of

Canterbury, was there to open the Conference. It was highly significant that he was the Conference's choice. It set the tone for what was to follow. Ramsay was sympathetic towards reunion with Rome. He had officially visited the Pope in the Vatican in 1966 and described the whole ecumenical enterprise as "the Holy Spirit working in us, uniting us in love and building us up in truth." He looked upon evangelicalism as sectarian, and even heretical, and took the opportunity afforded him by the conference to lecture a passive audience on their need to draw closer to Anglo-Catholics.

"Let us recognise," he said, "that amongst us Anglicans, some may have experienced the centrality of the Cross in ways different from others. For instance, those who value, as others do not, such things as sacramental confession or the Eucharistic sacrifice."

Bishop J.C. Ryle's warnings about the dangers presented by Anglo-Catholicism still echo down to us from the last century. The Anglo-Catholics, formerly known as the Tractarians, had long had a well-concealed plan for Church and nation to be reunited with the Church of Rome. Societies within their movement pursued this aim. They included the *Society of the Holy Cross,* the *Confraternity of the Blessed Sacrament* and, most particularly, the *Order of Corporate Reunion* – much of their business done in secret. At the end of the last century an article on the "Newest Fashions of Ritualism" appeared in a Jesuit publication, *The Month.* It declared that "At any rate the ritualists are doing a good work, which in the present state of the country, Catholics cannot do in the same proportion; they (the ritualists, or Anglo-Catholics) are preparing the soil and sowing the seed for a rich harvest, which the Catholic Church will reap sooner or later."

Cardinal John Henry Newman, hero and Saint to most Anglo-Catholics, and most influential leader of the Oxford movement, was said by Clifford Longley to have written the agenda of the Second Vatican Council from the grave. Newman's contribution to the cause of reunion with Rome is highly valued by the Vatican and he seems sure to emerge as the first Ecumenical Saint of the Roman Church. His defection to Rome in 1845 was described at the time it happened, by a future prime minister, as possibly the greatest religious crisis since the Reformation. How far things have moved since then!

Through the Anglo-Catholic movement, Newman's reformulation of doctrine (which is synonymous with continuing revelation) has had enormous influence inside and outside the Church of England. It has greatly influenced many Charismatics and liberals (and evangelicals too!) and provided good food for ecumenical believers. Newman's essay called *The Development of Christian Doctrine*, which he began as an Anglican and finished as a Roman Catholic, was the proof-text for those who helped put together the Agreed Statements of ARCIC (*The Anglican Roman Catholic International Commission*). As such it has helped to bring about the original goal of the Tractarians of convergence with Rome. The final ARCIC report, approved by the General Synod in 1986 and by the Lambeth Conference of Bishops in 1988, and the report's 1994 "Clarifications", show Anglican doctrine and practice on Ministry and the Lord's Supper to be reformulated in line with the Council of Trent. When Newman had met with Cardinal Wiseman in the Vatican in 1833 he had asked him on what terms the Church of England would be received back into the Roman fold. "By swallowing Trent whole" replied Wiseman. This has now been accomplished on behalf of the Anglican Communion. Only the issue of Women's ordination stands in the way of merger—or rather take-over—by the Church of Rome.

Whether such an outcome, such success for the Counter-Reformation was envisaged by those who determined the agenda at Keele is not known. But most of the facts and solemn warnings that I have referred to must have been well known to the evangelical leadership. But at Keele warnings of this kind were brushed aside by Dr. John Stott, who chaired the Conference. He and the other leaders were set on accommodation with the Anglo-Catholics. Earlier in 1963 a skirmish had been fought by these progressives with those who held fast to separation from doctrinal compromise. The Anglo-Catholic ritualists succeeded in a court action in making mass vestments and stone altars lawful. As a result of this many reformed evangelicals departed the Church of England at that time. Their loss made the task of those who were set on accommodating the Anglo-Catholics at Keele that much easier.

John Stott warned the Assembly at Keele that evangelicals had "acquired a reputation for narrow partisanship and obstructionism and that they needed to repent and change....The initial task for divided Christians is dialogue, at all levels and across all barriers. We desire to enter this ecumenical dialogue fully. We recognize that all who 'confess the Lord Jesus Christ as God and Saviour according to the Scriptures and therefore seek to fulfil together their common calling to the glory of one God, Father, Son and Holy Spirit [that is the *World Council of Churches* basis—Authors note] have a right to be treated as Christians, and it is on this basis that we wish to talk with them.'" This Statement made clear that the Keele Conference was accepting not only Anglo-Catholics and liberals as fellow Christians but Roman Catholics too. Let us just pause to consider the enormity of this. Thirty years ago the Church of England's most widely respected evangelicals, headed by John Stott, determined that ALL Roman Catholics are saved. It is interesting to note that it was 27 years before leading evangelicals on the other side of the Atlantic did the same, with *Evangelicals and Catholics Together.*

The influence of Billy Graham and his new evangelicalism played its part at Keele. Graham's apparently hugely successful ministry had long since accepted Catholics and liberals as fellow Christians. His example, in Martyn Lloyd-Jones words, "of Christian fellowship without agreement in the truth of the gospel, had shaken people's convictions as to what exactly it means to be an evangelical."

The sea change in the evangelical attitude to ecumenism ratified at Keele by Anglicans greatly influenced the other denominations. Dr Martyn Lloyd-Jones, probably the greatest preacher of the twentieth century, led the opposition to the departure from Protestant evangelicalism that Keele represented. Lloyd-Jones believed that far from providing the solution to the main problems of the church, Keele left the Church with much bigger questions to answer.

"What is a Christian?", for example, and "What is a church?". The abandoning of the stand of the Reformers against counterfeit Christianity and the downgrade of doctrine implicit in Keele's Statement meant in fact that true unity among evangelicals was no more. Addressing the *British Evangelical Council* in 1969 and citing the Scripture in 1 Corinthians 14, verse 8,—*"For if the trumpet gives an uncertain sound who shall prepare himself for the battle?"*—Dr. Lloyd Jones made clear that he saw the enemy as not just present, but rampant, in the camp. "Sound the alarm", he thundered, "Sound the alarm."

Opposing the new unity movement was a lonely task for him. So many of those leaders who had previously shared his views were shifting their position. For example, according to Iain Murray, Dr. J.I. Packer, once so close to the Doctor, changed his view between 1963 and 1965 to the very position that he had once criticised as inconsistent with evangelicalism. His endorsement of the Keele Statement was a telling blow to Dr. Lloyd-Jones, and others, with whom Dr. Packer had previously allied himself.

It was a very few years before, in 1961, that Jim Packer described the doctrine of justification by faith alone, *sola fide,* as, "like Atlas, it bears a world on its shoulders, the entire evangelical knowledge of saving grace." But his position on this defining doctrine changed as well, perhaps at that same time prior to Keele. His revised view has been recently demonstrated by his signing of *Evangelicals and Catholics Together,* the document that has rocked American evangelicalism. In a 1994 article, *Why I Signed It,* he refers to *Sola Fide* (faith alone) as "small print." He asked the question: "May ECT realistically claim, as in effect it does, that its evangelical and Catholic drafters agree on the gospel of salvation?" "Answer Yes and No." "No", Professor Packer says, "with respect to the 'small print.'" Thus *Sola Fide,* a burning issue for Reformation martyrs, and an issue which "bears a world on its shoulders", is relegated to "small print."

Martyn Lloyd-Jones felt that, by compromising with ecumenism, Anglican evangelicals were putting their denomination before the gospel and downgrading doctrine. Personal relationships, and superficial unity, tolerance and love were preferred to the confrontational truths of Scripture. He urged evangelicals to come out of the denominations united in the truth of God's word. How this was to be accomplished he felt was for others to determine, but he was convinced that it could happen and should happen. There had to be clarity—rather than the confusion that was overtaking the understanding of the gospel. "We should not be asking", he said, "'How can we have a territorial church', 'how can we have unity and fellowship' or 'how can we find a formula to satisfy opposing views?' We should be asking, 'What is a Christian? How does one become a Christian? How can we get forgiveness of sin and what is a church?'"

Keele legitimised compromise for evangelicals within the established Church. But, at Nottingham, the second *National Evangelical Anglican Conference* (NEAC II), which followed 10 years later, gave compromise its seal of approval. The ecumenical charismatic movement, which had begun in Britain in the early 1960s, had been opposed at Keele by that Conference's organisers. But at Nottingham it was highly praised. The Nottingham Statement declared: "We see a particular significance in the charismatic movement, especially in its strong witness to the primacy of God."

And it was at Nottingham that leading charismatic, David Watson, friend and mentor to John Wimber, spoke of the Reformation as "one of the greatest tragedies that ever happened to the church." He went on to tell the conference how he had come to sense the profound grief that God must feel at the separation of his body.

The Charismatic Renewal movement had begun in the United States in the 1950s and rapidly swept across the Christian world. It was widely seen as a great work of the Holy Spirit, a new Pentecost. Para-church groups within the movement like the *Full Gospel Businessmen's Fellowship International* brought Roman Catholics and Protestants together "under the banner of love" in what they called the "unity of the spirit." They placed emphasis on experiential testimony rather than Scripture.

It was less than two years before Keele that the Second Vatican Council gave its blessing to what they called this new movement of the Holy Spirit. The "separated brethren could now be welcomed back into the fold," announced Jesuit Cardinal Augustin Bea to the delegates in 1965. The heretics had become "separated brethren" and their abandoning of sound doctrine meant that they could come back to the Mother Church. The Vatican officially adopted its own renewal movement. To what extent this movement was spontaneous, or planned, we do not know. But with all the emphasis on gifts and experiences, it certainly helped to sweep aside doctrinal differences. At the same time it demonstrated, as did the Billy Graham crusades, what the evangelist called "the role in the Christian family of our Catholic brethren." With the reinstatement of Catholics as "brethren" in the minds and hearts of so many, the once secure fortress of biblical separation was breached. Keele was the formal surrender to the forces of new evangelicalism. Nottingham made the surrender unconditional.

The momentum from Keele and Nottingham and from the new evangelicalism seemed irresistible. The new spirit of tolerance and "love" outlawed arguments over biblical truths. Unity through compromise of doctrine was sought as the will of God to transform the church. The great doctrines of grace and reformed theology were seen as the province of those living in the past, fighting the same old irrelevant battles behind crumbling ramparts. Conservative evangelicals, who would have no truck with ecumenism, were marginalised, being seen as unloving and intolerant.

The decision by the Keele Conference of a majority of evangelicals to dialogue with ecumenism was of immeasurable spiritual consequence. It was extraordinary that such a momentous change should be brought about by those very Christians best placed to understand its implications and without serious protest too! In a very real sense evangelicals had ceased to be evangelicals. Doctrine had been relegated from its position of supreme authority to a lesser position. The high view of Scripture was abandoned: God's Word was no longer infallible. The part played in this by the acceptance of modern Bible versions in place of the King James was surely very considerable. "Thus saith the Lord" was allowed to give way to "depending on what version you have"—reminding us of the serpent's seed of doubt, "has God said?"

From Keele the slippery slope has rapidly led us downwards and we see the consequences today in the Church of England and in the other Protestant denominations too. During the past thirty years there has been such radical and profound change in the Church of England that this once great institution seems to have lost its very identity. The collapse of Protestantism at Keele and Nottingham had sold the pass to the new evangelicalism; and accelerated the downgrade of doctrine. The abandoning of our God-given Reformation heritage—enshrined in the 39 Articles and formularies of the Church of England—has "removed the ancient landmark, which our fathers have set."[1] The Scripture from Joel 2:17—"...*Spare thy people, O LORD, and give not thine heritage to reproach, that the heathen should rule*

---

[1] Proverbs 22:28 *"Remove not the ancient landmark, which thy fathers have set."*

over them: wherefore should they say among the people, Where is their God?" Where is their God? That question is now very relevant to our national church, to its Bishops, priests and laymen—so many of them so uncertain of their faith. It is a question that the nation is asking of itself as that once august body that many of us can remember falls further into disrepute.

At Keele and afterwards, the ancient landmark was removed; and our heritage was given to reproach. There was an act of betrayal. The legacy of those who gave their lives for the truth of the Word of God was abandoned. The verdict of Keele and Nottingham was that the martyrs of the Reformation were mistaken; they were party to one of the greatest tragedies that ever happened to the church. For all but a very few in the Church of England the flame of Hugh Latimer's candle was extinguished—the blood of the martyrs denied.

The same is true in the Free churches too. Free churches are no longer so free; indeed they are no longer so non-conformist. There is conformism—conformism to the spirit of the age—the spirit of tolerance and unity. We have seen even the Bible-based Baptist denomination succumb to this seductive spirit. Carried along by the stream that became a river that flowed from Keele, the Baptist Union gradually moved its position until in 1995 it routed those who remained in opposition and voted overwhelmingly to fully participate in *Churches Together in England.*

The new evangelicalism provides for love at the expense of truth. But this is not the expression of love of the bride of Christ, but rather of the harlot of Revelation 17. What has become of the love of truth, the jealousy for purity in doctrine and the hatred of idolatry? Where is the urgent concern for the souls of more than a thousand million religious Catholics, Orthodox and Anglicans in the ecumenical Church today, without assurance of salvation, in bondage to the sacraments and to a system of works and ritual? Where are hearts of compassion for those who seek truth and are imprisoned by deception? Where is the cry for the cleansing of the church and for deep repentance because we have failed them, our own kinsmen, by pretending not to see? Where today are the preachers who do not persistently avoid the clear message of Revelation 17; or "the man of sin" and "mystery of iniquity" of 2 Thessalonians 2; or the persecuting "little horn" of

Daniel 7, in the time of the fourth kingdom, "wearing out the saints of the most high". Where are the watchmen who sound the alarm? Why do they who hear the sound of the trumpet not take warning?

The fact is that in this land of such a precious heritage, very few pastors are prepared any longer to call to remembrance the sacrifice of the martyrs of the sixteenth and seventeenth centuries. The cause of those martyrs—of denying the sacrifice of the Mass as an appalling blasphemy, and the identification of the Papacy as Antichrist—that cause is now the preserve of the very few.

The Reformation provided Christians with two great truths—the just shall live by faith (and not by the works of Romanism or any other religion) and that the Papacy is the Antichrist as revealed in Scripture. If we lose the second we unquestionably do injury to the first, and that is being amply demonstrated today. Pastors won't preach it; they fear the disapproval of men—they should fear the disapproval of God. Few there are who scorn popularity and are ready to lay down their reputations, let alone their lives. But "evil abounds when good men stay silent."

At his enthronement as Archbishop at Canterbury in 1991, George Carey spoke of the example to us of former archbishops who were martyred. He named the Benedictine monk Alphege and he named Thomas a Becket, both of whom were canonised by the Roman Catholic Church; and then he spoke of William Laud. Both Becket and Laud sought to bring the Church of England under the authority of the Church of Rome and into her faith and practice. Conspicuous by its absence from George Carey's recollection of martyrs was the name of Thomas Cranmer, the Protestant martyr, whose quincentenary had been commemorated in a rather muted manner the previous year. George Carey's enthronement involved a commitment to upholding the *39 Articles of Religion* and the *Book of Common Prayer*, for both of which Cranmer was the man, under God, most responsible. The present Archbishop's commitment to the *Articles* and *Prayer* book has been borne extremely lightly. During his latest visit to the Pope in the Vatican, George Carey did have some good things to say in defence of the Reformation, but he continues eagerly to seek full unity with the Roman Church. This ambivalence illustrates and epitomises the leadership problem of today's church—man-centred and totally inconsistent.

As the Apostle Paul wrote to the Galatians: *"...so say I now again, If any man preach any other gospel unto you than that ye have received, let him be accursed. For do I now persuade men, or God? or do I seek to please men? for if I yet pleased men, I should not be the servant of Christ."*[2]

The same ambivalence and inconsistency is apparent in the Alpha course which is beginning to spread like a bush fire not just in the UK, but across the USA and Canada, too. In the spirit of Keele, doctrinal differences are glossed over; indeed Catholic theologians have endorsed the Course and, backed by Cardinal Hume, plan their own Roman Catholic Alpha courses in 1997. Alpha stems from Holy Trinity Brompton Church, which was first in the United Kingdom with the 'Toronto Blessing', as it was with the 'Kansas City Prophets'. Like ECT (*Evangelicals and Catholics Together*), in America, the Alpha Course is providing a highly successful means of reconciling the irreconcilable. The *Promise Keepers Movement,* another import from the USA launched in England in November '97 likewise builds bridges without foundations.

The consequences of surrender to ecumenism at Keele and elsewhere have been very apparent to the nation as well as the church. Given such a free hand, the Church of Rome with its mastery of the media has been positioning itself to take over when the Anglican Church has disintegrated beyond recall. To what extent the Church of Rome's agents are assisting in this process is not revealed to us, but history relates very clearly what lengths the Pope's followers will go to in order to further the cause of the "Mother Church." *The Catholic Herald* is now confident enough to predict: "The days of the Anglican Church are numbered, and most of its worshippers will return to the true faith of their distant mediaeval forbears." Many of them already have returned, at least in spirit.

Earlier this year *The Times* and *The Daily Telegraph* both gave front page coverage to the news that the Church of England has arranged for the return of the relics of St. Thomas a Becket, on loan from Rome, where they were sent for protection at the time of the Reformation. Fragments of bone and brain tissue, they are

---

[2] Galatians 1:9-10

the first relics to be displayed at Canterbury Cathedral since the Reformation.

The tomb of Thomas Becket in Canterbury and the spiritual presence of this "Saint" of the Roman Catholic Church in the principal Anglican Cathedral has proved important for the ecumenical movement, and will continue to be so. In 1982 Pope John Paul II and Archbishop Runcie prayed together at Becket's shrine, and in 1989, the Archbishop of York, John Hapgood, led pilgrims who had arrived for the first multi-faith gathering at the cathedral into the shrine as their final destination. The three strands of this fully ecumenical pilgrimage had earlier converged at another place, another "sacred site" where Henry II had paid penance to the Pope following Becket's murder in 1170. Services are now held annually across the country on the 29 December to commemorate Becket's "martyrdom" with unusual media attention. Becket's "martyrdom", which stemmed from his preferred allegiance to the Papacy rather than the Crown, may well prove to be important in the revival of the principle that the State should not have power over the Church.

The public perception of Becket's life and death has been greatly altered in this ecumenical century by plays and films like Anglo-Catholic T.S. Eliot's *Murder in the Cathedral*. Even more so in relation to Sir Thomas More, who, according to Foxe's *Acts and Monuments*, scourged and tortured in his garden "those guilty of reading the Scriptures and holding purely Protestant doctrines". Robert Bolt's film *A Man For All Seasons*, which has established Thomas More as a great and godly Christian man unequalled in his faith in Christ, is based on history rewritten, ecumenical propaganda. A year of "England's Christian Heritage" began in May 1997 with a celebration of the 14th Centenary of Saint Augustine's arrival in Britain. At his inauguration the Archbishop of Canterbury said that Augustine had brought Christianity to the British Isles from Rome. This is also no more than ecumenical propaganda. There is a wealth of evidence that Christianity had taken root in these islands at the end of the first century, and saints of Christ such as Alban and Patrick were martyred or persecuted for the sake of the gospel centuries before Augustine arrived to enforce papal supremacy. This year of Christian heritage that is said by its organisers to herald a "fresh spiritual breeze" and "a religious stirring" features numerous pilgrimages celebrating pre-Reformation Saints. The veneration or worship of Saints and relics is reversion to spiritism and necromancy, which are condemned in the Bible; but their practice is consistent with the Pope's recent advice to his flock "to call on dead ancestors for protection."

The accelerating reversion to pre-Reformation Christianity—to superstition and idolatry—is supported strongly by well-respected Catholic columnists such as Paul Johnson, who have prayed all their lives for England to be restored to Mary's dowry. The press has given extraordinary prominence to the very public conversions to Rome of public figures such as Ann Widdecombe, John Gummer, Alan Clark, Charles Moore, and, most significantly, the Duchess of Kent. So much has been made of these conversions, and yet, in this ecumenical age that we now live in, it's not supposed to matter.

Multi-faith worship has followed on—not unnaturally—for once the gates are thrown open all may come in. Reflecting this, the leading members of the Royal family have embraced other religions. The Commonwealth Day Service, especially dear to Her Majesty the Queen is no longer recognisably Christian, and she has not listened to the protests of two thousand evangelical clergymen concerned about the insult done to the unique claims and supremacy of the Lord Jesus Christ. It was Prince Philip who in 1989 launched the *International Sacred Literature Trust* to significantly contribute to inter-faith dialogue; and Prince Charles, the heir in waiting, whose allegiance is to faiths rather than faith, has gone out of his way to encourage Islam. The Muslims now plan to build 100 new mosques in the next three years—describing this project as "the biggest expression of religious faith in Britain for centuries."

In November 1992 the Church of England Synod deferred to the prevailing politically correct view and voted in the measure to ordain women. Dr David Samuel, who resigned his ministry in the Church of England as a result of the adoption of this measure, described something of his reaction at that time. "This was a decision that would have enormous implications and would set the course and direction of the Church of England for the future, and that course would be one of ever increasing divergence from Scripture, from its formularies, from orthodoxy and from truth. If the official doctrine of the Church of England can be changed arbitrarily by a show of hands in the Synod, then it has been undermined and revealed to be a fiction." It is likely that within a very few years there will be women bishops in the Church of England and archbishops too.

Then there is the "Christian" gay and lesbian movement. It was as long as twenty years ago that the NEAC Conference at Nottingham resolved that, "There should be a full welcoming voice in the Christian fellowship for the Christian homosexual." It was just a few months before that the Lesbian Gay Christian Movement was launched. The service at Southwark Cathedral in November 1996 "celebrated" its twenty-year anniversary. Protest at the Cathedral and across the nation was minimal. Informed observers in the General Synod now believe that the ordination of practising homosexuals is a foregone conclusion. Robert Runcie announced last year that when he was Archbishop of Canterbury this was already happening.

Once evangelicals allow compromise to enter in, and fail to stand their ground on the rock of Scripture, continuing retreat is inevitable. It is well known that leading evangelicals including John Stott convinced themselves that there is no literal Hell. Now just a few years later the doctrine of eternal punishment has been "officially" abolished by the Synod of the Church of England. Annihilationism is the reformulated doctrine of the Anglican Church—flying in the face of 2000 years of orthodoxy and the plain teaching of our Lord in Scripture. Another decision of the Synod is that cohabitation before marriage is now no longer "living in sin." The teaching of the New Testament in relation to fornication is crystal clear. But this is the new hermeneutic and the new evangelicalism. With the Synod legislating against the clear teaching of Scripture there must have been many who were reminded of the psalmist's question, *"If the foundations be destroyed, what can the righteous do?"*[3]

Meanwhile pulpits are physically disappearing, stone and other altars reappearing, crucifixes abound, roods are returning, as are confessions and "holy places" and "holy water"; and more and more ministers are styled as "priest" and "father", contrary to Scripture. The law is rarely preached in the church today. In the new ecumenical climate of live-and-let-live preachers do not want to run the risk of offending their congregations and losing numbers. It is

---
[3] Psalms 11:3

sobering to learn from the press that a 1997 survey has revealed that less than 25% of Anglican vicars now know the Ten Commandments. Without the law how does one properly preach the Gospel?

Within the Church of England the *Reform Group* of Anglican Evangelicals was formed from those who opposed much of what had been agreed at Keele. They expressed their disillusionment with the post-Keele direction of the church by advocating non-payment of part of the parish's share of the diocesan budget. They continue today to oppose some of the unbiblical trends in the Church of England. But they have no clear-cut position in relation to the ordination of women issue, nor do they take a stand with regard to separation from the ecumenical movement. *The Church of England (Continuing)* separated from the Anglican Church after the Women's Ordination measure was passed by General Synod in November 1992. It seeks to preserve the real identity of the Church of England through the Authorised Version of the Holy Scriptures, the *39 Articles of Religion*, the *Book of Common Prayer* and the Ordinal. David Samuel, the Presiding Bishop, has described these texts as the identity card of the Church of England without which those who belong would be mere vagrants in Christendom.

In bringing this brief survey to a conclusion I feel I must speak of the very real danger, both political and spiritual, that confronts us as our new government and those behind the scenes who influence it weaken and dismantle the Union and prepare us for submergence into a federal Europe. To what extent the retreat of Protestant evangelicalism, epitomised by Keele, has been responsible for the drift into abandoning our cherished independence, only the Lord knows. But as I have sought to argue, our precious and God-given heritage has been betrayed; the lessons of history and the far-sighted precautions of our forefathers in protecting our liberty—enshrined in the Bill of Rights, the Act of Settlement and the Coronation Oath—have been sidelined, sadly not least by the Queen. And the malign experience of the Papacy in our nation's affairs in the past has simply been ignored.

We know that as a nation we deserve judgement. The defection of evangelicals from their Protestant Reformed legacy has, not surprisingly, paralleled that of the Monarch and her Parliament. At her coronation Her Majesty recognised the authority and supremacy of Holy Scripture: "This is the most valuable thing this world affords. Here is wisdom. This is the royal law. These are the lively oracles of God." She then promised to "maintain to the utmost of her power the Laws of God, the true profession of the Gospel and the Protestant Reformed Religion established by law."

In other words, the Queen committed herself, and the Crown-in-Parliament, to upholding the statutes and laws of Holy Scripture and the Christian faith. However, during her reign, we have seen the royal assent given to radical legislation totally opposed to Christianity as revealed in Scripture, and plainly fostering immorality. Bills facilitating divorce, legalising abortion and homosexuality as well as encouraging adultery and pornography have laid the basis of today's moral crisis in society. There are many signs that we are reaping the whirlwind of God's righteous anger and judgement, not least in the devastation being brought about by collapsing family values which has been experienced by the Queen herself. What we are seeing unfolding at breathtaking speed is the withdrawal of the grace and blessing of God that many of us had come to take for granted—as a result of our national apostasy. As a nation we may be about to pay a very heavy price.

Our religious liberties are at stake. As Adrian Hilton, in his 1997 book, *The Principality and Power of Europe*, writes: "Evangelical Christians are classified by the European Union as a 'sect', and any group that does not belong to the majority church (Roman Catholic) is viewed by many MEPs with suspicion." This classification is nothing new. The early church was branded an heretical sect, and this was the earliest basis of persecution. Of course, any impending persecution will not be on overtly religious grounds: an enlightened European Union would consider this abhorrent. Persecution will be political, as it was with the early church, with accusations of "disturbing the peace" or "inciting sectarianism" as in the Book of Acts chapters 16 and 17. David Hallam MEP has confirmed that a European resolution on sects and cults permits the European police force Europol to carry out surveillance on such group's activities. He adds: "In Europe this could include Christians."

With Protestantism's surrender, Apostate Christendom is swiftly unifying world religion, which under its veneer is as intolerant and bloodthirsty as it ever was. Once religions of the world combine with the New Age to form one great ecumenical and multi-faith monopoly, God's little flock will yet again be as lambs to the slaughter. Bishop Ryle's words encourage those evangelicals who will not compromise: "This is the church which does the work of Christ on earth. Its members are a little flock and few in number, one or two here and two or three there—a few in this district and a few in that. But these are they that shake the universe; who change the fortune of kingdoms by their prayers; these are they who are the active workers for spreading the knowledge of pure religion and undefiled; these are the lifeblood of the country, the shield, the defence, the stay and the support of any nation to which they belong." Let us be encouraged therefore and "stand fast in the liberty wherewith Christ hath made us free."[4]

---

[4] Galatians 5:1 "*Stand fast therefore in the liberty wherewith Christ hath made us free, and be not entangled again with the yoke of bondage.*"

D. The Monarchy In Peril

Elizabeth II at Her Coronation Service, June 2, 1953[1]

"I, Elizabeth do solemnly and sincerely in the presence of God profess, testify and declare that I am a faithful Protestant." *[H.M. The Queen's first address to Parliament, November 4, 1952]*

[November 30, 1995 marked the day Her Majesty the Queen attended a Service of Commemoration at Westminster Cathedral to mark the Centenary of the building of this spiritual centre of Roman Catholicism in Britain. In doing so Her Majesty belied the declaration above as well as her Coronation Oath. Her attendance was intended to underline ecumenical reconciliation and unity. In fact it symbolised the continuing retreat of the Protestant identity of our nation and anticipated the likely imminent removal of the *Act of Settlement* and the resulting constitutional redundancy of the monarchy. It was the latest in a series of events in the

---

[1] < http://www.filmworld.com.au/htm/collections/collections_archival.htm>: Film World.

ecumenical process that, step by step, was and is pulling up the historic roots of the Protestant Throne.]

1993 - The Year of the Maastricht Treaty and the "Annus Horribilis" - "Is it Time for a Conversion of England?"

"1993 may turn out to have been a fateful and historic year in the long tale of Christianity in this country," wrote Roman Catholic columnist, Paul Johnson, in the *Catholic Herald*. "I am coming to believe that the days of the Anglican Church are numbered and that most of its worshippers will return to the true faith of their distant medieval forebears."[2]

Mr. Johnson and other zealous Catholic commentators had good reason for such confidence. In 1993, for the first time since the Reformation, the spurious sacrament of "penance" and the hearing of confessions began again within the Palace of Westminster. Previously the Roman Catholic Primate, Cardinal Basil Hume, had preached before Her Majesty the Queen, the first time that a Catholic prelate had done so since the seventeenth century. The protest of over two thousand Church of England clergy, who were concerned by the insult done by the multi-faith worship at the Commonwealth Day Service to the unique claims and inviolable supremacy of the Lord Jesus Christ, was ignored by the Queen. On April 21, 1993, the Queen's birthday, a High Mass took place at Westminster to receive Junior Social Security Minister, Ann Widdecombe, "crossing the Tiber" from the Church of England to the Roman Church.[3]

There were other high-profile conversions that year and there have been several since, including most significantly the Duchess of Kent, the Queen's cousin by marriage, as well as Princess Diana's mother, Mrs Shand Kydd; Conservative Ministers, John Selwyn Gummer and Alan Clark, and the then Sunday Telegraph Editor, Charles Moore. All these conversions or desertions from Canterbury to Rome, in an ecumenical climate in which it wasn't supposed to matter (and for the majority of people today it didn't and doesn't), had been very public and had received extensive press coverage. Without question,

---

[2] *Catholic Herald* Christmas 1993
[3] After her conversion Miss Widdecombe adopted the name Hugh, partly, incredible as it might seem, 'in remembrance' of the great Protestant martyr Hugh Latimer!

public opinion was being managed and manipulated by grossly unbalanced coverage of religious conversions in the media. An illustration of this was Prince Philip's reversion back to Greek Orthodoxy from the Church of England which attracted no press coverage whatsoever.

"Annus Horribilis"

In that same year, 1993, the fortieth anniversary of the Queen's reign[4] and her "annus horribilis," the prince of Wales' adulterous relationship with Camilla Parker-Bowles surfaced in the media. Mrs. Parker-Bowles was by then amicably divorced from staunch Roman Catholic, Andrew Parker-Bowles, "Silver-Stick in Waiting to Her Majesty the Queen", and it seemed that there was a campaign in the press to legitimise her relationship with the Prince. It was widely believed at that time (1996) that both the Queen and the Prime Minister favoured changing both the Royal Marriages Act (1772), and the Act of Settlement (1701), so that the heir to the throne, if divorced, can remarry, and he or she can be married to a Catholic if that is the choice.

The departure of the royal family from their constitutional identity and duty as faithful Protestants had been seen in their fraternising with Roman Catholics. Prince Charles had attended Mass on more than one occasion with Catholic friends and was prevented from participating in the Pope's private Mass only by command of the Queen. Princess Diana's closest friends seemed to be Roman Catholics. They included Mother Teresa, with whom according to press reports, she has a special rapport, Rosa Monckton, wife of *Sunday Telegraph* Editor, Dominic Lawson, Lucia Flecha de Lima, wife of the Brazilian Ambassador and James Gilbey of the "Squidgy telephone tape." At the end of 1992, the tabloid newspapers reported that the Princess was taking instruction from a Dominican Priest, at a secret Oxford address, to convert to the Roman Catholic faith. With the Princess so open to such influence and with Camilla Parker-Bowles' children attending Catholic schools, it is hardly surprising that Prince William very nearly found himself in the one house at Eton College with a Roman Catholic house-master.

Prince Charles had made it known that his allegiance was not to

---

[4] Forty years (or days) is a time of testing in the Bible

the Protestant faith, but to all faiths. It would be impossible for him to swear exclusively to maintain the Protestant religion in his realm given that by his bedside he kept a rosary given to him by the Pope. As the *Sunday Telegraph* reminded its readers in providing this information:

> "How changed is our country. Even 30 years ago the news that the future Supreme Governor of the Church of England practised what would have been considered Popish superstition would have provoked outrage. A century before it might have provoked revolution. The news about a mistress would have attracted far less attention."

Maastricht and Monarchy – The Nation's Loss of Direction

It was also in 1993 that the Maastricht Treaty was signed and the EEC became the European Union. This treaty effectively laid the Crown-in-Parliament at the feet of those who rule in Brussels. Despite John Major's professed Euro-scepticism the reality was that, in spite of the opt-out, the Treaty committed Britain to ever-closer union, with federalism sure to follow. The conveyor-belt "process" of Maastricht, inevitably leading to total abdication of sovereignty, can be stopped only by the exercise of massive and unprecedented political will. Meanwhile the desired expression of the will of the people for a referendum has been brushed aside, and no amount of rational and passionate argument, nor warning signs, nor adverse publicity, nor bad behaviour or breaches of trust experienced with our European partners, seem able to restrain the compulsion to merge and abandon our independence and identity. The recent rejection of the proposed European Union Constitution by the French and Dutch people has made little difference to the process. The British people have had no say, and the EU Constitution is being implemented, by stealth, anyway. If the process is completed, and we are integrated into a federal Europe, sovereignty will no longer rest with the people of these islands, nor with their Queen, who will simply be a citizen of Europe like the rest of us; and her Parliament will be seconded to the European State. In fact all this has already happened. The reality is concealed from the people, until the EU Superstate fully reveals itself as a fully legal entity.

There is today a collapse of moral and political confidence in Britain and a loss of faith in our institutions the like of which we have not seen before. The Church of England, increasingly intent on following the fashions of the world and the lunacy of "political correctness," has lost the trust and regard of the people and seems destined for disintegration. The police service and the courts of justice have repeatedly been discredited or maligned, and the modest proportion of corruption or fraud that has actually been detected in the business world is on an unprecedented scale. The young have scant respect for their elders, reverence towards anything is rare, and *"there is no fear of God before their eyes."*[5] The mounting crime wave and the sheer nastiness of so much criminal (and other) behaviour are deeply worrying for all of us.

There is now no national consensus on virtually any issue, "one-nation" polity is impossible with no general agreement that we should remain a sovereign and united kingdom. Patriotism is widely despised and loyalty to our institutions unfashionable. The one great certainty that marked the fourth consecutive Conservative Administration was that the Maastricht Treaty, which seemed to have had most of the Cabinet and Opposition leaders mesmerised, had to be forced into law. Tony Blair and his "New Labour" government have carried on in the same vein, whisking the Amsterdam and Nice Treaties through Parliament and signing the proposed Constitution without consulting the people; and there is a sense in which events seem to have been orchestrated—so swift and relentless has been the assault on the nation's institutions, not least the monarchy and the Protestant Throne.

The Religious Dimension

The predominant religion of the confederation will be Roman Catholicism and its spiritual head will be the Pope. At the time of Maastricht, among the European leaders who were most influential in furthering the federalist agenda were Jacques Delors and Dutch Prime Minister Ruud Lubbers, both Jesuit educated, as well as German Chancellor Kohl and Prime Minister Felipe Gonzales of Spain, also devout Catholics. These four leaders were products of the Roman Catholic Social Movement, which believes that "there is

---

[5] Romans 3:18

no nobler task than the unifying of our continent." The concept of European Unity was championed by the founding fathers of the EEC—Monnet, Gaspari, Spaak, Adenauer, and Schuman. Konrad Adenauer, first Chancellor of West Germany, was Privy Chamberlain to the Pope, and declared in 1953 that "Germany had a divine mission to save Western Europe." Robert Schuman, founder of the Franco-German Coal and Steel Federation, was the leading visionary, who pointed ahead to a federation of Europe. His cause for Sainthood is in process of advancement in the Vatican. The European Union from its inception, was an idea in the mind of the Vatican to re-Catholicise the continent of Europe and into the bargain re-Catholicise this country.

Departure from Biblical Christianity

When, at her Coronation Service, Her Majesty the Queen took the Bible handed to her by the Moderator of the Church of Scotland, the Archbishop of Canterbury, and the Moderator expressed that which lies at the very heart of Protestantism and at the heart of the institution of the Monarchy—the recognition of the authority and supremacy of Scripture:

> "This is the most valuable thing that this world affords. Here is wisdom. This is the royal law. These are the lively oracles of God."

Her Majesty then promised "to maintain to the utmost of her power the Laws of God, the true profession of the Gospel and the Protestant Reformed religion established by law." Then laying her hand on the Holy Gospel she added: "The things I have here before promised I will perform and keep. So help me God."

Her Majesty, who at her Coronation promised "to maintain to the utmost of her power the Laws of God, the true profession of the Gospel and the Protestant Reformed religion established by law" visits Pope John Paul II, wearing black, which is symbolic of the Anglican Church's submission to the Church of Rome.[6]

In other words, the Queen committed herself, and the Crown-in-Parliament to upholding the statutes and laws of Holy Scripture and the Christian faith. However during her reign, we have seen the royal assent given to radical legislation totally opposed to Christianity as revealed in Scripture, and plainly fostering immorality. Bills facilitating divorce, legalising abortion and homosexuality, and "liberating" adultery and pornography laid the basis of today's moral crisis in our society. *"If the foundations be destroyed, what can the righteous do?"*[7] There are signs that we are reaping the whirlwind of God's righteous anger and judgement, so very apparent in the devastation brought about by collapsing family values, which have been experienced by the Queen herself.

Church leaders do not speak for God from Scripture as they once

---

[6] Photo courtesy of <http://boston.com/news/specials/pope/galleries/retrospective?pg=10> The Boston Globe.
[7] Psalms 11:3

did, but God's Word is not silent about what has happened in our land. What we are seeing unfolding at breath-taking speed is the withdrawal of the grace and blessing of God that many of us had come to take for granted as the inevitable result of our national apostasy.

The History of Christianity in Britain – Misrepresented

At his inauguration, Archbishop of Canterbury, George Carey, said that Augustine had brought Christianity to the British Isles from Rome. This is not true; rather it is simply ecumenical propaganda. There is a wealth of evidence that Christianity had taken root in these islands at the end of the first century, and saints of Christ such as Alban and Patrick were martyred or persecuted for the sake of the gospel centuries before Augustine arrived to enforce papal supremacy in A.D.596.

The rule of Rome was established after a century of opposition from indigenous Christians at the Synod of Whitby in A.D.664. The church in Ireland retained its freedom for nearly 500 years, and sent out another saint, Columba, to evangelise Scotland and Northern England from his community base in Iona. Henry II was commissioned by the Pope to invade Ireland and bring the Christians there under papal control, which was accomplished at the Synod of Cashel in A.D.1171.

Britain's Christian Heritage

Our forefathers who carefully drafted the *Bill of Rights* and the *Act of Succession* were at pains to protect and defend the Biblical Christianity rediscovered at the Reformation and thus consolidate the basis of our parliamentary and individual freedoms. They saw the Roman Papacy as a proven threat to the safety and liberty of the realm and the practice of Roman Catholicism as an affront to true New Testament Christianity. This was apparent in the Sovereign's Coronation Oath sworn by every monarch up to the time of King George V:

> "...I do solemnly and sincerely, in the presence of God, profess, testify and declare that I do believe that, in the Sacrament of the Lord's Supper, there is not any Transubstantiation of the Elements of bread and wine into the Body and blood of Christ, at or after the consecration thereof

by any person whatsoever; and that the invocation or Adoration of the Virgin Mary or any other Saint, and the Sacrifice of the Mass, as they are now used by the Church of Rome, are superstitious and idolatrous."

At that time, memories of the burning of godly men, who would not compromise their faith in Christ and the infallibility of Scripture (such as Hugh Latimer and Nicholas Ridley at Oxford and George Wishart in Scotland), were still precious to the majority of the people and their children at school. Relativism had not taken root, nor had tolerance stretched the bounds of morality beyond the limits of Scripture. Truth really mattered. Our great Christian heritage, firmly guarded by the national church and enshrined in the *39 Articles* and the other great Protestant Confessions of faith, was treasured by the whole nation. Reminders of the wonderful deliverances from papal power were included in the Prayer Book, and are still to be found in the preface to the Authorised Version of the Bible.

England had repeatedly experienced plots, conspiracies and assaults against both Throne and State carried out by the Jesuits in the sixteenth and seventeenth centuries. The Ridolphi Plot, the Babington Plot, the Spanish Armada, the Gunpowder Plot, and numerous other attempts to advance popery during the time of the Stuart kings culminated in the "Glorious" and bloodless Revolution and to the securing of the Protestant Throne in 1688.

The Jesuits, ever zealous in their conviction that the end, of establishing the rule of Rome, justifies whatever the means, went underground. They were banned from nearly every country in Europe including our own, until they were able to re-emerge just before the launch of the *Oxford Movement* in the 1830s. The success of the Tractarians and the man described by previous popes as the founder of the ecumenical movement, Cardinal John Henry Newman, in building up the "High Church" or Roman Catholic wing of the Church of England, sowed the seeds for the departure of the denominational structures from true Christianity in the twentieth century. *Vatican II,* in the early 1960s, convinced and continues to convince many Protestants that Roman Catholicism had changed and was looking for agreement and compromise. This is not so. Cardinal Basil Hume claimed that the Roman Church "possesses all of God's revealed truth and all the means of grace and will not accord that status to others." Gullible Christians longing for unity have swallowed a red herring. The dogmas of the council of Trent, which pronounced anathemas on "the heretics" of the Protestant Reformation, were upheld by Vatican II. The language has changed but not the substance. Protestants have become "separated brethren", but "subsidiarity," a Jesuitical term of "Vaticanspeak" first used in the pontificate of Pius XI early in the last century, can mean whatever those at the centre of power choose it to mean. "The single market" and the "social chapter" are also concepts that derive from Roman Catholic social thinking. This does not bode well for our future freedoms.

The Faith that Made Britain Great

As a nation we have turned our backs on God and denied and squandered our great Christian heritage—the faith that won us the freedom to read the Bible (and indeed any other book) and that so many martyrs sacrificed their lives to defend; the religion that sent missionaries out to all corners of the world, winning countless souls and laying the foundation of the greatest empire the world has known; the Christianity that withstood the constant threat of papal Rome and gave us our Protestant Reformed Throne and national identity. That faith given to us by the grace of God maintained the freedom and safety of the realm. Under King George VI, when that freedom was threatened by Nazi Germany, the nation was repeatedly called to prayer. Several times during the Second World War, just as at the time of the Spanish Armada, "the people of the book" cried out to Almighty God for His deliverance. He has always answered the nation's prayers and these islands have long been free from invasion by an alien power.

The Way Forward

As the government continues to yield powers to Brussels in the Maastricht "process;" as the proposed Constitution is implemented without the people's consent; as the Monarchy and the established Church together with their shared Protestant Reformed identity crumble; and as the moral landslide gathers momentum; once again **as a nation** we need to repent and cry out to Almighty God for mercy and deliverance. *"Where there is no vision, the people perish."*[8] We need to look to Scripture to rediscover, as the Reformers did, the simplicity of the Gospel, repentance and the promise of a personal relationship with Jesus Christ.

> *"As it is written, There is none righteous, no, not one: There is none that understandeth, there is none that seeketh after God. They are all gone out of the way, they are together become unprofitable; there is none that doeth good, no, not one. ... There is no fear of God before their eyes. ... For all have sinned, and come short of the glory of God; Being justified freely by his grace through the redemption that is in Christ Jesus: Whom God hath set forth to be a propitiation through faith in his blood, to declare his righteousness for the remission of sins that are past, through the forbearance of God;."*[9]

Martin Luther, who saw corruption and depravity all around him, found the answer of individual salvation, free and totally unearned, which in the past has resulted in corporate and national blessing, in such verses of Scripture from the third chapter of the book of Romans.

For those who understand what God has done for this nation in the past, the implications of Parliament's decisions to sign both the *Treaty of Rome* and the *Treaty of Maastricht* transcend economic considerations. In addition, the prospect of revision of the *Coronation Oath*, as well as of the *Act of Settlement* and the *Royal Marriages Act*, threatens to further undermine our national identity, as well as the freedoms that we cherish. It is imperative that we remember the lessons of history and respect the prudence of our forefathers in protecting posterity. *"O God, our fathers have told us, what work thou didst in their days, in the times of old."*[10] Let us pray that God will stay the hand of the politicians, and grant the people of the British Isles the opportunity to decide these things; and in His mercy He will give them the wisdom to once more *"ask for the old paths, where is the good way, and walk therein."*[11]

---

[8] Proverbs 29:18
[9] Romans 3:10-12, 18, 23-25
[10] Psalms 44:1
[11] Jeremiah 6:16

E. How Understanding the Doctrine of Election Changed My Life: Testimony of a New York Homemaker

I was raised in a Lutheran church, but it was not until I was about 23, and read "Steps to Peace with God", a tract by Billy Graham, that I desired to know the Lord Jesus Christ. I went through the "steps" and began my life with Christ.

Throughout my walk, I always had a fear of God, as I was raised with that, and I always wanted to please Him. However, I also thought of Jesus as my friend, causing my relationship to be casual. Something was missing—a certain intimacy was just not there. There was no desperation to know Him—there was no hunger for His Word—I would read it, simply because I knew that I should, but I would get nothing from it. I presumed that somehow this was my fault—I must have had some great sin that was in the way. I began to ask the Lord to show me what I had done and why I was not desperate.

One night, not long ago, I went to the home of a fellow sister in the Lord to study the Word together, and, while she had been called to the telephone, I asked the Lord again to show me what was wrong. He showed me myself in a fire, and His pulling me out. I thought of Zechariah 3:2, which says in part, "*...is not this a brand plucked out of the fire?*" I was horrified at my response, which I saw next. Saying, "Thanks, Lord," I stood up, brushed myself off, and went on my merry way. This was much too casual. I could see that there was pride there, but I didn't know the root of it. Still I knew that somehow, this was at the heart of that which was the obstacle.

From this point on, I thought I needed a revelation of hell—a fuller understanding of what I had been saved from. I began to pray earnestly for this. What I received instead was a revelation of the cross.

I suddenly had part of what I'd asked for—a hunger for the Word of God. I began to read the gospel according to John, where I began to "hear" the doctrine of election coming through. I understand that I did not save myself, and my salvation had nothing at all to do with the "steps" I had followed back when I was 23. Once I understood this, the Word opened up even more, and I began to see more. James 4:6, which says in part, "...*God resisteth the proud, but giveth grace unto the humble.*" suddenly opened up to me, and I understood what that meant as well.

I understood that even repentance wasn't possible without Him, as He had to first show me what I needed to repent of, He had to turn my heart to Him in brokenness. It was His goodness that led to my repentance, as it says in Romans 2:4 ("...*the goodness of God leadeth thee to repentance...*"). This was what I needed to finally destroy my pride and rid myself of any notion that I had saved myself.

In my life I have gotten married, I have given birth to children, I have lost a parent, I have "walked" with the Lord Jesus for fourteen years, but nothing has ever impacted my life as knowing that He chose me. Knowing He is sovereign assures me that He WILL do all that He has promised. I know that He doesn't have to depend upon me for anything—not even to respond toward my own salvation—and this gives me peace I have never known.

Nothing in my life will ever be the same.

Acknowledgements

~

This book has taken a long time to write. It grew out of *'All's Well' or Sound the Alarm,* a booklet about the wellbeing of the church which was distributed in the early 1990s. I want to thank the many supporters of Spirit of '88/ Dorchester House Publications and others who offered suggestions and constructive criticism and have given much encouragement over the years. Most especially, I would like to thank Ralph Brockman and Jean Shepherd who have faithfully prayed throughout that time.

I would also like to single out Richard Bennett, a special brother in the Lord, who has helped me a great deal on a number of issues. Also to Lynn, Richard's wife, who has given me wise advice and much encouragement as well. I owe a lot, too, to Derek Owers, who had much to do with the writing of the third section of the book.

For editing the text I am extremely grateful to Barbara Merz (and members of her church) who also so willingly helped me a great deal with research. Without Barbara's help, it is difficult to know by when I could have finished this book.

Michael de Semlyen
September 2006